TAKE A YEA

Chris Cotton

Illustrations by Nick Beringer

TiA Publications

A CIP catalogue record for this title is available from the British Library

ISBN: 978-1-5272-5998-0

Cover and all illustrations by Nick Beringer
Author photograph by Chris Cotton

TiA Publications
Training in Action Ltd
Lyndale House
6 The Avenue
Truro, TR1 1HT

This book is dedicated to my adorable grandchildren
in the hope that it may both inspire and amuse.

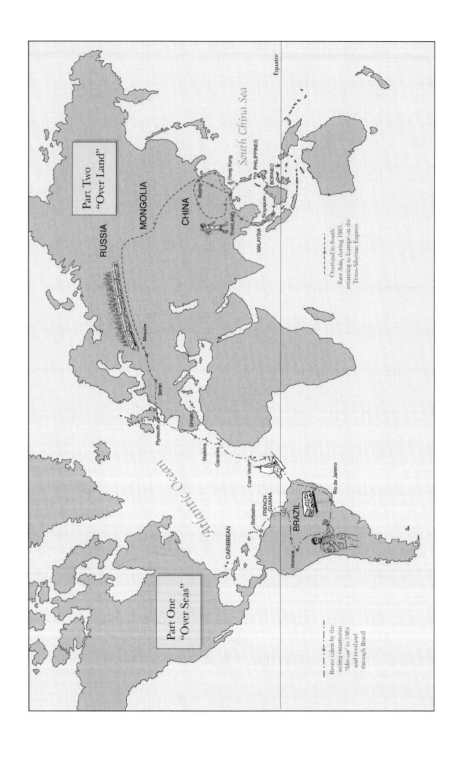

Part Two "Over Land"

RUSSIA

MONGOLIA

CHINA

Moscow

Berlin

Plymouth

SPAIN

Madeira

Canaries

Cape Verde

Atlantic Ocean

CARIBBEAN

Barbados

FRENCH GUIANA

BRAZIL

Manaus

Rio de Janeiro

Part One "Over Seas"

Hong Kong

South China Sea

PHILIPPINES

THAILAND

MALAYSIA   Singapore

BORNEO

Equator

→→→→ Overland in South
East Asia, during 1985,
returning to Europe on the
Trans-Siberian Express

—·—·—· Route taken by the
sailing catamaran
'Moksha' in 1984
and overland
through Brazil

CONTENTS

Introduction

Life is a tapestry of experiences. Some of these come without invitation – for better or for worse we are forced to play the ball that is thrown our way. Other life experiences involve more choice. They are opportunities for us to pick up or let pass. This book describes the choices which I made as a younger man, open to adventure, and is intended to inspire the reader to say 'yes' to opportunity when it comes knocking.

The manuscript was originally written as a travel journal in the form of letters home, in a time before the internet or mobile phones, when 'keeping in touch' was complicated and correspondence relied on a sometimes infrequent postal service. Some of these letters were written at sea, being tossed around in the ocean, desperately fighting to keep my manual typewriter from bouncing across the cabin. Other letters enjoyed the leisure and luxury of a transcontinental train journey, but mostly they were letters scribbled longhand on airmail paper whilst sitting on the side of the road waiting for a lift, or in a hotel bedroom waiting for a storm to pass or dawn to break.

The year of my journey, 1984, was a remarkable year. George Orwell's famous novel by the same name was written in 1949 but describes an imaginary future, the year 1984, when much of the world has fallen victim to perpetual war, intrusive government surveillance and flagrant propaganda. As I travelled around the real world of 1984, it was with this story in mind that I tried to interpret what I saw – whether it was the extraordinary control of the Communist Party in China, just emerging from the grip of Mao Zedong, or the crazy bureaucracy of a newly formed African country like Cape Verde. At home in the UK, the country was virtually at war with itself. Margaret Thatcher was in her second term as Prime Minister and the miners' strikes were in full flood – arguably the most ugly struggle for political supremacy for half a century. As I travelled from country to country, Orwell's predictions for 1984 resonated on many fronts!

Now reviewing my letters home, and an earlier attempt to draw them together as a complete story, it strikes me that, at the time, I did not appreciate the significance of what I saw and experienced during my 'year out'. Perhaps it was the innocence of youth that allowed me to accept things as 'normal' even when looking back they were anything but. How else could I now justify the decision to be smuggled across the China Seas by pirates or to spend a night tempting a vampire bat from its lair in the Amazon jungle, just for a dare!

Yet all of these were choices, fuelled by a desire to grab life and experience it to the full. To say 'yes' to opportunity and to create my own rich tapestry of experiences – experiences which would remain with me for life.

Take a Year Out is meant as a challenge – a gauntlet thrown down – to anyone pondering the opportunity, but in particular it is dedicated to my grandchildren, for whom the book of life is just beginning, with pages ready and waiting for them to write. My hope is that this book will inspire and encourage them to fill those blank pages to the brim and to experience life in all its richness and wonder.

Chris Cotton, December 2019

PART ONE

Over Seas

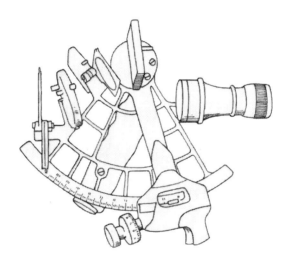

CHAPTER ONE

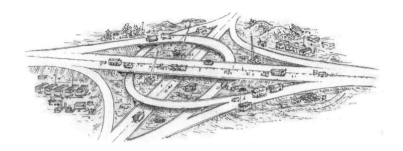

The Decision

It began one miserable Tuesday morning in late March 1984. The rain
had been falling all night, and as I sat in the damp and grimy site hut
looking out through steamed up windows I could see the men, huddled
under the shelter of one of the great dumper trucks, urgently debating
with the General Foreman. I couldn't make out what was being said but
I had a fair idea of the gist. The M25/M4 motorway interchange was a
prestige job and the main contractor involved in the construction had
settled for an extremely tight programme.

To continue working in the conditions which prevailed that day would
be to run the risk of doing more damage to the site than if we all went
home and left the rain to do its worst. But there were wages at stake as
well as programmes and I guessed that this was the real issue under
debate outside.

I shared my office with half-a-dozen other civil engineers, using the
place more as a base for our outside duties than as an office in the
conventional sense of the word. Consequently, the state of the hut inside
was little better than conditions outside, as men trudged in and out
bringing large quantities of mud from the brown 'soup' that had begun
to form over most of the site. Even in the summer, conditions are little

improved since the mud is replaced with clouds of dust pushed into the air by the machines as they thunder past the offices.

It must be said that for all of this I used to enjoy my time on site, working out of doors in all weathers, organising the 'muck shift', as the earthmoving side of the operation is known in the trade. However, on that Tuesday morning I seriously wondered whether I would want to be a part of it for the rest of my life. The other engineers in my office were making their way in from the canteen, muddy hands clutching plates of steaming sausage sandwiches – the conventional construction worker's breakfast. We were all in our mid-twenties, some a little younger, and all of us wore the same, ubiquitous black 'donkey jackets', which were the uniform of our trade.

I stopped staring out of the window, content that the issue being discussed was bound to be resolved in favour of some sort of compromise, meaning that no one would go home and a general 'odd job' day would be declared. From the hole which had once been a drawer (my desk having suffered the ravages of years of hard service on sites up and down the country) I took out a copy of *Yachting Monthly* which I had borrowed from a friend the previous day. The weather was depressing me and I knew that browsing through the pages advertising sunshine, crystal waters and beautiful beaches would help me justify my self-indulgent feelings of hardship and misfortune.

I was also feeling less than happy that morning for another reason, completely unrelated to the rain which continued to run down the outside of the window or the drips falling from the ceiling onto a pile of incomplete calculations which still demanded my attention. In under a month's time I was to take my professional examinations, turning the muddy boot engineer of some seven years' experience into a Chartered Engineer – one qualified to '... harness the resources of nature for the benefit and use of mankind'.

I was confident about passing the exams, but at an absolute loss as to what I should do with the qualification. Did I really want to pursue a career in civil engineering? It had hardly been a burning ambition. Indeed, I had no real idea what a civil engineer did until I was half-way through my degree course. I have always envied those who wake up one morning with the vision of becoming a lawyer or a doctor or such like, and for whom life is a simple matter of pursuing a clearly defined path, getting the right 'A' levels, taking the right course at university and then entering their chosen profession without the slightest doubt that it was absolutely the right thing to do.

For me, it was far more a case of stumbling through a maze of generalities, trying to identify a few values which I held dear and then attempting to mould a career around them. How then, with such a haphazard approach to life, was I ever to be sure that I had made the right choice? I flicked through the pages of the yachting magazine, mulling it all over in my mind and not really concentrating on the magazine itself.

Over the previous few weeks I had tried to explore a few options – questions which might help me to decide on a sensible direction to follow after the exams. After all, if I was so unsure whether or not I was suited to civil engineering and it to me, then the logical course of action would be to go off and try something else for a while.

I felt there was a whole world of different careers 'out there', and that to carry on in the same direction simply because I had started, was really dodging the issue. Consequently, during the previous month, I had made one or two enquiries to various business schools using the logic that it would allow me the opportunity to undertake a thorough appraisal of my long-term objectives, in an environment shared with others from a wide variety of career backgrounds. Then, if I felt that a change of career was right, the business qualification would help open the door to my new, chosen field.

However, on the other hand, if a year out simply confirmed that I really did want to remain a civil engineer, then the education in itself would be no bad thing. And anyway, it wasn't as if I would be missing much by taking a few months leave. For years now it had become increasingly obvious that the country was producing more and more civil engineers and providing fewer and fewer jobs. Consequently, there had been a general slow-down in progress that any one person could make up the career ladder.

The traditional 'bottom rung' of that ladder had always been a year or two of 'setting out' or 'peg bashing' as it is known to those who do it. This is where the young engineer learns the tools of the trade and has the opportunity to observe the job at 'the sharp end'. It seemed to me, however, that this period was now being dragged out as companies struggled to accommodate their new recruits within the true management structure.

All these things had become real issues as I contemplated my future, weighing up the pros and cons of any one course of action. If I were to go to business school it made little sense to stay on after my exams in May, given that the school term would not begin until September. And if this was to be the case then what could I do that would be really worthwhile in the intervening four months? I'm not the type of person to waste such opportunities!

As my mind churned through the tangled logic of the situation, I turned to the personal column of the yachting magazine.

'Crew required for a sailing expedition to the Amazon, shared expenses, no experience necessary.'

The short advertisement went on to say that the expedition would be leaving on the 1st of June from Plymouth, and that it aimed to be at the mouth of the Amazon by the end of July. Perfect timing! My qualifications for the post were impeccable since I had had virtually no previous sailing experience. A fortnight's flotilla sailing in the tranquil waters of the Mediterranean was the nearest I had ever been to working onboard a yacht.

My fellow engineers were still tucking into their sausage sandwiches. The mud was beginning to dry on their boots, falling off in large chunks, to be trodden into the lino floor of the office, along with all the previous days' mud – the cleaners refused to even attempt our particular office while the weather was poor. I looked around our pigsty of an office and through the window once more. The rain seemed even heavier now.

Then I stared back at the advertisement in front of me. '... the Amazon ...' I would be a fool not to grasp such an opportunity.

The following few days saw a flurry of activity. I contacted the skipper of the boat and arranged a time for me to visit him in Plymouth. Then I phoned the business school at Cranfield and secured a provisional place on the course for September 1984.

I found that reaction to my decision was mixed. Amongst my colleagues at work some felt that having left the profession I would never be able to get back in, whilst others thought that a change of environment could only be to my ultimate advantage and anyhow to pass up the chance of the sailing trip would be madness. I tended to agree with this latter reading of my situation, satisfied that the dissidents among them were either jealous or lacking the slightest spark of an adventurous spirit!

From my friends outside of work, and my parents, I received tremendous support. My parents had long given up expecting me to lead a 'normal' life. Ever since I wandered off by myself in the Welsh mountains at the age of four, it had been clear to them that my life and travel were fairly firmly bound together. Indeed, travel has been an absolute passion with me for as long as I can remember. As a teenager I would never squander money on records and tapes (as they were in those days), and I still think that spending money on clothes is scandalous, and yet I thought nothing of blowing £300 on a return flight to Mozambique during my second year at university when I was invited to spend Christmas with a friend whose home was in Maputo.

Since those days, and up until I set sail for the Amazon, a combination of work and leisure had taken me to South Africa where I lived and worked for a year, and to North America, India, Nepal and Egypt, as well as most of the Western European countries. In this respect I suppose the concept of leaving the UK for foreign parts was not new to me. However, this time, the ground rules were going to be very different.

At this stage, with a place at business school secured for the coming September, I was only anticipating a four-month trip culminating, I hoped, with a short time in the Amazon before returning to the UK to resume a normal life and my quest for my true vocation. I hadn't even considered the possibility of extending my self-awarded 'leave of absence' by a further few months, let alone until the following September.

Indeed, although that is precisely what did happen, I am sure, looking back, that I would never have been able to screw up enough courage to have decided in favour of such a radical move. Four months seemed reasonable and not excessive. To have committed myself for over a year at that stage, would, I think, have proved so daunting a prospect that I would never have embarked upon this adventure at all.

My brief meeting with the skipper of the yacht in the tiny Cornish village of Millbrook, where the vessel was moored, confirmed my belief that all was well with the world and that this was the right thing for me to be doing. By profession Tom used to be an English teacher and his love of literature had never left him. Indeed, I often had the impression that it was partly because he never found enough time to indulge his passion for reading that he eventually gave up teaching and took up sailing as a fulltime occupation.

At the time of the expedition Tom was in his early fifties and had been building and chartering yachts from his base in Cornwall for the best part of ten years. He looked the part as well! A grey flecked beard, 'salty', weather-beaten face and an appalling dress sense. In all the time I spent with Tom over the months that followed, I don't believe I can recall more than one occasion when he was ever dressed in anything more respectable than an old pair of corduroys and a rough check shirt, and that was on his wife's total insistence!

However, Tom knew the sea and he knew his vessel. He had built *Morvran* in 1982 to take charters across the Channel and back. Some 36-feet in length, the vessel was a sloop-rigged catamaran by design and constructed almost entirely of timber and plywood with a GRP skin. Having built the boat himself, Tom had been able to incorporate a number of features which were to prove invaluable over the months ahead. An extra high coachroof for one, which allowed for a spacious saloon in the centre of the vessel, and a work bench built into one of the hulls complete with a vice and hand drill.

Two boats were to take part in the expedition, *Morvran* and one other. This second boat was skippered by a man of previous circumnavigation sailing experience. Like Tom, Pat had also designed and built his boat. For Pat, however, yacht design and construction was a profession and the expedition was an opportunity to put his latest design to the test. The boat's name was *Ocean Winds*, and she too was a catamaran.

The word 'expedition' implies a purpose, a reason for doing what we were doing which stretched beyond a simple desire just to 'do it for its own sake'. In this respect, I don't think that the Ocean Environment Expedition ever really qualified as a fully-fledged expedition. Ostensibly the aim of the expedition was to navigate a passage across the centre of the Amazon Delta, a two-hundred-mile-wide maze of channels and backwaters which wind their way through some of the most inhospitable jungle in the world. However, the Amazonian stage of the trip was to be couched in a much wider itinerary. Our route to Brazil, for instance, would take us many miles further south than most trans-Atlantic crossings, with the dual purpose of avoiding the hurricane belt and enabling us to conduct a plankton and squid-sampling project for the Marine Institute in Plymouth.

April and May sped past. It was as if I was closing down my past and opening up a brand new future. My letter of resignation was tendered and my possessions sold. All that was left to do was to pack a few things into a box and make my way to Plymouth.

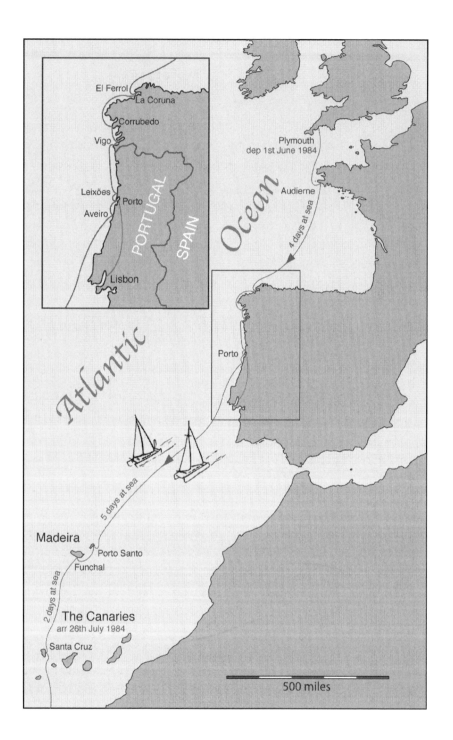

El Ferrol
La Coruna
Corrubedo
Vigo
Leixões
Porto
Aveiro
PORTUGAL
SPAIN
Lisbon

Plymouth
dep 1st June 1984
Audierne
Ocean
4 days at sea

Atlantic

Porto

5 days at sea

Madeira
Porto Santo
Funchal

2 days at sea

The Canaries
arr 26th July 1984
Santa Cruz

500 miles

CHAPTER TWO

Onboard *Morvran*

It wasn't until we actually cast off that the enormity of what lay ahead fully landed. Decisions taken on impulse are a bit like that I find. I make a decision and then get swept along by the chain of events without ever sitting down quietly to weigh up the pros and cons. I suppose it's a kind of defence mechanism. If 'gut feel' tells me I'm right then I act, knowing full well that if I were to analyse the decision too closely I would simply end up talking myself out of it. The expedition to the Amazon was a classic example.

Once I had phoned Tom and told him that I would join him I stopped thinking about the 'whys and wherefores' and simply concentrated on the 'hows'; all those little things which needed doing before the June 1st deadline. Even during the two days which I spent on the boat prior to departure I never really came to terms with it. I had joined Tom early to get all my bits and pieces stowed onboard and to lend a hand with last minute chores, but with a close friend living in Plymouth my commitment to the task had been half-hearted to say the least.

The boat itself was moored across the water from Plymouth in the little Cornish fishing village of Millbrook. There, during those final couple of days we brought the last few boxes of supplies onboard and gave the boat a good thick coat of antifouling. This ghastly substance has the consistency of something between treacle and gloss paint and is applied to the underside of the boat in an effort to ward off the worst of the inevitable marine growth that would otherwise attach itself to the hulls and create drag – a problem which in warmer waters can become severe.

A whole day's antifouling and a night in a damp berth was sufficient to persuade me that a couple of days to settle in was perhaps excessive, and so leaving Tom to work through the pre-departure checks for the 'nth' time I took the ferry from Millbrook to Plymouth to spend time with close friends, home cooking and the security of four walls. I was feeling decidedly unadventurous!

The 1st of June 1984 was not at all bad by British weather standards. A nice force three to four blew from the West and the sun shone down on Plymouth Sound through a 'cotton wool' sky. I had agreed with Tom that instead of returning to Millbrook I would wait for him to bring the boat across to Plymouth where he had to clear customs and load up with duty free. As chance would have it, Sutton Harbour was full that particular morning and so Tom had been forced to tie up outside the inner harbour, right alongside the very steps from which the Pilgrim Fathers had departed on their epic voyage to the New World.

There must have been great crowds of people at the quayside on that famous day in 1620, all waving and shouting tearful cries of good luck to friends and loved ones. There might even have been a seventeenth century equivalent of a brass band to send the settlers on their way. However, on the 1st of June 1984, there were no brass bands or crowds of people, just a disgruntled customs officer and a few close friends. We cast off and motored out into the Sound, then the sails were set and the engine cut. Silence. We all looked back to the shore. My friend, Vicki, stood alone on the end of the harbour wall. A miniature figure waving a white scarf. Behind her, on Plymouth Hoe, people were rushing back and forth, going about their normal business completely unaware of the poignancy of the moment. Their activity should have captured my attention but all I could see was 'home', slowing receding into the horizon. It was then that the enormity of the undertaking suddenly hit me.

It was as if my subconscious had suddenly lifted the shutters on a previously taboo subject. Here was I, a civil engineer, and not even a good one at that, with no real knowledge of the sea, setting sail in a 36-foot wooden boat with a crew I'd never met, on a voyage which was to take us 6,000 miles, across the Atlantic Ocean and into uncharted waters of the Amazon. It had to be madness – or simply the true essence of adventure? By now we had drawn out into the middle of the Sound and the crowds of shoppers and tourists had become little more than dots on the landscape. I turned seawards and then went below to make some coffee.

In all there were nine of us in the expedition, three people on *Ocean Winds* and six on *Morvran*. Each of the two skippers had been responsible for selecting his own crew and, in addition to his wife Jean, Tom had settled on four newcomers to the sailing world: Karin, Jeanette, Barry and myself. In the original plan we had all intended to meet up at least a month prior to departure but in the end, finding a completely free weekend in everyone's diary had proved impossible and so even up until the day of departure only Tom had met us all.

Karin, Jeanette and Barry had joined the boat and said all their farewells to friends and loved ones in Millbrook the previous evening, and so by now had worked their way through all the preliminary introductions and potted life histories. As we stood in the cockpit sipping our coffee, and while the boat gently jogged its way down the Cornish coast, the stories were told once more for my benefit.

Next to Tom, Karin was undoubtedly the most qualified for the position, insofar as she had enjoyed quite a lot of dinghy sailing in her native Norway. I say 'native Norway' since that is where she lived. Although with a Norwegian mother, British father, Norwegian husband and British passport her specific allegiance was somewhat dubious and subject to the vagaries of circumstance. Karin, who like myself was in her mid-twenties and nicely settled into a career, was nevertheless also an opportunist and had managed to negotiate six months 'leave of absence' from her husband and her work in fish farming to take what we all then believed to be a once-in-a-lifetime opportunity. For Barry the wrench was less dramatic. A few years older than me, Barry had all the qualities in a man that I strived for yet lacked. In his early thirties and looking like he was still in his late twenties, Barry had life 'sewn up' and I took an instant liking to him.

After leaving school, Barry had begun an inspiring career in accountancy with the promise of a comfortable life in his hometown of St Helier, Jersey. However, a mortgage, wife and 2.2 kids had not been Barry's idea of a future and so, flying in the face of all advice to the contrary, he bought a one-way ticket to Australia and began afresh. Travelling back overland some two years later he had found himself a temporary job in a ski resort restaurant in Switzerland where he worked his way up to the position of head chef. With his winters tied up in Switzerland, Barry felt that the least he could do would be to reward himself with a little sunshine in the summer and so, on the proceeds of his life as a part-time chef, he bought himself a little cottage in the Greek islands where he became an expert in the art of doing very little. I don't say this lightly as the ability 'to do very little' is indeed an art and a very valuable one, as anyone who has spent seven months at sea can tell you. This summer, however, Barry had chosen a more active pastime than quietly quaffing ouzo!

Of all the crew Jeanette seemed the most unlikely candidate for a trans-Atlantic expedition. While Karin adopted a practical, down-to-earth outlook on life and Barry a more *laissez faire*, relaxed approach, Jeanette (who was also in her mid-twenties) struck me as being the sort of person who might be more at home in the busy sophistication of a London ad. agency than scrubbing out the heads in a choppy sea. Yet, however unsuitable she might have been, Jeanette had 'guts'. She suffered violently from sea sickness during almost all the crossings we were to make and yet never once baulked from standing her turn on watch. Had it not been so sad, her appearance in the cockpit at the start of her watch with her chalk white face and contrasting shock of bright auburn hair could have been amusing. As it was, we all pitied her for her suffering, which we all shared to varying degrees.

None of us had much time to get sea sick on that first short leg as the wind had turned southerly and we were forced to abandon our planned crossing to France and divert to the little village of Lerryn, some five miles up the river from Fowey in mid Cornwall. In many ways the postponement was a blessing in disguise as it gave us all a breathing space between the frantic preparations of the previous week and the fairly intense sailing programme which lay ahead. The weather stayed with us as well and so while the wind remained stubbornly south, we all enjoyed a couple of days 'exploring' the beauties of our own shores. It seems a strange thing to say now, but in retrospect, although my travels over the year that followed were to take me from the jungles of South America to the plains of Mongolia, I can't honestly recall a much pleasanter spot than that quiet little anchorage at Lerryn.

Isolated from the rest of the world by a maze of country lanes, the village of Lerryn is nestled at the bottom of a gently sloping river valley, gushing in summer greenery and deciduous woodland. It had a couple of pubs, as I recall, a shop and an atmosphere of quiet contentment. However, on the third day, the wind veered sufficiently for us to attempt a channel crossing and so with reluctance we heaved the anchor back onboard and wound our way back to Fowey and the open sea. I had never before been at sea in a small boat at night and so had never experienced that peculiar mixture of feelings which can overwhelm you. Sitting alone in the cockpit of *Morvran* with blackness all around, half my mind sensed only fear and awe, the 'tiny boat in an enormous ocean' syndrome.

Experience has taught me that with time these feelings of vulnerability subside and begin to give way to a curious sense of great privilege. It's almost as if you become absorbed into the very fabric of nature itself, breathing with the wind and rising and falling with the ocean swell. It's an intimacy that becomes like a love affair, an experience which can be so personal that in the end you simply don't want to share it. Solitary watches soon, therefore, became the order of the day, though more from a point of view of maximising on sleep than any romantic notion! In terms of weather the passage was uneventful. Indeed, by dawn the next morning the wind had come round enough to allow us to hoist the square-sail and run with the wind on our quarter.

The square-sail was a rather novel idea which both Tom and Pat had adopted for downwind sailing. Made by dividing a parachute into three parts – one part for each boat and the third for patches – our 'square' sail was secured along its upper side or 'head' to a horizontal pole or 'yardarm' which we hoisted up the forestay to the top of the mast using the foresail halyard. Each end of the 'yard' was steadied by braces that were fed back through blocks attached to the shrouds (which tension the mast from either side of the boat) and into the cockpit.

The bottom corners or 'clews' of the sail were controlled by sheets (ropes) in the normal manner. When set, the square-sail would add two or three knots to our speed meaning that in a force-three wind we could make six or seven knots of speed with ease.

The romance of downwind sailing under square-sail was enhanced during that particular crossing by the presence of some fifteen-or-so porpoises which stayed with us for almost all of the second day. By nightfall of the second day we were safely moored at Audierne on the Brittany coast of France. Our first significant passage was complete.

Tom was a very competent, level-headed sort of man and in all matters nautical or otherwise he ruled his ship in a fairly autocratic fashion. It was his boat and therefore his prerogative and, since most of his decisions accorded with my likes and dislikes, I saw this as no bad thing. However, such accord was not universal!

One of the most amusing and yet at the same time annoying things about our communal life onboard was the general appreciation, or rather lack of appreciation, which was shown for the ship's music. Karin, Jeanette and Barry disliked 'mainstream' classical music, loathed Gilbert and Sullivan and abhorred opera. Yet Tom could not grasp that anyone should not be put into raptures at the sound of a male voice choir and so continued to fill the boat with what I would call beautiful music, sending the renegades to the farthest corners – never more than thirty-six feet away!

On Saturday the 9th of June the weather forecasts were good and so during the afternoon the two skippers made the decision to 'go for' the Biscay crossing. Our first night's watches were made all the more interesting by the onset of thick fog and frequent encounters with French fishing fleets which would loom up out of nowhere and then disappear into oblivion just as quickly. I felt a kind of intimacy with other vessels which we passed during a dark night after perhaps hours with no sightings.

After a day's sailing we were still only a quarter of the way across the Bay and the weather had been overcast for several hours. Under normal circumstances this would have made navigation very difficult but our eleventh-hour purchase of SAT-NAV had changed all that. This pocket-sized onboard computer took bearings from overhead satellites and converted them into position fixes at the touch of a button. One direct benefit which this gave to an operation like ours was that mid-passage destination points or 'way-points' could be fed into the machine which were then computed to give us a continuous assessment of distance and bearing to any particular point. The advantage of this technology when sailing in company was, that in the event of the two boats losing contact with each other, the way-points would provide a convenient mid-ocean meeting point.

Many references will be made to our SAT-NAV in the coming chapters, and the reader should bear in mind that whilst this technology may be commonplace nowadays, in 1984 it was in its infancy and very experimental.

Now that the trip was well under way I had begun to feel much happier about my decision, and the doubts which had overwhelmed me as we cleared Plymouth had slowly become a thing of the past.

At first I had thought that I would easily become very bored. However, as it turned out, it became difficult fitting everything into the day. There was a lot to do on the boat in the way of sailing and domestic chores, so that it was almost a matter of squeezing in the 'teach yourself Spanish' course which I had sworn to master before reaching Spain. Consequently, by the time we approached the Spanish mainland I had only reached the stage of being able to order a beer or ask my way to the post office.

We eventually arrived in Spain after what turned out to be an extremely fast night's sailing. However, as we started to cross back on to the continental shelf, the force-five winds which had been giving us such a good passage during the night, turned the sea into quite a chop, putting the yacht through its paces. *Morvran* rose to the challenge magnificently, proving to us all that she could not only cope with such conditions but that she positively thrived on them. So, by the way did I, much to my surprise, and no longer with the aid of 'the tablets'!

After the long night watches and the cold Easterly winds which took us across most of the Bay, our leisurely passages along the coast of Spain, from one cove to another, were pleasantly relaxing. The temperatures were in the upper seventies and life alternated between siesta and food – oh, and drink of course, the great lubricant of all types of holiday. With Vivaldi playing somewhere in the background, the sound of water slopping against the side of the yacht and bottles of tonic trailing over the stern (cooling for the evening glass of G&T) who would not be relaxed!

We cleared customs in the busy port of El Ferrol and stayed on for a further three days to carry out some necessary maintenance work before continuing southwards, dotting from port to port in a pleasant week of coastal sailing. I want at this stage to set down a typical day at sea and to compare it with a typical day of coastal sailing.

Whilst at sea we maintained a constant watch. This meant a turn on deck of two hours at night or one hour during the day, either at the tiller or, if the self-steering was working, just being vigilant and doing the odd bit of navigating. Between watches there were a limited number of options. The yacht carried an old typewriter which I was trying to master and so typing was always one possible option, but a frustrating one with all the pitching and rolling. Anything social was difficult as we were never all together at any one time.

In the end, reading tended to be the main preoccupation. That and sleeping! Indeed, the night watches tended to break the night up to such an extent that one needed to use much of the daytime for sleeping just to keep 'on top'. Initially, meals were a little irregular, with Jean (Tom's wife) not feeling too much like cooking and few of us really feeling like eating. However that soon changed, and meals became one of the few times when all but the watch-keeper got together. After the evening meal everyone would turn in, often even before the sun had set. Although we drank the odd glass of wine with the evening meal no social drinking was done. This was partially because getting up at three o'clock was difficult enough without having to struggle through the onset of a hangover, and partially because none of us was, at that stage, willing to jeopardise our new-found sea legs.

Once we arrived at a port, however, the emphasis changed dramatically. Although usually moored alongside each other, the crews of both yachts had developed enough of a sense of family spirit, or loyalty, for each yacht to live a relatively independent life. A good wash was the number one priority and since the water tanks usually needed a top-up we would often find somewhere to come alongside where there was access to a hose and a customs official. With the decks shipshape and after everyone had had a chance of a hose-down on the foredeck the next priority was to find a bar. Almost as if to counter the inconveniences of life at sea, life when coastal sailing was one of total convenience.

We would rarely be up much before nine, starting the day with a jog along the shore or a swim. Being the lazy type, and provided we weren't in some filthy harbour, I would usually opt for the latter as it doubled as a good wash. Breakfast was taken individually in the cockpit. Unless we were staying put for the whole day, we would normally aim to weigh anchor and get under sail in time to get around the corner and into the next bay for lunch. In contrast to when we were at sea, lunches when coastal sailing were taken seriously, largely due to the popularity of Jean's freshly baked pies and bread. With a generous allowance made for aperitifs and wine, lunch usually had to be followed by a siesta under the canopy which sheltered most of the deck while we were not actually sailing. Then a quick swim to freshen up before getting under way for our night halt, possibly four or five hours' sailing away.

During the journey, when no actual sailing was required of the crew, there were usually plenty of related tasks ranging from stitching on sail hanks to fashioning wooden braces to strengthen the cockpit floor. Having reached our night halt, the activity for the remainder of the day depended on whether we were moored out in a bay or tied up alongside a quay. It was our policy to avoid large towns or marinas and wherever possible we would stop at a small fishing village.

If we were able to come alongside then our evening meal would usually be followed by a sortie into town for a drink or, in the spirit of Tom's passion for music, a square dance on the quayside! There were four of us onboard who could play a musical instrument and our capabilities encompassed accordions, guitars, an electric organ, and two recorders. The drawback was that due to our limited numbers it was difficult to provide both dancers and players and so we would generally have to resort to using the yacht's cassette player to provide accompaniment while we encouraged astonished bystanders to 'strip the willow' or join us in an eightsome reel!

On the whole these efforts were well received by the locals who saw the arrival of our two strangely-shaped yachts as something of an event. Once it was established that our intentions were simply to have fun we usually found that there were quite a few people who were prepared to launch into the fray and run the risk of making fools of themselves.

By midnight the dancing, drinking and singing would draw to a close and the quayside would return to a sleepy quiet backwater, with just the gentle slap of water against the hulls to lull us all to sleep.

On the morning of Saturday the 16th of June we were making a short passage further down the Spanish coast, again through thick fog, and in company with our sister yacht as usual. The wind was only the merest whisper of a breeze and the sea was flat calm, when suddenly we went through one of those memorable little moments which were beginning to characterise the trip. With no warning at all the sea off our port bow suddenly broke into a foamy whiteness, as a school of about twenty dolphins, some up to eight feet in length, cleared the surface. When it became obvious that the dolphins were intent on joining us, Ann (one of the two crew on *Ocean Winds*) who combined a flair for the romantic with a degree of scientific curiosity when it came to all things animal or vegetable, took up her recorder in an attempt to see if they could be lured, Pied Piper fashion, nearer the yacht. Imagine the scene; the hazy outline of a yacht sailing through the mist with the shape of a young woman just visible, like a figurehead, playing to a school of dolphins as they swam and cavorted beneath her. I am just about enough of a romantic to believe that it was indeed the music that had lured them closer!

Our progress up to now had been quite good, all things considered, but as we made our way down the coast of Spain we began to be plagued by a spate of engine problems. On one of these occasions we found ourselves in the port of La Coruna, tied up alongside the main quay. More of a city than a town, La Coruna provided a refreshing change from the industrial atmosphere of El Ferrol. Typically Spanish, with long, narrow streets packed with barrow markets ending in large shaded plazas, it proved as pleasant a forced stop as any forced stop could be. Two days later our engine was repaired but our problems were not over. After very little progress along the Spanish coast we were again obliged to return to port with engine trouble, this time on our sister yacht *Ocean Winds*.

Disillusionment began to grow like the mould on our clothes. With a September start at Cranfield Business School still in mind I dispelled any idea of touring Brazil when we arrived in Belem and became concerned about even having enough time to make the Atlantic crossing itself. When at last the repair was complete we were prevented from leaving by the same force-seven winds which drove us into port when the engine inherited its problems.

I began to learn that adopting a true attitude of *laissez faire* when living at sea was as important as learning to tie a bowline. Unfortunately, this was a most difficult lesson to learn and having deadlines to meet didn't help the trying. Nevertheless, there were certain realities to face and one of them was that to make Belem on time we were going to have to engage in a fairly intensive sailing programme, the like of which we had not experienced to date. Left to their own devices I felt that the two skippers would have liked to abandon our published schedule and take life more as it came. However, both agreed that in taking on crew they also took on the responsibilities of setting and keeping to a rough itinerary, even if this meant cutting out a number of ports of call.

There was no hard feeling about our falling behind on schedule especially since it really only affected *me* at that stage and, as long as we weren't pottering for pottering's sake, there was little more one could ask.

With the wind showing no sign of abating and with due regard to the delay suffered with engine problems, we made a prompt start the next morning, heading out into the bay in a following wind blowing force six, gusting seven. The yacht responded like a young stallion. It took off across the sea at a full eight knots with water crashing and foaming behind it. Sadly, the weather did not stay with us and we were soon back to slopping about in a windless sea. As the day drew on, however, a good sailing breeze picked up and we made our destination by mid-evening. The bay in which we anchored had been chosen for the ideal shelter which it offered against northeasterly winds.

Some two miles across, it was forested on its southern side, duned to the east and dotted with the most delightful selection of red-roofed cottages which went to make up the village of Corrubedo on its northern flank.

The next morning was plagued by thick fog and no wind, but at least by resorting to our engines we made some limited headway. However, my concern for our progress remained, as I understood that the next three days would be spent in Vigo having parts machined for one of *Ocean Winds'* engines.

I remember that when talking with friends about the pros and cons of doing this sort of venture (that is to say buying a yacht; devising our own journey; and advertising for our own crew) getting someone who was mechanically minded onboard was recognised as essential in case of engine problems. I now firmly believe that it is in fact a case of not 'if' but 'when' the engine goes wrong, as all our problems at that time seemed to have revolved around things mechanical or electrical!

Our stay in Vigo lasted only one-and-a-half days. The broken crown wheel from *Ocean Winds* could not be machined locally so the phone call was made to England and we arranged to meet up with the flown-out parts, a few days further down the coast, in Porto, Portugal.

On the morning of Saturday the 30th of June, the yachts were at anchor off the port of Bayona, a small tourist town about ten miles south of Vigo, where we had decided to wait a couple of days before completing our journey to Porto. Tom, Jean and the girls had rowed ashore to do some shopping for the weekend. Barry was fishing for lunch off the stern and I had just completed half-an-hour's rehearsal of the tenor parts to 'The Merry Month of Maying' and 'Lit'le Lisa Jane' for a madrigal session which had been planned for that afternoon. I was beginning to enjoy this life of ease. Before Jean had left for the shore she had removed one of her very special courgette pies from the oven to cool and the smell of it, as it drifted up into the cockpit, was making the prospect of waiting for Barry to catch his first fish before declaring 'lunch' less and less likely.

Jean's energy and patience in the face of all our individual likes and dislikes had done much to smooth troubled water over the past week or so of engine problems and associated frustrations. She was one of those people who never seemed to stop – the sort of person to whom boredom would have been a novel experience, and yet she was no sailor and took very little pleasure in the long sea passages.

In port, however, Jean came into her own, organising our daily routines and concocting the most marvellous meals from her sorties into local fish and vegetable markets. In short, Jean became a surrogate mother to us 'youngsters' and concern grew at the thought of her leaving us in August, when her teaching duties would recall her to England.

The next morning at six o'clock the wind was the merest whisper, and in the wrong direction at that. However, it was decided that we had to make an attempt, even if we were going to be turned back. After one hour out at sea the wind direction changed to northerly and increased to a steady force four. The Gods were with us. We hoisted the square-sail and, making an average speed for the whole journey of five knots, we arrived twelve hours and sixty miles later in Leixoes, Portugal, just north of Porto.

The idea of making for Leixoes was prompted by the discovery that the British Consulate in Porto had recently been closed down and we had thus decided to have our engine parts sent to Leixoes Yacht Club instead.

That day's sailing was just as sailing should be: a following, stiff breeze, excellent visibility and sensible times for departure and arrival. How few days actually turn out like that! By the beginning of the next day we were starting to regret our decision to stop in Leixoes and await the parts as the town was little more than an international shipping terminal, and so with the knowledge that we had at least a week's wait on our hands we decided to sail the five miles round to Porto.

Porto is Portugal's second city and home of the drink of the same name: Port. Having crossed the sand bar, which now precludes most large vessels from entering the mouth of the river, we sailed for about two miles up the Rio Douro with the red-roofed houses of Porto sprawling over the steep hillsides on either side. When we were as near to the city centre as the river allowed, we tied up alongside a wharf with *Ocean Winds* rafted alongside us. The area immediately adjacent to the river was not unlike some parts of Naples as I remember them. It was distinctly 'southern European', consisting of narrow cobbled streets with bird cages and laundry hung from balconies three or four storeys above, and grimy street urchins, mangy dogs and a prevailing smell of rotting vegetables.

On the morning of the 4th of July, American Independence Day and my birthday, I was woken by the harsh noise of life on the quayside, the sunlight as it streamed in through my cabin skylight and the smell of sewage – it being low water. I pulled myself through the hole in the saloon bulkhead, which was our only access, and out on to deck to see what all the noise was about.

A Frenchman was standing on the quay arguing with an official, his arms working in that gesticulative manner which is the hallmark of a Frenchman wherever he is in the world. It appeared that he had brought his yacht in late the previous night and had rafted up against a ferryboat which now wanted to leave. He was therefore being told to move his yacht onto the quayside. It all seemed pretty rational to me.

His indignation, it transpired, arose from the fact that he did not possess any kind of ladder and had been relying on the ferryboat as his only means of scaling the quayside. In the end, a local fellow from one of the quayside cafes lent him a ladder and I helped him walk his vessel, the only other yacht we had seen down the whole length of the river, adjacent to ours. After all the commotion had subsided I realised that I hadn't, as yet, done anything more than don a pair of swimming trunks since getting up and so I went below to wash and have some breakfast. What a way to start a day, and a birthday at that!

I should perhaps say a word or two about the layout of the boat, which was my home for almost seven months.

In essence our 36-foot by 16-foot world was divided into three areas: the port and starboard hulls and the bit in-between. *Morvran* had been designed as a working boat with plenty of space both on deck and below. Each of the two hulls divided into three parts. The aft section, both port and starboard, contained double berth cabins whilst the middle section of the port hull housed the galley and the corresponding section of the starboard hull was given up to another double berth. Forward in both hulls were large storage areas accessible through deck hatches and these spaces were used for storing sails, the inflatable dinghy and the odd pieces of 'bric-a-brac' which we collected *en route*.

Between the hulls was a seven-foot wide area which extended the length of the boat and which again divided into three parts. The middle portion acted as the saloon, spacious enough to seat ten people comfortably and with almost enough headroom to allow you to stand without developing neck ache. The forward portion, which was accessed through a waist high hole cut in the bulkhead, provided yet more accommodation in the form of a twin berth cabin. This I shared with

Barry. The aft section housed a small but most serviceable chartroom and the external cockpit. In addition to all this, the toilet or 'heads' and a well-equipped work bench had been squeezed into the access ways of the starboard and port hulls respectively.

The Frenchman was still tidying away his lines by the time I had finished my breakfast in the saloon and so with almost half of the morning already gone, I joined Tom and Jean on a trip to the market to pick up some bulk vegetables for the next few weeks.

That night of my birthday was marked by a feast of Christmas Day proportions with plates of roast lamb and jacket potatoes and a sweet of strawberries with cream. After the meal the local harbour master, Antonio, who possessed the rare quality of becoming a nuisance through his over-enthusiasm to assist, took us to a nightclub in the centre of Porto to hear some Fado music. Fado is a traditional Portuguese genre of music. The word itself refers to singing but it is accompanied by instruments not unlike the bouzouki or large lute to look at, but with twelve strings. Predictably, the music sounded like a cross between traditional Greek and Spanish.

The following day, having explored Porto, four of us hired a car and set off into the interior. Like a typical British family, Tom, Jean, Karin and I loaded the little Renault 5 up to the gunwales with picnic baskets, cameras and the like, and headed north into the lake district of Portugal.

It was nice to be inland again and even nicer to be away from the yacht for a while. The roads were generally in an appalling condition, making the effort of avoiding potholes greater than that required for actual motoring. The construction of most roads was of a non-conventional nature, generally granite setts topped with a thin layer of black tar. The potholes had formed where the setts had become totally dislocated and removed, thus causing an extremely vicious 'wheel trap'.

Once clear of the coast, the scene became predominantly rural, each little village having its own elegant parish church, washed in china blue, with its own music-box-like chimes which would ring out on the hour and half hour. The whole area was much more green than we had expected, being not unlike parts of the lake district of Northern Italy.

The night was spent in a *pension* at a most reasonable price, more than could be said for the price of the hire car. The following day we returned to the yacht.

I was determined that this week, which had been forced upon us, was not to be wasted and so the morning after our return from the country I took a bus to the outside of town and with a rucksack suitably provisioned for an overnight stop, began hitching a ride south.

There had been enthusiasm from some of the other crew members but unfortunately we made an odd number and so I decided that if any progress was to be made at all it would have to be made alone. Well, the idea was admirable, however hitching didn't seem to be as readily acceptable here as it was across the border in Spain and so instead of sticking rigidly to my original plan of heading for Lisbon, I took whatever I could get in the way of lifts and soon found myself scudding down the coast road using a number of small rides with long waits in between – but at least it was southwards. This northwest coast seemed to be quite a popular little 'riviera' with the Portuguese and the miles of sandy beaches made it easy to see why.

Anyhow, by five o'clock I decided that enough was enough. I was bored with my own company and had no real motivation to make an overnight halt just for the sake of it, so I made my way to the nearest train station and paid the incredible sum of twenty-five pence for the one-hour journey back to Porto. The following day, down but not out, I spent washing and typing and then headed up to the station again. I had noticed, during my travels the previous day, billboards advertising a bullfight in one of the small towns through which I had passed and I felt that the effort had to be made to return.

The bullring at Espinho was not a very grand affair from the outside but was everything a bullring should be inside. The golden, swept carpet of sand which made up the floor of the arena, the band and trumpeters ready to herald the arrival of the picadors and matadors, and that unmistakable atmosphere of tense expectation.

A Portuguese bullfight is conducted in a very different manner from its more famous Spanish counterpart. For a start, the bull is not actually killed. The 'fight' begins with the bull facing a mounted banderillero, I don't know what the correct name is for him but he would be dressed and mounted on horseback like a picador but armed like a banderillero, with three-foot-long barbed darts or banderillas. The horsemanship which these men displayed in getting the darts secured to the bull's nape surpassed anything which I have ever witnessed. At times the horse would be made to lead the bull at a canter with the bull so close to the horse's rump as to be almost – but never quite – scratching it with its horns. Then the horse would veer away, circle and turn in on the charging bull, approaching it head on, swerving left and right in order to create confusion.

Just as the bull was upon the horse, the horse would double step like a footballer in a tackle, leaving the deadly horns only a hair's breadth from its totally vulnerable flank and enabling the rider to place the dart gracefully and accurately in the bull's nape. In placing the dart, the rider would simultaneously snap off the shaft about a foot from the barb. This would release a fan or similar decoration rather like a clown producing a flower from his jacket. This performance would be repeated four or five times depending on the skill of the horseman, with matadors playing the bull in the usual way in between attempts.

When the bull was suitably adorned with flags and fans, the horse would be ridden off to be replaced by a team of about ten men looking a bit like a circus troupe of tumblers. With the bull against one side of the ring they would arrange themselves, with one fellow in the centre of the ring facing the bull, another about ten paces behind and with the remainder bunched behind him, on the opposite side of the ring to the bull. Unlike in Spanish bullfights, the bull at this stage is still extremely lively and so when he turns to charge the fellow in the centre of the ring, who is shouting taunts at him, it is with no half-hearted effort.

The man in the centre stands his ground and then, as the bull is upon him, he launches himself through the horns, grasping the bull around the neck, his legs still dangling over its head. The job of the remaining troop is to act as brakes to stop this charging mass before it reaches the far end of the ring. Having stopped the charge, the whole team suddenly break loose as one, and the bull is now free to be led out by half a dozen cows which are herded in and then out of the ring. As with Spanish fights this performance is then repeated with five more *toros bravos*.

Encouraged by the success of this last little venture out on my own, I decided the next day, the 9th, to take an early train and travel the one hundred and eighty odd miles south to Lisbon. Arriving around lunchtime and leaving during the early part of the same evening, the day proved an all-round success. The travelling was relaxed and Lisbon turned out to be quite a pleasant city in which to be a tourist.

Portugal's capital city is not the sort of place which makes an instant impression on you for anything in particular: like Venice for its canals; New York for its skyscrapers; or Paris for its wide boulevards. Yet it was a memorable city if only for its overall pleasantness. From a tourist's point of view, Lisbon is split into two parts. The first is the sixteenth-century part, of which little is left except the Tower of Belem and the Jeronimo Monastery. These alone though were worth the bus trip out of the centre. Close to this old area is Lisbon's greatest (or at least most obvious) landmark: a huge steel suspension bridge so similar to the Golden Gate bridge in San Francisco as to look almost out of place.

The second area to be visited as a tourist is the city centre and this comprised the major part of my visit. Fairly compact and rectangular in layout, the newer part of the city produced a pleasing blend of old-style buildings within a modern framework. The effect, however, was almost nicer from above than from ground level. The bird's eye view can be achieved by climbing up through the narrow, winding, cobbled streets which lead from the city centre up towards the old pre-Christian castle. From here the view was magnificent. The whole city spread before you with the river, and finally the open sea, beyond. A very pleasant day's sight-seeing, with just enough time for a cool beer under the shade of a tree in a small cobbled square in the old quarter, before heading back to the station.

By the time I had taken my day trip to Lisbon we were getting towards the end of our vigil in Porto. However, I did manage to squeeze in a day on the beach before we left. This meant returning by train to one of the little seaside resorts which I had come across on my hitch-hiking trip. These last few months must have had some effect on my overall temperament since I could now spend a whole day on the beach and require little else in the form of diversion. Something which would have been unheard of before the trip!

On the 12th of July we finally cast off from our quayside home in Porto and headed out to sea, first only to Leixoes to pick up the engine parts, and then southwards to Aveiro, Portugal's 'little Venice'.

Although prior to our departure from the UK in June much of my time had been taken up revising for and subsequently sitting my professional civil engineering exams, I had left both my job and the country without knowing the results of my seven years of effort. Whilst in Aveiro, I discovered that my confidence and optimism had been well founded. However, hearing the news that I had passed my exams was one of the biggest anti-climaxes I had ever experienced. In the space of a two-minute phone call all the anxiety and anticipation which had been building up over the preceding months suddenly dissipated, leaving a great void. I couldn't even bring myself to fill it with joy. Instead, I went back to the yacht, told the others in a matter of fact way and went out into the cockpit to sit alone with my thoughts. After many years of taking exams I have come to the conclusion that there are few things which are more intensely personal than a hard-fought battle for qualifications.

The stop in Aveiro was just long enough to dry out and reconstruct the various bits and pieces which went to make up the new crown wheels and shaft for *Ocean Winds'* engine. Then we were off again, but not quite as promptly as we had planned.

Our first attempt at crossing the bar had to be aborted and we ended up anchoring just inside the river mouth to wait for the turn of tide at five o'clock the next morning. The countryside around us consisted of vast marshlands, not unlike the Camargue in southern France, all draining through an inlet a few hundred yards wide. It was therefore not surprising that the tides across the bar were terrifying and so timing was essential. However, on our second attempt we were better prepared and once across the bar the open water of the North Atlantic stretched before us. We trimmed sails and set a course for Madeira.

For the first day or two we were favoured by a good force-five wind and we made an average speed of six knots. Unfortunately, we also suffered an unduly large beam sea (that is to say, a sea that approaches the boat side-on) some sixteen feet from trough to peak, and I have to admit that for the first day and a half I had to resort back to the old pills to ward off seasickness.

Seasickness is a most curious problem which seems to strike quite arbitrarily, with little rhyme or reason. Some, like Tom, have never suffered from it in all their life at sea. Others, like Jeanette or Jean, rarely went to sea without suffering. Personally, I fall somewhere in between these two extremes. During our first two months at sea I suppose I felt queasy at some stage on just about every passage, though generally when the boat was moving through a beam sea or alternatively when the boat was bashing its way to windward, causing it to see-saw, back and forth, often crashing with alarming force down into the waves before shuddering and then lifting itself clear. Then suddenly the seasickness would stop and for four months I wouldn't suffer the slightest discomfort until one day, quite out of the blue, back it came again. Anyhow, thankfully after our third day out from Aveiro the wind veered, settling down to a steady force three on our starboard quarter – a far more comfortable motion in that the wind is neither directly in line with the direction of travel nor side-on, but comfortably between the two.

I took advantage of this particular leg of the journey to get to grips with astro-navigation, a subject which had fascinated me since the days when my father would tell me bedtime stories of his life as a navigator on merchant vessels during the war. The sextant at my disposal was a 1914 model not unlike my father's which now sits in my study at home. Yet this old instrument was still in an extremely good condition and capable of giving me morning, noon and afternoon sights, resulting in position fixes which agreed with the SAT-NAV to within a couple of miles.

My whole day now revolved around getting good 'shots' at the sun, providing me with an interest which kept me as happy as a sandboy!

One night during the passage, to my secret delight, the marvellous SAT-NAV went down, due to a fault in our electrics. Suddenly all my diligent calculations became relevant. Two hours later, however, our electronic friend was back on its feet again, and once more I slunk back into antique obscurity, clutching my sextant and dividers.

During the last night of this five-day passage I had some unexpected company on my watch. At around fifteen minutes past midnight I began to notice the phosphorescence of breaking water where no breaking water should have been, and then a couple of feet off our starboard quarter the familiar noise of a dolphin exhaling – but was it? With no moon to see by and knowing that something was out there, something large, and that we were in whale waters, the experience was a little unnerving! However, the one dolphin was soon joined by others and now that it was clear that we were not about to be bumped, the company was most welcome.

Land was sighted at four o'clock on the 20th of July. Unfortunately, the navigator was not the first to spot it as he was asleep in the sun on the foredeck! That evening we arrived at the island of Porto Santo in the Archipelago of Madeira. All the islands in the group rose starkly out of the Atlantic, forming a dramatic backdrop as we lay at anchor in one of the few little bays which provided shelter outside the island's man-made or developed harbours.

Any journey of more than a day left everyone feeling in need of a good night's sleep and a good wash, so the following day we spent swimming and sunning ourselves on the shore. The rocky nature of the coast had given rise to some very good diving grounds just offshore, teeming with fish, so the more aquatically minded of us donned flippers and goggles in the hope of pulling up some octopus for lunch. The attempt was only thwarted by the fact that there was no octopus to be seen.

By mid-afternoon with everyone suitably refreshed, we set sail for the main port on Porto Santo, a fishing village of the same name as this seven-mile long island. Here we were sheltered enough from the Atlantic swell to carry out a more thorough repair to our forestay which had broken dramatically during the last few miles of our main passage to the island. Thankfully the yacht had twin independent forestays and was cutter rigged so the damage, however dramatic it may have sounded when it came crashing onto the deck, did not affect the safety of the mast.

After a short and uneventful trip ashore and a restful night at anchor in the harbour, we set sail the following morning for the largest island of Madeira, some twenty-five miles away. Funchal is the main town on the island housing two-thirds of the population of the whole group of islands. It is every bit the tourist spot with a splendid marina and a wide seafront boulevard with cafes and white-aproned waiters. It was here that we had that extra special treat of mail and here that I made my decision to stay with the expedition beyond September, deferring my admission to Cranfield by twelve months to the following September.

Once again it was one of those 'spur of the moment' decisions, since until our arrival in Funchal this alternative hadn't really been a serious option. Yet suddenly it seemed foolish to have invested so much time and energy only to abandon the expedition on its arrival in South America, even before the main purpose of the journey, our trans-navigation of the Amazon delta, had been attempted. With the decision made, all my concerns regarding our progress evaporated and I slipped into 'low gear' once more.

In order to gain a better overall impression of the island we decided, on the Monday afternoon, to be good tourists and take a bus trip up into the interior. We found the island to be much greener than its smaller counterpart, with thick forests of pine and eucalyptus growing on the steep volcanic slopes and giving off the most gorgeous aroma.

The island as a whole had a sub-tropical feel to it, the main crop being bananas, followed by vines for the famous Madeira wine. All crops were grown on narrow terraces painstakingly won out of the mountainside, reminding me distinctly of Nepal. Our trip inland ended with the compulsory visit to a wine cave to taste the 'real' Madeira and to nibble at some Madeira honey cake.

With a firm impression of Madeira in our minds and the prospect of limitless travel ahead, we set sail on the 24th of July to cover the two hundred and forty miles south to the Canaries. It had been our intention to sail to the Canaries via the deserted islands of the Selvagens (these islands lying only thirty miles off our course) but no sooner had we cleared the coast than the wind sprang up and the sea with it, making any thought of landing there impossible, so the idea was shelved.

It was rare that we ever managed to get a weather forecast before making a crossing. The day we set out from Madeira, however, we phoned the local airport and were given a favourable report of winds force three to four, northwest. The force seven gusting eight which subsequently hit us from the east was therefore a mite unexpected! During the day it moderated to a five, gusting six, which then remained with us until twenty miles off the island of Palma.

Seasickness again hit all of us bar Tom and so it was with much relief that we eventually sighted the island of Palma in the chain of seven islands which go to make up the Canaries. The attractive red roofs of Madeira were here replaced by the starker profile of the concrete apartment block, and in truth the sight of Santa Cruz de la Palma as we approached it (in need of the soothing sight of palm-fringed beaches and the fishermen's nets) did nothing to un-edge everyone's already fragile temperaments. The silver lining to this cloud, however, arrived in the form of a friendly expat who swam up to the boat soon after we had anchored.

Juliet was a teacher in her mid-forties who had been living on the island for the previous two years. The island is not noted for tourism because of its relative inaccessibility, and so English visitors were a rarity. Keen, therefore, to make the most of us, Juliet invited us to join her and some friends for a meal that evening in one of the local restaurants. It appeared that of the ninety thousand inhabitants on the island of Palma, about two hundred were British, and most of them were involved in the observatory which was jointly run by Spaniards, Dutch and British.

The soiree proved immensely enjoyable, and useful to us as new arrivals, as by the end of the evening we had secured a chamber concert for the following evening, a trip up to the observatory and an evening of dancing at a village fiesta south of Santa Cruz. During the days that followed, we got to know Juliet better and went with her and her friends to visit the island's attractions: pretty little churches, local pottery shops and some of the most splendid vistas. In the evenings when we were not dancing or concert going we would go out to one of the little mountain restaurants to sample the island's culinary offerings.

The day trip to the observatory was perhaps the most memorable of all as it gave us the opportunity to put the island into perspective. We hired a car for the day, along with a Dutch couple who held fairly senior positions at the observatory. The site for the observatory was chosen for its clear, stable air and, needless to say, these conditions were best at the highest point on the island. It took us around two hours of driving along dirt track roads, roughly hewn out of the mountainside, to climb the 8,000 feet from sea level to the site. The terrain was less forested than Madeira but bananas and vines were being grown in quantity on the terraced slopes. As we motored up above the tree line, leaving a cloud of fine dust behind us, I could not help feeling just a little homesick for South Africa and in particular the tiny village of Louwsburg in the Natal, which is where I had last struggled up dirt track, dusty roads to a mountain top site as a fledgling civil engineer. Dust, I think, lends a lot to a dry landscape, blending greens to browns and producing a most beautiful softening effect.

Close to the site, the volcanic landscape had been fashioned by nature to produce a terrain of the most exaggerated proportions; sheer drops of thousands of feet divided by narrow craggy ridges along which our road precariously wound.

The visit to the actual telescope was no less awe-inspiring and had the added advantage of being accompanied by a steak lunch. My only previous experience of telescopes had been the use of one belonging to my grandfather which, having a lens of almost two inches, thrilled me with its magnifying powers as I gazed up at the stars as a child. The observatory on Palma housed a telescope with a lens some 2.5 metres wide and at the time, construction was well underway for a 4.5 metre telescope on a neighbouring site.

Two days after our visit to the observatory, and tempted by the beauty of the island's interior, I took off once more. This time, hitching to save the car-hire fees, I headed south to visit the volcanoes which are a feature of the southern tip of the island. The largest of these, St Anthony's Volcano, is perfect in shape and form, rising bare-sloped from the sea and affording a commanding view of the peninsular from its rim. I hasten to add that this particular volcano was last active in the seventeenth century, not the case with its smaller neighbour which exploded into existence in 1971.

Having gratified my curiosity, I left this barren landscape of lava rocks and ashes behind and headed back once more through the banana and tobacco plantations. I had forgotten to mention the tobacco, when I was listing the island's agricultural interests, and am only prompted to mention it here because of the lasting impression which the large trays of home produced cigars, handed around in the restaurants, made on me.

All in all, when we set sail on Saturday the 4th of August for Cape Verde, we did so with warm memories of the island of Palma, its people and its customs. It seemed strange but pleasant, after such a short stay, to be able to bump into friends in the street or in cafes, or to visit a restaurant in the evening and be greeted by the proprietor or serenaded by a Spanish guitarist in a manner more usually reserved for long-standing friends than for acquaintances of only a week.

One of the last things I did before we set sail was to visit a doctor, who, through the medium of an interpreter friend, explained that the large and painful lump on my backside was in fact a haemorrhoid. This was bad news but not altogether surprising as moving around had become gradually more and more uncomfortable over the previous two or three days. What I really felt I needed then was twenty-four hours of remaining relatively still. What I got was something quite different!

Tristan Jones, in writing his sailing novels, is noted for the fact that in his stories he always seems to set sail in storm-force winds. I am, however, in no position to condemn this flair for the dramatic as it is something which I am beginning to recognise in my own account! Our departure from the Canaries was no exception. Two hours out of harbour and we were again flying along in a following wind of force seven to eight with me clinging to the guard rail, desperately trying to brace myself, and wincing as the boat pitched and rolled beneath me.

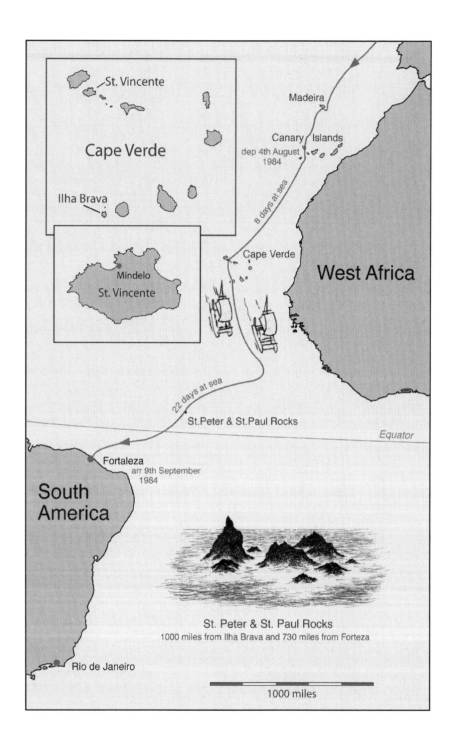

St. Vincente

Madeira

Cape Verde

Canary Islands
dep 4th August
1984

8 days at sea

Ilha Brava

Mindelo
St. Vincente

Cape Verde

West Africa

22 days at sea

St.Peter & St.Paul Rocks

Equator

Fortaleza
arr 9th September
1984

South
America

St. Peter & St. Paul Rocks
1000 miles from Ilha Brava and 730 miles from Forteza

Rio de Janeiro

1000 miles

CHAPTER THREE

The Atlantic Passage

The gale-force winds which we experienced on leaving Palma appeared to be fairly common around the islands. Whether or not this was simply due to the channelling effect of the islands I was unsure but, for whatever reason, the weather stayed with us for the remainder of the first day and most of the second. However, with the islands almost a hundred miles behind us the wind settled down to a pleasant force three and the sea with it. From then on we ambled along making about ninety miles a day, much of the time using self-steering and alternating our sails between the square-sail and two small genoas flown goose-winged from the forestays, that is to say one sail out to starboard and the other out to port. In general, we found that the square-sail gave more drive but always at the expense of steerage control, necessary for efficient use of the self-steering.

With no one suffering from seasickness, life onboard settled down to a quiet routine of eating, sleeping and standing watch. Jean had left us in the Canaries to return to her teaching job in the UK and so we were now having to fend for ourselves as far as food was concerned. This meant a three-day duty cook with the remaining four of us handling the watches, three hours at a stretch. When the sea is calm, the night warm and clear, and when the self-steering is working, a three-hour watch can pass very pleasantly. But in stormy conditions where every ounce of one's concentration is needed to keep the yacht free from broaching, that same three hours can leave you feeling totally drained.

To help pass the time on these extended watches I began using my personal stereo, taking Bach and Mozart into the cockpit with me. I was all the while terribly aware of the effect that the salty atmosphere has on all things vaguely electrical and so I used to take exceptional care to keep the unit dry and protected. In the end, however, this excellent form of entertainment fell foul of my own stupidity when, one day, I forgot to check the voltage setting on the ship's variable adapter, sending a full twelve volts through its four-and-a-half volt system. From then on music on watch was restricted to the noises of wind, water and strained rigging.

Fishing had always been a pastime and we must have baited, trailed and hauled in our multi-hooked line through nearly 2,000 miles of ocean since we left England, but by this time we still hadn't caught a single fish. All this didn't bode well for the squid-jiggling which we were about to begin.

Squid jiggling is the unlikely term used to describe the process by which squid are lured to the surface and caught. Ideally it is performed at night with the boat stationary, using a long line and a strong torch beam which is shone vertically down into the murky depths, highlighting the lure that is being 'jigged', or pulled up and down in a series of regular jerks, by the person in the boat at the end of a thirty yard line. All this was being done in the name of science, as along with the plankton sampling, which had been going on since Madeira, it formed the major part of a work programme we had agreed to do for the Marine Institute in Plymouth.

The programme, which was in essence just a data collection exercise, had been encouraged because of the particular route we were taking. Most trans-Atlantic sailing traffic leaving the Canaries prefers to head straight across in late October, after the Caribbean hurricane season has passed. Therefore, on hearing that our route would be taking us some two thousand miles further south, the Institute jumped at the chance of obtaining a few samples and equipped us with specimen jars, nets, strainers and preservatives, as well as some ingenious squid lures.

Despite our notable lack of success with the rod and line, fish still formed a major part of our diet. This we carried with us in the form of dried cod which hung suspended from the galley ceiling, a safe distance from the dried ham. Once soaked and cooked, the fish provided a tasty alternative to packet dried meat or soya. Now that we were getting so far south, very little food would keep for more than a 24-hour period. Fresh meat certainly had to be cooked the day it was bought, and fruit rarely lasted more than a few days. Indeed, a fruit crumble which was made up during a day of calm sailing and then not cooked because of a surprise storm, had begun to ferment overnight, so that by morning the crumble was visibly bubbling in the dish.

The passage to Cape Verde was notable for its lack of other vessels and in the eight days that we took over the voyage I think I only spotted two other ships on the horizon. There was, however, an increase in visible wildlife.

Flying fish were our constant companions, skimming across the waves in shoals, or 'flocks', of thirty or more at one time. There were no whales though, which was a little disappointing despite the fact that their great bulk close up to the yacht would have been a little unnerving. At night, the sea had other things to offer. Occasionally, whilst on night-watch, one's attention would be snatched by the sudden appearance of large numbers of bright flashes of light in our wake, light blue in colour and up to two feet in diameter, each flash lasting for up to two seconds with a dozen or more flashes appearing at one time. Interspersed by showers of sparkling phosphorescence the display had more in common with a personalised firework display than with the Atlantic Ocean. No one onboard either yacht had experienced the blue flashes before and we finally concluded that they must have been a form of jellyfish.

However, for me the night was beginning to take on another dimension as I started to get to grips with obtaining dawn fixes from the stars. I got enormous pleasure from learning celestial navigation especially since we were now beginning to depend more and more on the sextant for determining our position and progress. Although perfectly serviceable, the SAT-NAV took quite a lot of power and in down-wind sailing conditions this could put quite a strain on the battery. The root of the problem lay with the wind generator that we were using to keep our batteries topped up.

Looking rather like a miniature windmill this excellent device would generally be able to meet all our power requirements for free, negating the need to waste diesel running the engine for a couple of hours a day – our only other way of charging the batteries. In a down-wind situation, however, the apparent windspeed (that is to say, the real windspeed less the speed of the boat) was considerably reduced, meaning that our 'little windmill' would do little more than tick over. Thus, whenever we became involved in a long down-wind leg the SAT-NAV would be switched off and out would come the sextant.

As time drew on we, as a crew, began to bind together much better as a family. We would joke very freely about each other's complaints and ailments and nude sunbathing soon became accepted for those who were willing to risk an uncomfortable dose of sunburn! The maintenance of personal space however, remained of prime importance.

In this respect, I had expected many more cases of individuals retreating to their cabins, feeling the need to be alone for a few hours. In fact, this rarely happened; everybody seeming quite happy to be sociable for almost all of the time. I nevertheless began to wonder how this might change as the more prolonged confinements of the Atlantic crossing came into play.

During these long days at sea, each of us reverted to his or her own way of filling the time. For me this meant navigation and typing. Tom often used to read one or two books a day while Karin busied herself with articles that she was writing for a Norwegian journal. Jeanette (when she was not being sick) would read or sleep; and Barry, poor soul, used to fish. This being (on the whole) a most fruitless and frustrating occupation, he would concentrate the remainder of his efforts on carving a chess set from driftwood which he collected as we went along. This particular project proved amazingly successful and promised to produce quite a first-class chess set and perfect souvenir of the trip.

The ship's radio played quite a major part in our daily lives at sea. It was, after all, our only means of communication with the other yacht. Generally the conversations were fairly business-like, concerning navigational matters and speed adjustments required to keep the boats within sight of each other. Occasionally, however, we would abuse our monopoly of the airwaves to discuss lighter matters; like the day, much earlier in the trip, when Pat called up Jean to ask her to dictate a recipe for apple fritters, or later that week to sing her 'Happy Birthday' over the airwaves. Sadly on that occasion Jean was being sick over the stern, but the gesture was appreciated!

On the 8th of August we made our fastest daily average to date – one hundred and fifty-five miles, noon to noon – and as if to celebrate the achievement, our fishing exploits suddenly took a turn for the better. Not that we caught anything, just that during the night two flying fish landed on deck providing us with bait for our ever-available tuna line. Sadly, this move failed to turn the tide of our success and I began to think that we should give up the fishing altogether and settle for eating the flying fish that landed in our saucepan. I'm told they are not unpleasant but very bony.

The health of all onboard tended to be just about as topical as the weather. As Tom had predicted, constipation was a major offender. I believe this to be due to the fact that our stomach muscles were constantly tensing up, unconsciously, to cope with the motion of the boat. The unusual and unaccustomed nature of life at sea affected all of us in different ways. Normal bodily cycles became disrupted, obviously having a more direct effect on the girls than the boys onboard, but even with us the constantly changing daily routine caused by a rotating watch system seemed to throw the body generally off balance, resulting in upset stomachs and compounding the constipation problem.

This must seem extremely trivial. Perhaps it is. Yet, in the maelstrom of everyday life on land, the problems which make themselves most apparent are those concerned with the little things in life; trivia. At sea, or at least in a closed environment such as a yacht, the problems imposed are no different. At sea, one's whole life is made up of trivia. Sometimes the fact that we were on an expedition to the Amazon seemed totally incongruous with what we spent ninety-nine per cent of our time doing.

Around midday on Saturday the 11th of August, we sighted the islands of Cape Verde, or the Republic of Cabo Verde to give the country its official title. The visibility had been bad for the previous twelve hours and a good fix had been impossible. SAT-NAV had blinked off during the night due to a battery failure and so we only had dead reckoning (based, I might add, on very little local knowledge of currents) to determine our exact position. Consequently, we found ourselves in a bit of a quandary as we sat staring at the mass of featureless rock which lay shrouded in haze two or three miles dead ahead.

The problem arose from the fact that the archipelago of Cape Verde consists of ten main islands, three of which could constitute our present landfall. After much debate, comparing contours found on the chart with what lay before us, we proudly concluded that we had arrived at the correct island. It was a bitter moment when a few hours later we had to resign ourselves to the fact that we were wrong. Suffice it to say that by nightfall, having beaten up around some of the wildest coastline I have ever seen, we crossed the Canal Sao Vicente and dropped our anchor in three fathoms off the town of Mindelo on the island of St Vicente.

The islands of Cape Verde get their name from a green (verde) cape on the west coast of Africa some three hundred miles to the east. Looking at the islands before us we couldn't help feeling that the name was highly inappropriate. The landscape was classic mountain desert. Though the islands of Madeira and the Canaries rise steeply out of the Atlantic, neither could compare with the precipitous nature of these shores.

Not a tree nor a shrub nor even a blade of grass could be seen as we scanned the mountain sides. Where verdant valleys should have been the wind had made sand deserts and these areas constituted the only level ground that could be seen. We learned later that the island of St Vicente had not seen rain for over ten years.

Although the terrain for the other nine islands was said to be similar, not all the islands suffered the same drought conditions as St Vicente. It was here, however, that Cape Verde had its administrative headquarters and therefore to St Vicente that we had to come to clear into the country. It is often said by those who travel extensively in the third world that a newly independent country's greatest industry is bureaucracy. Cape Verde bears out this theory wonderfully. It took us two days of repeated visits to the port official's office to clear into St Vicente by which time Pat and Tom, who had taken the brunt of all the nonsense, were quite ready to leave.

Cape Verde had been an independent country for about nine years at the time of our visit. Before this time they had had five hundred years of Portuguese rule. Like their Mozambique comrades, the Cape Verdians had replaced Portuguese democracy with African communism, for although Cape Verde is three hundred miles out into the Atlantic, this is still very much Africa. Indeed, it took no effort at all, as I wandered around the dirty, beggar-ridden streets of Mindelo to imagine myself back in Maputo, Mozambique.

Mindelo is the largest town on the island and it takes about ten minutes to walk from one end to the other. Beyond the main town lay Africa's interpretation of suburban sprawls; miles of gaudy coloured, corrugated iron shacks set in debris-strewn, sandy plots, with hosts of snotty-nosed, jet black children playing with dogs and chickens or chasing after the odd truck as it trundled up the sandy track overloaded with people as they returned home for the evening.

Here lived the vast majority of the island's forty-five thousand population, a figure which represented a sixth of the whole country's population. Communication proved possible in many cases through the medium of French, and we were soon learning a lot about these people and their land. As the Portuguese left so did many of the jobs which had supported the community. What remained was a population living on a large rock where it was impossible to grow anything but the smallest amount of market garden produce; where unemployment was at a staggering seventy per cent; and where, until recently, water had to be brought by ship in containers. Nowadays a desalination plant provides drinking water.

In the marketplace there were more reminders of Mozambique. Nowhere could we find a fresh meat stall, and what vegetables and fruit we did find was limited to about four items: bananas, mangoes, green tomatoes and sweet potatoes. We were all grateful for the decision to stock up for the Atlantic in La Palma, as provisioning here would have been impossible. Wherever we went on shore we were escorted by two or three locals, generally children but often adults.

Unlike in India, where you felt fair game for anyone and everyone who wanted to sell things, buy things, beg things or just generally be a nuisance, here there seemed to be some sort of system. Dozens of kids would meet us on the shore as we rowed from the yachts but just who watched the boats for us and who followed us up into town seemed to have been pre-agreed by our welcoming committee before our arrival, as it all happened automatically and we never had any choice in the matter.

The two escorts who adopted me for our entire stay were Caesar, a fifteen-year-old, intelligent looking boy who had a very cool sense of humour and who spoke tolerably good English, and Fredo, a younger lad who wore a permanent and very welcome smile and with whom I spoke French. French, by the way, is the language these children are taught in school with English coming a poor second. At the time of our travels this had also been the state of affairs in Spain and Portugal.

Partly because of the difficulty of going anywhere ashore on one's own, and partly because whatever was available in the shops tended to be extraordinarily expensive, we found ourselves spending more time on the yachts than usual, making purposeful visits only to the town, rather than just wandering as we might have done in the Canaries.

There were, however, two notable exceptions to this and I shall now relate their stories. The first is a fishing tale. One of our escorts, a chap by the name of Rodriguez (who had earlier solved our washing problem by carting it all off to his mother's), put us in touch with a local boat owner. A shipping lawyer and one of Cape Verde's newly hatched middle class, this fellow had bought the boat, a twenty-foot timber proa (that is to say, a single-hulled vessel with one outrigger), from an Irishman who had sailed it there two or three years previously. Anyhow, the man, whose name I never did learn, invited us to join him on a fishing trip which he had organised for some friends the following morning.

The pilot for Cape Verde had many interesting pieces of advice to offer the would-be navigator, not least of which was a warning about the danger of shark attack within the harbour at Mindelo. This had done much to heighten our enthusiasm for a fishing trip and so at six o'clock the following morning, Karin (our fish enthusiast) and myself (a through and through opportunist) rowed over to join our friends from the previous evening, armed to the teeth with hooks, bait and expectation.

There were nine of us in all: our captain and host, four of his friends, two hired hands for the donkey work, and ourselves. I can't help smiling a wry smile whenever I come across this sort of situation in a 'new free democracy', especially an African one. Had this fishing trip taken place ten years previously, our host and his friends would have been white Portuguese and their act of hiring a couple of local 'blacks' as servants for the day would have heralded howls of righteous indignation from the 'thinking' black Cape Verdians. Yet straight into dead men's shoes step those very protestors in the guise of our goodly lawyer and his friends. Perhaps it appears that I am objecting to our host's behaviour. I am not. The bone I pick is with those who would condemn an act as being racially discriminative when, in fact, the issue is not black and white but classist.

Nevertheless, on this particular morning the sun was warm and shining, there was a cool refreshing breeze blowing and our host was offering the rare treat of cold beer, so I allowed political wrangle to take a back seat, and I settled down to enjoy a quiet morning's fishing.

The yacht was a joy to sail, though its rigging was extremely basic. Fortunately for us, the skipper was no sailor and was quite happy for Karin and me to handle that side of the trip. It was a great morale boost for us both, applying our slowly acquired knowledge on another vessel, successfully. In terms of the fishing, we trailed lines as we sailed and then anchored off a small rocky island for about an hour to fish and enjoy a beer. By the end of the morning we had amassed a total of around a dozen four-pound tunas, a few 'flatties' and a couple of red fish of about three pounds in weight which I took to be snappers. Sadly, only one of these fish was caught by the *Morvran* contingent.

It had always been my intention to see something of the interior of this island before we sailed on and so, with the fishing trip having rekindled the spirit of adventure in me, we returned to *Morvran* and rallied a shore party aiming to walk and hitch our way around the island spending the night under the stars.

By one o'clock in the afternoon our party was ashore with rucksacks full of provisions heading out of town on the desert road. I think that the locals thought we were mad. I too, began to question the impulsiveness of our decision, especially since we were navigating by a compass and a few garbled instructions from a local who had half-a-dozen words of German and even fewer of French. There were no maps of the island to be bought for love nor money and signposts were something one had learnt not to expect. Two hours out and we were passed by a truck heading for the airstrip at the extreme western end of the island. He stopped and offered us a lift. We accepted.

Despite the heat and the aridness of the terrain, it was good to be out of the town, away from our escorts and experiencing the harshness of what little life the island had to offer. From the airstrip, barely distinguishable from the desert floor into which it was set, we walked the remaining half-mile or so to the western extreme of the island. Here we found ourselves at the end of a blind alley. Ahead of us lay the Atlantic Ocean, while within half a mile to our left and to our right the desert gave way to mountains which we had seen on our approach to the island a few days previously. We were left with no choice but to return to Mindelo and then to head off in a different direction to the one we had just taken. This we achieved through a series of lifts (very easily obtained) until we arrived, just as the sun was setting, at the foot of the island's highest peak.

Sunset is swift in these latitudes, but we made what little use we could of the available dusk to clamber up away from the road and seek shelter for the night behind a rocky outcrop. As luck would have it, our sanctuary afforded us the most perfect view of the bay in which we had left the yachts and as the moon rose the wide Atlantic took on a silvery sheen in stark contrast to the blackness of the desert mountains which rose from its shores like the ruined steps of a Roman amphitheatre. The night air was cool but not cold, and we all slept well under our starry canopy.

At dawn, we arose and after a small breakfast, set off for the summit in order to reach our destination before the sun's heat became too intense. Our route took us along a well-laid track providing access to the transmitting station which took advantage of the summit's commanding position. As it happened, our precaution of an early start was unnecessary, since the mountain was acting as a focus for gathering cloud which would occasionally drop down sufficiently to wrap the top of the mountain in a curtain of mist. Fortunately, the mist was intermittent and our walk was rewarded by a most impressive vista stretching the whole width of the island. As the eagles soared around us, carried by the desert thermals, I could almost hear a small voice behind me reciting the words of Matthew 4, tempting me, from the highest mountain, with all the kingdoms of the world. The desolation of the land which lay before us was total; not a plant was to be seen nor an insect to be heard. Indeed, during the night when a fly had taken off from the rock above our heads, the silence which it had shattered had been so absolute that the noise had actually woken us up.

Our return to Mindelo was uneventful save for the well-earned drink that we treated ourselves to at the town's poshest hotel. The following morning, after gathering together what vegetables we could from the market and topping up the fresh-water tanks (calculated to give us half-a-gallon per person per day for our Atlantic crossing), we set sail from the island of St Vicente heading due south. With luck and a fair wind we hoped to fetch either the island of Fogo or the island of Brava on this course, both of these being part of the archipelago of Cape Verde and both lying about one hundred and twenty miles due south of the island of St Vicente.

The passage was straightforward with light and variable winds for the first forty miles and by the second night we found ourselves approaching Ilha Brava. However, our approach was made somewhat more difficult than it might have been by the fact that the lighthouse showing the northern-most point of the island had not been maintained and was therefore nowhere to be seen. The difference between what was marked on the chart and what existed in reality was becoming quite a problem as we worked our way around these tropical backwaters. This was an entirely different ballgame to navigating in the English Channel! And whilst it is easy enough to make this observation with hindsight, it is not so easy to break a life-long habit of navigating from buoy to buoy, or light to light, as the average British yachtsman is able to do. Thankfully, Tom was not your average British yachtsman, and so having given the helm the instruction to head due south for the Ilha Brava until the loom of Cima light came into view, he then made sure he was back on deck by the time the light was due and, seeing that it was not in view, checked his dead reckoning, concluded that the light had been put out, and hove to. Would I have sailed on until I hit the island of Brava itself, putting more faith in the Admiralty Chart before me than in my own rough calculations? I wonder.

'Heaving-to' is a manoeuvre which entails balancing the mainsail against a backed foresail, leaving the boat just off the wind and virtually stationary – in other words 'parked'! In this position we bobbed up and down and waited for dawn before making our final approach to the island.

Ilha Brava is about half the size of St Vicente which makes it around six miles north–south and four miles wide. The chart showed only two anchorages which offered any protection at all from the Atlantic swell. Both shelved steeply with very little room to swing, and so with apparently little to choose between them, we chose the first we came to. As we approached our anchorage with the morning sun just clearing the mist from the mountain slopes, it seemed that here at last was the ocean yachtsman's reward. Brava consisted of the same precipitous rocks which we found in St Vicente but here they were blessed by water and with water, life. Half a dozen houses lined the shore and behind them was a backcloth of palm trees and laboriously-constructed terraces, where banana trees and sugar cane could be seen growing.

Having anchored and made a little breakfast we went ashore to explore, very aware that our presence was a great novelty. For almost three hours we followed paths up mountain streams; paths which could have been lifted from the slopes of Annapurna. Then sweating like the proverbial pigs, we made our way back to the boats and here our euphoria was doused; bureaucracy had struck again.

It always amazes me that no matter how small the place or how far from civilisation it is found, officialdom in all its pomp and regalia will always search you out. So it was this fine morning on the Ilha Brava. It transpired that, on our arrival, a runner had been sent to the next village, where the island's constabulary lived, to inform them of our presence. Two of their number (or perhaps this was their number) then leapt upon their Russian motor bike and sidecar and, armed with malevolence, headed round to where we were anchored. Here, having examined our exit documents for St Vicente which stated that our next port of call was to be Fernando, Brazil, they told us to up anchor and leave. To reinforce the point, they commandeered a local fishing boat and proceeded to shout at us from the water until we eventually did, reluctantly, haul the anchor up and leave. I am willing to admit that this maybe a somewhat biased account, but I can't stand someone spoiling my fun! Thus it was that on the 18th of August 1984 at around half past three in the afternoon, we began our Atlantic crossing.

Weather in the Atlantic Ocean is governed by two large high-pressure systems, one north of the equator and one south. In the north, Atlantic winds and currents rotate about the centre of this pressure system in a clockwise direction, while in the South Atlantic they rotate in an anti-clockwise direction. Where the two systems meet, there exists an area of light and variable winds known as the Doldrums. In making our passage from Cape Verde to Brazil we had to pass from the northern weather system through the Doldrums and into the southern weather system.

Being still some five hundred miles north of this division we left Ilha Brava expecting the full benefit of the northeast trades and the corresponding current. The disturbing effect of the islands, however, dominated the first fifty miles of our journey, giving us fluky and light head winds. A most frustrating start to the long voyage ahead.

The southerly winds were with us for so long in fact, that we began to wonder whether the doldrum belt hadn't pushed five degrees further north than usual. However, two days out the northeast trades reasserted themselves so that, for a while at least, we made good progress south with a comfortable force three on our quarter.

In order to fetch the St Peter and St Paul rocks, which lie more or less bang on the equator in a direct line between the Cape Verde islands and Fernando, we had to steer a 'dog's leg' course juggling the equatorial counter current to give us as much easting and southing as possible, so that when we eventually reached the southeast trades we would not find ourselves faced with a beat to windward in our attempt to find the rocks.

The pilot book, *Ocean Passages of the World*, now in its third edition having been first published in 1895 advised that in August, on our present course, we could expect to meet with the doldrum belt at between ten and twelve degrees north of the equator. On the 22nd of August as we sailed across the 11th parallel, the northeast wind which had been dying away during the night, was replaced by a gentle southerly breeze, while in the distance we could see the gathering thunder clouds of our first doldrum squall.

The pilot describes the Equatorial Trough or Doldrums as having the following features: light and variable winds alternating with squalls, heavy rain and thunderstorms. A mixed bag at the best of times! One minute clear skies, brilliant sunshine and light southerly breezes, the next minute the yacht would be thrashing away under a working jib with rain falling so heavily that in less than an hour we were able to replenish our entire fresh water supply. During these squalls, the sky would be alive with blinding flashes of sheet lightning, which at night would flood our ocean stage with dramatic effect, as our two small boats pitched and tossed their way through the driving rain and seas. Yet in an hour the wind would die away to nothing and the menacing clouds would disappear as quickly as they had appeared. Other days the skies would remain overcast all day and light rain and drizzle would drive everyone to their beds. Such was our passage through the Doldrums.

Since leaving Cape Verde, we had noticed a marked change in fish life. In our passage south from the Canaries we had become accustomed to large shoals of flying fish, turning the waters white as they broke the surface in their hundreds, or landing on the deck at night, to be found stiff and dried by the morning. But after leaving Cape Verde these extraordinary little fish were seen only occasionally, and in far smaller numbers than before.

In their place, porpoises, dolphins and the odd pilot whale were now more frequently encountered. Often during a heavy downpour, dolphins could be seen throwing themselves clear of the water landing with an almighty splash on their backs. To my mind, this most extravagant behaviour was just playfulness, though I am told that the fresh rainwater helps dislodge unwanted parasites and that it is for this reason that the dolphins jump. On a long night watch their company was especially welcome.

I remember one evening in particular, when the phosphorescence was spectacularly bright and I was visited by a number of dolphins. The sea exploded into a thousand tiny particles of brilliant white light as the creatures broke the surface and then, as they dived to pass under the boat they trailed a beam of phosphorescent glow behind them like a laser beam from a science fiction movie or a scene from *Life of Pi*. As the water temperature increased, I had expected to see more evidence of shark activity. However, the only shark that any of us saw during the crossing was a four-footer which the crew of *Ocean Winds* noticed, to their horror, swimming around the boat while they were having a quick dip by way of a bath one afternoon.

While we were in the Doldrums, washing was no problem since we were guaranteed a shower at least once a day in soft refreshing rainwater. As for keeping clothes clean, life had never been simpler. My entire wardrobe for the crossing consisted of a sarong which I knocked-up from some material bought in Mindelo – I'd become quite a dab hand at the old sewing machine by then – and a tee shirt, which I would occasionally slip on for a night watch. The sarong, simply a rectangular piece of material which is gathered around the waist and tucked in, was wonderfully suited to the climate since it provided cover from the burning sun but at the same time did not cling – and so allowed perfect freedom of movement.

As the days drew on we all settled into our own routines again, enjoying the luxury of having a whole ocean to ourselves. Barry by this time had taken upon himself the role of chief cook, and with no one feeling in the slightest bit sick he was having to bring all his culinary expertise and imagination to bear on the problem of feeding us.

Soya-bean 'nut roast' with roast potatoes became a speciality and the evening meal was the focal point of the day. Many-a-time I would sit in the cockpit enjoying the evening sun, sipping my warm gin and tonic (now without lemon), debating whether or not dinner would fall before my watch (allowing me to enjoy it in peace) or whether I would be forced to perform nautical gymnastics – dashing between the saloon and the cockpit to check the self-steering and our relative position to *Ocean Winds*. It was a hard life at sea!

To make the best use of the prevailing winds and currents, the pilot book had advised us to keep a southerly course from Cape Verde until we hit the doldrum belt at between ten and twelve degrees. Here, we should expect to find the northeast trades dying away to be replaced by variable, but prevailing southerly breezes and the pilot advised that we accommodate these on starboard tack, thus making a southeasterly course. This we should hold until latitude five degrees north, where we could expect to find the east-going equatorial counter current replaced by the west-going current of the southeast trades. The southeast trade winds themselves should also have asserted themselves by then, giving us a broad reach on port tack all the way to St Peter and St Paul where the wind should back to an easterly allowing us a run for the remainder of the trip across.

'Fine', I hear you say, 'I can follow all that without too much of a grimace', but did it actually happen like that – did it heck! The light southerly breeze which we encountered on entering the doldrum belt at latitude eleven, soon veered to give us SSW allowing us a touch more southing in our dog-legged course than we had hoped for, but it remained like that as we sailed past five degrees north, then four degrees, then three ... by now things were getting beyond a joke, we were still on starboard tack heading further and further away from our destination with every hour that passed and still the wind did not back. Where were the trade winds? In the end we decided that this southerly wind which by now had become a stable force four was in fact the southeast trade blowing from the wrong direction, so on the 31st of August at latitude three degrees north, we put in a tack and began heading just south of west, slowly eating up the hundred or so miles which the last few days on starboard tack had cost us.

We continued sailing on that tack for four days and four nights, close-hauled in an effort to lay the islands of St Peter and St Paul, despite the trades. Bashing and crashing through the North Atlantic, constantly having to bear away as the wind headed us, we moved slowly further and further west.

During the night of the 3rd of September, at a position of 00° 50' north, 28° 00' west, the wind backed to the southeast. We heaved a sigh of relief, eased the sheets and relaxed into the more comfortable motion of a beam reach as we completed the last hundred miles to the islands.

I use the word 'islands' since that is the term we used whenever we referred to St Peter and St Paul. Indeed, the pilot wouldn't have you believe otherwise. It referred to 'a seven-fathom bay' and 'safe anchorage in calm weather', terms suitable enough to conjure up visions of a restful couple of days with perhaps the odd barbeque on a palm-lined beach. The pilot, chiefly constructed from reports submitted by square-riggers and published in the nineteen twenties, confined itself to the facts, and in that respect it could not be said to be wrong. Indeed, the position which it gave for the rocks was extremely accurate and we all felt a glow of self-satisfaction as they appeared on the horizon at the appointed time and dead ahead. Our enthusiasm, however, soon paled as we drew closer to our landfall and began to realise the true extent of these 'islands'.

Gnarled and jagged, like the half-eaten rocky remains one might find off a storm-wrecked peninsular on the Cornish coast, the rocks of St Peter and St Paul broke the Atlantic swell over an area three hundred yards by one hundred yards. Between the peaks, the highest of which was no more than sixty feet, the sea crashed through in foaming cascades. Any hope of shelter was soon forgotten. On the lee-side of the island the rocks were so placed as to form a very small but distinct bay. All around its narrow mouth, however, jagged rocks, like the teeth of a barracuda's jaw, stood threatening those who would be over-intrepid.

As we lay off the rocks, hove-to in a force three with very little swell, we tried hard to imagine a square-rigged vessel lying at anchor in that pitiful excuse for a bay. We could only conclude that the ravages of time had taken their toll and that when this valiant vessel had made its bid for the record books the conditions must have been considerably more favourable.

As the sun was about to set, and the seabirds were returning to their exclusive haunt, we turned our backs on the 'islands' of St Peter and St Paul and set a course for the Brazilian mainland, still some six hundred miles away.

Our southeast wind, to be truthful, had more south in it than east, and it soon became apparent that to lay a course for Fernando was going to be impossible. This was a disappointing blow, since we were all hopeful of mail there, but the wind is the final arbitrator in all such decisions, and so on the 6th of September we adjusted our course to lay Fortaleza, a city of some one-and-a-half million people, three hundred miles further up the Brazilian coast. On the evening of the same day we parted company with *Ocean Winds*, who, because of a self-steering problem, had opted to steer a more indirect route to the port.

That last few hundred miles seemed to take an eternity, although in fact we made some of the best average speeds of the journey. During the morning of the 7th of September the wind backed sufficiently to allow us to bend on our trusty square-sail, the first such opportunity since leaving Cape Verde. The current too became more evident as we approached the coast, and for much of the time we were achieving a speed over the ground in excess of seven knots.

On the evening of the 8th the wind finally came around to the east and we ran before it as we sailed over the edge of the continental shelf to begin our final approach to Fortaleza.

The shelf off the east coast of Brazil falls away dramatically into the Atlantic, so that at one moment we would be sailing with two thousand fathoms of water under the keel, while the next there would be only thirty or forty, and then as little as fifteen – a fathom being six feet. This point of transition is very apparent as the swell of the Atlantic is suddenly forced into relatively shallow water. This has the effect of pushing the seas up to form a steep foam-crested sea in the slightest weather. So it was, that with a force four wind blowing over our stern, we surfed and yawed our way across the last thirty miles of our ocean passage.

As soon as we had crossed over, onto the continental shelf, the seas around us became as busy as the Isle of Wight in Cowes Week. These boats, however, were all fishing vessels, presumably out of Fortaleza and throughout the night we steered our way through them and their nets. By dawn, the industrial spread of Fortaleza was visible on the horizon and we edged our way gently through the shoals which afflict this coastline, keeping a careful eye on the echo sounder until we emerged into the safety of the navigation channel.

By lunchtime, our time, boat time, GMT, we were at anchor off a sandy beach which ran along the waterfront of the old part of Fortaleza. The red roofs of the old quarter went well with the lush green of palm trees and others which lined its streets and squares, and indeed the picture was not unduly spoilt by the backcloth of modern Fortaleza, which towered above and all around this nucleus. After a pleasant lunch and a well-deserved siesta, we weighed anchor and made our way round to the main port area to face the rigours of bureaucracy once more.

Since leaving Ilha Brava in Cape Verde, we had travelled 1,950 miles which, for a journey time of twenty-two days, works out at an average speed of 3.7 knots. The rhumb line distance or straight-line distance via St Peter and St Paul is 1,520 miles.

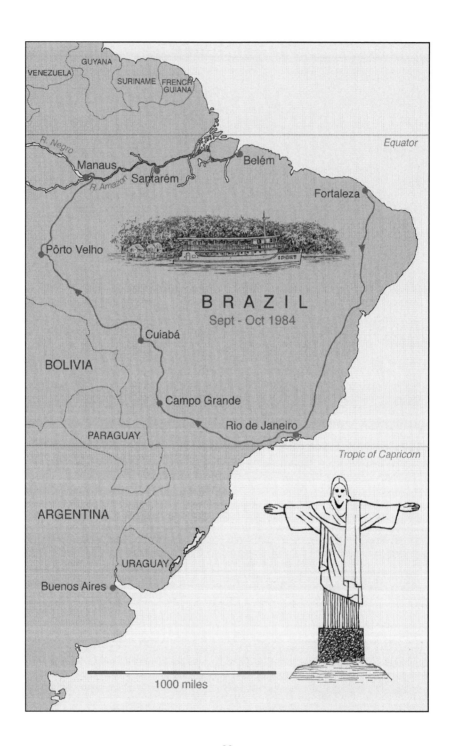

VENEZUELA

GUYANA

SURINAME FRENCH GUIANA

Equator

R. Negro

Manaus

Belém

R. Amazon Santarém

Fortaleza

Pôrto Velho

B R A Z I L

Sept - Oct 1984

Cuiabá

BOLIVIA

Campo Grande

Rio de Janeiro

PARAGUAY

Tropic of Capricorn

ARGENTINA

URAGUAY

Buenos Aires

1000 miles

CHAPTER FOUR

Brazil

Fortaleza was, at the time of our visit, a city of about one-and-a-half million people which, having grown out of a very small old quarter, now spread itself for almost twenty miles along beautiful sandy beaches.

Here you could sit under the shade of a palm tree and enjoy the warm sea breeze with a cold beer or coconut juice. In fact, ordering your first coconut drink is quite fun because a guy just shins up the tree you're sitting under, cuts one down, lobs the top off it with a machete, sticks a couple of straws in it, and presents it to you as coolly as if he had just pulled you a pint of beer. These are, I hasten to add, green coconuts which is to say they are full to the brim with juice, very little of it having been turned into flesh. Later the milk will form flesh and the green outer husk will fall away or be turned into mats. The brown, hard shell with which we are more familiar, will then be exposed.

The old part of Fortaleza was quite interesting with lots of markets and narrow streets and, on the whole, the place was quite clean. But the real focus of attraction was its seafront, with mile upon mile of gorgeous beaches, skyscraper hotels and all the other trappings of a seaside town. Further along the coast, on the outskirts of town, was the yacht club, and then close-by to that, the local fishing fleet and finally the port of

Fortaleza. The yacht club appeared to be primarily a social club as there were no local yachts there at the time and only two other foreign yachts.

During our first few days we had a great deal of contact with the local fishing fleet as we beached the boat to re-do the antifouling and repair a few leaks. The fishing boats which are used along the Brazilian coast are called 'jangadas' and are a raft-type sailing boat with very little freeboard and a disproportionately large sail area. The sail, made of cotton, is supported on a huge boom which pivots on a short mast. When sailing, the boats, which varied in length between twenty and thirty-five feet, look similar to large arab dhows and present a most majestic sight as they sail back into the bay in the evening, having navigated themselves thirty miles out to sea and back without the aid of a compass. On arrival these boats are hauled manually up the beach on logs with the aid of twenty or so bystanders. In keeping with the rest of the 'design', the anchors used by these vessels consist of a quantity of rocks contained in wicker baskets.

The Fortaleza fleet was quite large and its crews were very friendly and so we were never short of hands for manoeuvring *Morvran* into a suitable spot on the beach to carry out our maintenance work. However, unlike in Europe, no one spoke anything other than Portuguese, making even the simplest tasks a great trial. Eventually we found ourselves approached by a Brazilian fellow by the name of Armondo who could speak good English and who promised to take up our difficulties and play 'host' for our stay.

Armondo, who was secretary of the fishing cooperative in Fortaleza, was full of little gems of information, like the fact that up until five years before our visit, Fortaleza's one-and-a-half million population relied entirely on septic tanks for sewage disposal. The achievement of installing a complete piped sewage network is celebrated in a magnificent piece of modern art which dominates the sea front. A closer inspection reveals that it is constructed from a large piece of one-metre diameter sewage pipe. How much more appropriate than a statue to some bloody General! According to Armondo the main industry in Fortaleza was cashew nuts, which were grown locally and exported. Its second major interest was the processing and exporting of lobster. At the time, Brazil was the second biggest producer of lobster and all of it was fished and processed in Fortaleza, some 2,000 tonnes per year.

Whilst running around with Armondo in an effort to get some materials for the boat, I had the privilege of being shown around one of the larger processing plants where the lobster and red snapper were being prepared for the American market. It is worth recording that the standards of hygiene which I noticed during this tour were equal to any that I have seen in British food factories.

Cleanliness everywhere in Fortaleza had been impressive and nowhere more so than on the beaches. The Brazilians are great beach folk and seem to take a zealous pride in their foreshore. However, it is not hard to see why they are so beach orientated as I have never in my life seen such pure sand on a beach. Without any fear of exaggeration, to run your hand over the sand on these beaches is just like running your hand through pure silk, the particles are so fine. And yet, these grand beaches also provided evidence of the great divide between rich and poor in Brazil. Beach-buggies were a craze, typical of the time, driven by the wealthy 'playboys' of the city. Indeed, the rich appeared to live very well in Brazil, but their lives contrasted very starkly with those of the poor, who lived in shanty towns built amongst the shifting sand dunes on the outskirts of the town.

After eight days in Fortaleza we still hadn't managed to get very far away from the city, and I could see a golden opportunity to visit Brazil's interior slowly slipping by. So, having sweet-talked Tom into taking *Morvran* up the coast short-handed, Karin and I set out to make a four-week condensed tour of the interior. Our first leg was an 1,800-mile, 48-hour coach journey south to Rio de Janeiro.

The standard of coach was our first surprise. I had undertaken a good deal of coach travel in both Europe and the United States, but nowhere had I ever encountered a more luxurious vehicle than the one that we had just boarded. Twice as much legroom as National Express and with an onboard 'loo' which surpassed anything that British Airways had yet designed. Mind you, with nothing much to speak of in the way of a railway network and such large distances involved, the coach system was required to meet the majority of the country's public transport needs.

At first, the scenery was very much akin to the African bush with dry shades of greens and browns. Sisal was being grown as a cash crop and everywhere there were cacti to be seen – the variety being what one might typically expect to see in a cowboy movie. Outside the farms one would more often find horses tied up than cars and much of the porch would be given over to the drying of tobacco and sisal.

Every couple of hours or so the coach would stop for a break in order for everyone to stretch their legs and get a bite to eat. When these stops occurred in towns, it afforded us the opportunity for a quick walk around. A characteristic of all towns in Brazil appeared to be the prominent role played by the common black vulture. Far from being expelled from the community, he was actually encouraged and formed an essential part in the disposal of waste. Thus, wherever we were near people and dwellings, we generally found flocks of these large, clumsy-looking creatures.

As we passed from the state of Bahia into Minas Gerais, the bush landscape gave way to more lush vegetation with pastures replacing the acres of sisal, and rolling hills with craggy outcrops breaking up the horizon. Further south, coffee plantations began to dominate the scene in the same way as vineyards do in Burgundy. With the increased lushness came an increase in apparent prosperity. Farm buildings began to look far more grand and extensive, and gardens were adorned with a most colourful and varied selection of plants and trees.

Just as the land around was starting to take on the appearance of rural England, we emerged from the state of Minas Gerais and began climbing into the mountains which characterise the state of Rio de Janeiro. This last stage of our journey to Rio provided some of the most stupendous scenery that we encountered on the whole of our trip through Brazil. Fold upon fold of thickly forested 'sugar loaf' mountains. Tucked away, in picture postcard settings, we caught glimpses of the homes of Rio's rich and elite, but the real glory remained with the mountains. Few of the world's major cities can boast of such a backyard.

We arrived in Rio at the beginning of the rush-hour but managed to keep our cool through a trying hour of battling with buses and searching for hotels. Success was eventually rewarded with a room full of cockroaches and a shower which electrocuted me twice before allowing me the luxury of a cold wash. The cockroaches' two inches of body, preceded by a further two inches of feeler, we learnt to live with. And the shower, we learnt to use. So, with the considerable advantage of the price and the hotel's central position we were, by morning, quite pleased with our accommodation.

Breakfast was typical of all the cheap hotels in which we stayed in Brazil; coffee, rolls and butter. In this respect, Brazil seemed to have developed ahead of its European cousins, for where in France we British had come to accept the absence of bacon and eggs as a necessary constituent of breakfast, in Brazil we were required to accept that the jam or the marmalade must go too.

Rio is a city which, penned in between high mountains and the sea, has been forced to spread sideways. Each new area of development is linked to the last by a tunnel, since each new area is in fact the next bay down the coast. Thus, each area has its own beach around which all life revolves and after which each area is named. Hence the famous Copacabana and less famous but more exclusive area of Ipanima.

Our hotel was by Flamengo beach and thus in the area of Flamengo, which is the nearest area to the original downtown – our first port of call after breakfast. Downtown Rio was much as 'downtown' anywhere. Wide caféd boulevards and extensive shopping malls, but pleasant enough all the same. To get things into perspective, however, one had to view Rio from a distance. This meant either getting into a boat or climbing into the mountains behind the city. We opted for the former and took a ferryboat to the Ilha de Paqueta.

Few skylines can equal that of Manhattan when seen from the sea, but Rio has a jolly good try. As you pass under the nine-mile-long Rio to Niteroi bridge you have a splendid view of the bridge, with the city behind. The cable car can be seen rising to the top of Sugarloaf Mountain on one side of the city, whilst to the right of the city as you are looking, the famous statue of Christ the Redeemer stands high above the hustle and bustle below. The Ilha de Paqueta itself is a pleasant little island only a few miles across, inhabited at the time entirely by a few fishermen and those in Rio who could afford it as a second home. No cars were allowed and so a quick tour of the island was conducted by tandem cycle.

With time in hand at the end of the day, we decided to complete our views of Rio from a distance by taking the cable car up to the top of the Sugarloaf or Pao de Acucar as it is known locally. Vivid memories of the James Bond movie were relived as we made our way to the top. From the cafe on the summit, we scanned the city, picking out and naming the beaches which form the nuclei of this most curious city. In many ways it might be likened to a string of pearls, each pearl an entity unto itself, but connected to the next by a strong thread which, by passing through all the pearls, forms a necklace. The thread, in the case of Rio, being its tunnel and road network which connects up all the bays. Sadly, we had chosen a rather misty afternoon to make our trip up to Sugarloaf, and so with our curiosity satisfied, we headed back down into the city without much delay. The evening was marked by the most splendid meal of steak *fillet mignon*, as cheap a meal in Brazil as liver and bacon in England. However, in Brazil, they cut their steaks with a fork!

The following morning we rose early and took the bus to the foot of the funicular railway which would take us up to the summit of Corcovado or the Hunchback Mountain, where the one hundred-and-twenty-foot statue of Christ the Redeemer stands guard over this, Brazil's most prized city. The ride up takes you through some beautiful forest and the view from the top is staggering. Sitting at the top looking out, the weather having vastly improved since the previous night, and with a cold beer in hand, we planned the remainder of the day.

To find out what really makes Rio tick, you have to look to its beaches and its nightclubs. Sadly, with our limited resources, the nightclubs would have to remain undiscovered until a future visit. However, nothing was going to stop us spending the afternoon on the beach and so, with the compulsory visit to the Jesus statue firmly 'in the bag', we set off for Copacabana.

Early the following morning we left Rio for Campo Grande in the heart of Mato Grosso. This particular leg of the journey, some nine hundred miles, took twenty-three hours and was conducted in the same luxury to which we had become accustomed on our way down from Fortaleza. The scenery, however, was less than impressive despite a promising start with some beautiful stretches of mountain terrain. Nearer Campo Grande the land became much flatter and cattle ranches began to appear again. The state of Mato Grosso is very much the forgotten outback of Brazil. The scenery is monotonous and the area cried out for development. It is the state which borders with Bolivia and in many respects it seemed to have more in common with that country than with Brazil. Yet despite all appearances to the contrary, it is still a part of Brazil, and so the ram-shackled wayside cafe still served freshly ground coffee and the toilets were still furnished with toilet paper. And we still paid for it all at an electronic checkout, despite all the looks of impoverishment.

With only a short while in Campo Grande before our next bus, we took a stroll into town and bought some breakfast. Once again, not a blob of *confiture* was to be found. It appeared to us in the short while that we were in the town that considerable effort had been put into achieving some standard of architectural excellence in the town centre, but that this was in sharp contrast to the shabbiness further out, which was perhaps more typical of the region as a whole.

Three hours after arriving, we were aboard the bus again bound for Cuiaba, the capital of Mato Grosso. This journey, a total of four hundred and forty miles, was to take ten hours. The road from Campo Grande to Cuiaba skirts along the edge of the Pantanal, a swampland and naturalist's paradise about the size of Wales. However, we were not to see anything of the swamp until we were the other side of Cuiaba. Instead the terrain around us consisted of large rolling plains of bare red soil, dry but workable. We saw tractors here, the first since leaving Fortaleza; and ostriches, the first I'd seen in the wild since South Africa.

Cowboys too were back in evidence, a sight which enhanced the appearance of the small 'outback' towns that we passed through on our journey north.

Where the land was not ploughed, it reverted to scrub savanna with local areas of dense woodland, not unlike areas of Bahia. We kept the wide arable plains with us all the way to Cuiaba. Towards the end of the journey sugar cane became the predominant feature in the landscape, which by this time was being lit up by the most spectacular thunderstorm.

We eventually arrived in a very wet Cuiaba at about seven o'clock in the evening and began the search for a hotel. The drains were not coping with the downpour and the streets were consequently awash. Most restaurants and cafes had seemingly given up for the evening and were closing down, but by nine o'clock we had succeeded in finding a hotel to suit our budget, and so settled in for our first real night's sleep since leaving Rio.

Before finally turning in I made a phone call to a local American missionary, by the name of Dave Snyder, whose number we had been given by another missionary *en route* from Campo Grande. We had wanted to find out something of what lay ahead, as official information only covered the stage upon which we were about to embark. Indeed, at this point in the journey we were not even sure whether the road to Manaus was passable, let alone whether or not there existed a bus service along it.

Dave, it turned out, was equally in the dark. However, he was able to impart some local knowledge by telling us that the storm which we had experienced the previous evening was the third that they had had in a week, and that it was widely accepted as being the beginning of the rainy season. He also told us that the road which we had hoped to take the following morning into the Pantanal was not served by public transport, since it was frequently being washed away. In the morning we attempted to arrange to visit the area privately, but the costs were prohibitive so we abandoned the idea and caught an earlier bus out of Cuiaba heading north again for Porto Velho, an 880-mile, twenty-four hour journey.

Luck plays a great part in any trip like this where information is scant and knowledge of the language is even scantier, and on that particular morning as we motored out of Cuiaba, she was on our side. Quite unbeknown to us and in defiance of what would seem to have been logical, the bus route took us into the northern borders of the Pantanal and across to within twenty miles of the Bolivian frontier, before eventually heading north towards Porto Velho. So it was that we ended up seeing almost as much of this great nature reserve as we might have done had we succeeded with our original plans.

In appearance, the Pantanal was very similar to the French Camargue. Large expanses of marshy plain supporting some cattle and a wide variety of wildlife. Most abundant were the Ibis and Egret. It is well worth remembering though, that what we saw was the smallest portion of an area which is over five hundred miles long and two hundred miles wide.

We saw no signs of arable farming north of Cuiaba, at least not on the scale that had been so prominent a feature south of the city. Instead, the landscape was hilly, with thin bush or scrub. As we travelled further north the bush became thicker and the trees more substantial. We were approaching the great Amazonian rainforest, a landscape which was to become so familiar to us over the following weeks and months. Indicative of our approach to Amazonas was the appearance of a number of bush huts. These were similar in construction to those I remember seeing in a Zulu kraal, but rectangular in plan and fitted with hammocks slung either inside the hut or out on the 'stoop'.

Once firmly in the jungle, we came onto a section of road that had only been open a matter of a week or two. They were, in fact, still in the process of putting the finishing touches to the rainwater run-off channels. As we motored past one group of workers, I was amazed to find the foreman seated on horseback. In the circumstances I had to admit that there did not exist a more practical means of keeping an eye on things, however, it did create a rather contrasting image to the life I had left behind on UK construction sites!

The scar which this new road made on the landscape was profound. The shimmering black road surface bordered either side by the pale reds and yellows of the natural earth looked like a flesh wound which had been scored through this vast carpet of green. I can remember many years ago seeing a photograph of just such a road constructed through some other part of the Amazon, running straight as a die for as far as the eye could see. The photograph made a big impression on me at the time, and I can remember vowing someday to see such a sight for myself, horrified that by a single stroke we can create such wanton destruction in our beautiful world. Now I had seen it for myself, and the impression would still live with me for years to come.

At about three o'clock on the morning after leaving Porto Velho we passed from the state of Mato Grosso into Rondonia, a small state wedged between Mato Grosso and the state of Amazonas. However, before crossing the border we were all required to disembark and receive a yellow fever vaccination – or prove that we had had one already.

Thankfully we were able to do just that. But, queuing at the dead of night outside a small roadside hut in the middle of the jungle was to be as interesting as the jab was to our fellow passengers. The racket that issued from the jungle around us was deafening. Above our heads as we stood in the queue were paraffin lamps which had attracted the most extraordinary selection of moths, some as large as sparrows. I gawped like a half-brave puppy at these harmless, but unfamiliar, creatures of the night!

Our luxury coach was now acting as a local bus service, picking up passengers at every clearing. Sometimes whole families would get on, complete with all their possessions – our coach providing the only cheap removal service. By mid-morning we were down to 'standing room only' and still they piled on.

From the Rondonian border northwards we saw much evidence of pioneer farming. For the majority of the route, a half-mile of jungle either side of the road had been put to the torch (some areas only recently) and some attempt at farming had been made. Usually a small wooden shack had been established and a few Brahman cattle with their familiar white humps would be grazing the newly cleared ground. These areas were characterised by charred, bare tree trunks rising one hundred and fifty feet into the air, with new palms asserting themselves, a feature of the jungle and the first plant of any size to re-establish itself in the cleared land.

For the last sixty miles of the journey to Porto Velho, we were once again on a newly-constructed bituminous road. The new road meant new areas could be opened up to settle and so we found ourselves with the opportunity to witness, first-hand, true pioneering.

As we drove along the continuous line of jungle, it would suddenly be broken by the smouldering remains of what a few hours ago had been dense rain forest. In the midst of the clearing, which would always be a neatly defined rectangle of between one and two acres, there would stand a newly constructed hut, the palm roof of which would still be green, and somewhere among the charred timbers would be the figure of a solitary man, hacking at those parts of the jungle not fully defeated by the fire, with a machete. Here was today's frontier. The little towns and villages that we came to, reflected this frontier atmosphere. Being rarely less than sixty miles apart, they formed the centre for trade for a large number of settlers. Every other shop was either a general store or a hardware store, stocked with chain saws, machetes and the like.

We arrived at Porto Velho around midday and the heat hit us like a wall. With the rain forest all around us, the humidity was extreme and even the slightest effort induced a river of sweat. With all of the following day to kill before the bus left for Manaus, we invested in an air-conditioned hotel room. Like mad dogs we chose the middle of the next day to conduct a quick tour of Porto Velho.

Only once in my life had I ever been subjected to the kind of humid heat which suffocated us that morning in Porto Velho. The experience conjured up memories of mid-summer in Miami, Florida – only there I had had the luxury of an air-conditioned car in which to escape. Here we toured on foot. My only clear memory of Porto Velho is sitting in the shade of a railway museum gazing out over the Rio Abuna before trudging back into the town centre in search of another few glasses of guarana – a non-alcoholic drink made from the fruit of the same name which is native to the Amazon Basin. In taste, guarana is a curious blend of guava and passion fruit, but nearer guava than anything else.

On the evening of the 27th of September, we boarded the bus for Manaus. The standards were beginning to drop by now and the luxury coach that we had become used to was at this stage replaced by a very high-wheelbase, battered contraption, with a reinforced chassis and a large heavy-duty tow bar fore and aft. Needless to say, the inside 'loo' had long been removed. Night fell as we drew out of Porto Velho and a drunk began to sing at the back of the bus. He sang all night.

The road to Manaus had been surfaced ten years before with two inches of tarmac. Now this surface was old, and in many places broken up where the jungle had fought to regain control and had won. The rains had completed the job in these places by removing the broken pavement, completely exposing the sandy clay subsoil to the thunder and rain which now crashed around us as we drove through the night and the teeming rain.

Where the surfacing had been removed, the bus would lurch off the tarmac and into the clay, with a crash of the chassis as it caught the trailing edge of the blacktop. Slithering, sliding and rocking to get through the ruts, it would then crash back onto the road surface at the other end for a further one hundred yards of clear motoring before lunging through another fifty yards of clay. Often the bus was forced off the road altogether and into the bush to negotiate ruts. Though the jungle loomed impenetrable on both sides, the trees were not as substantial as I had expected and were not always dripping with lianas.

By this stage of the journey our coach had been joined by other vehicles, including another coach, heading for the same destination. The logic for travelling in convoy soon became clear as the quality of the clay surface was so bad in places that each coach would occasionally be needed to pull the other out of trouble, with the assistance of a lorry at the head. The traffic load on this the only road to Manaus from the south, was about one vehicle per hour – all lorries or buses – and so these points soon became great social gatherings and a chance for a chat.

At other places, where the road had been built on an embankment, for instance across a boggy area, half the road would frequently be found to have collapsed, complete with surfacing, leaving a perilously narrow strip of the embankment across which to negotiate the bus. At one such point we found a fully laden lorry completely overturned and lying by the side of the road with its glum-faced driver sitting on the top of his upturned chassis.

It was a long day and a night's drive to a town of any substance and the chassis of our bus was hitting the ground more frequently by now; each time the blow shaking the whole structure of the bus. In the rainy season this road becomes impassable and we began to feel that we had only just made it in time.

For every ten areas of cleared land adjacent to the road, nine had been abandoned leaving the skeleton framework of the palm-clad building, now half buried in new jungle. Of the one in ten smallholdings that was making a go of it, the majority were cultivating bananas, and people could be seen working their two-hundred-yard-wide strip as we drove past. Somewhat to our surprise, the people working the land were not Amazonian Indians adopting a change in life-style, but Brazilians from the south, the characteristic slight slant to the eyes, flat nose, round face and dark chocolate complexion of the Indian being mixed in with European traits – the mark of a liberal-minded Portuguese rule.

All bridges across the creeks on our route were made of wood, and often two or three failed bridges would be found adjacent to the one that we used. There was clearly a 'build again' rather than 'repair' policy, which seemed to indicate poor original foundations. In addition to the bridges, there were six ferry points on the road from Porto Velho to Manaus. The ferries were large pontoons capable of taking up to three buses at a time. These were steered from one bank to the other by means of a small tugboat. The tugboat would be connected to the pontoon, mid-way along one side, by a single pin fastened in the bows in such a way as to allow the boat to pivot through 180 degrees. There were always long delays at these ferry points, not through the volume of traffic but simply because the ferry would invariably be on the other side of the river with the ferryman at lunch or asleep!

The locals always took great advantage of these delays to sell you fruit or coffee. Many of the fruits were a complete mystery to us, and so wherever possible we tried a selection. One particular strange fruit which I remember, but whose name I have forgotten, tasted more like a sweet potato than any fruit. It even possessed the same fibrous inside as a yam or sweet potato but, to look at, it bore a great resemblance to a yellow plum. Pineapples were always a favourite at these times. Having made your choice, the fellow selling the fruit would deftly use his machete to strip the sides, slice off the base and dissect the pineapple from its base as far as the stalk. The stalk, still being attached to the pineapple, served as a perfect handhold when the two halves were devoured, rather like a lolly on a stick.

By the third of the six crossings, the journey was beginning to get tiresome, with little sleep being possible due to the constant bouncing. At the fourth crossing point the same casual delays were encountered. It was here, however, where the executive decision was taken to try for the eight o'clock ferry to Manaus. This ferry represents the final crossing and is located where the Solimoes and the Negro meet to form the Amazon. At this point, the river is some five or six miles wide and thus large enough to warrant a timed ferry crossing. The eight o'clock ferry was the last one that night and to make it was going to require some hard driving. First, on forty miles of reasonable road, and then twenty miles of exceptionally bad road. Oh joy!

All went to plan until the beginning of the twenty-mile stretch, when the bus was pushed just a little too hard. On hitting one of an innumerable number of potholes flat out, the whole frame of the bus cried out, shuddered and became engulfed in a cloud of black smoke, heavy with the smell of burnt rubber. Our front near-side wheel had sheared off its axle and now lay alongside the bus, which had somehow managed to hobble to the edge of the road. Now I understood the real reason why the buses always travelled in convoys of two! We all grabbed bags and piled into our sister bus and roared away leaving our poor driver to keep watch on our erstwhile transport until help could be sent in the morning.

Amid sighs of relieved anticipation of yet another night on the bus, we arrived at the last ferry bang on eight o'clock. Needless to say, we didn't actually slip our moorings until nearer nine o'clock – this was, after all, Brazil!

During the journey from Porto Velho we had made friends with a most curious couple. He, Romeo Angelo, was Brazilian, very tall for a Brazilian and with a long black beard smothering an otherwise friendly face. She, Sandra, was Danish and of the 'flower power' era in terms of the way she dressed, though neither of them was much more than thirty-five. She was also six months pregnant. For once, communication was no problem, as they used English to talk to each other.

Angelo introduced himself initially as a doctor, though this was progressively diluted to homeopath, and then bush-doctor. The true definition of this final label we were only to find out much later. However, their relevance to this part of my tale derives from the fact that – having spent the last few months in the jungles of Peru – they were on their way to a little village called Bonfim on the mountain border between Brazil and its northern neighbour, Venezuela, but planned to spend a few days in Manaus at a cheap hotel, to which they were prepared to guide us. Such an offer, when arriving in a strange town late at night, is not lightly shunned.

We were forced to complete the six-mile journey from the ferry terminal to Manaus central by taxi, since there had not been room for the bus itself on the ferry. Our second desertion in one evening. The hotel was ideally situated; only two blocks from the river Negro, (Manaus being slightly upstream of the confluence of the Negro and the Solimoes rivers) and a further two blocks from the town centre. The rooms were bare, save for the beds and the single fan which offered some relief from the stifling heat, but the hotel staff were cheerful and friendly and that makes up for many a material discomfort.

As had been our experience in all the hotel rooms to date, the cockroaches had first to be temporarily banished and the holes in the mosquito netting over the window plugged before unpacking for the night. The only drawback with all of these rooms were the bed bugs that interrupted each night's sleep and caused infernal itching all the next day. This, however, was a tolerable price to bear for the benefit of paying only £3 a night per room in an otherwise expensive town.

After a reasonable night's sleep, which was interrupted only briefly by a powerful thunderstorm, we began our exploration of this most unusual city. Until recently the place was completely inaccessible by road, its sole line of communication being the Amazon river. Yet since the end of the nineteenth century, during the height of the rubber boom (Manaus's *raison d'etre*), this city has boasted an opera house which was supported by a social elite whose lifestyle rivalled Paris and London for opulence. All this in a city whose isolation was so complete as to be a thousand miles inside the largest and wildest jungle in the world.

When the focus of the rubber industry moved to Ceylon (now Sri Lanka) the effect on Manaus was catastrophic and the city began a steady decline. However, a few years before our visit, the Brazilian Government had declared Manaus a free port, meaning that foreign goods would not incur import tax and could thus be traded much more cheaply than elsewhere in the country. This move initiated a second and equally powerful boom in this jungle-locked phenomenon.

Our first task for the day was to secure a berth for the next stage of our journey – the riverboat trip to Belem. I set off into town with this as my aim, leaving Karin with her foot propped up on a pillow, it having swollen to an alarming proportion from bites which had turned septic. First, I went to the Post Office to check that Tom had not telegraphed us to advise of any change in plans and then I pressed on towards the quay.

To call this area of embarkation and disembarkation a 'quay' instantly gives a wrong impression of its construction. In essence, the quay was little more than a floating steel pontoon some five yards by twenty yards which was secured end-on to the shore. The mooring strategy being employed by the riverboats tied up to the pontoon was nothing short of chaotic. Stern-to, alongside or stuck at forty-five degrees to the quay, these boats, varying in size from thirty to a hundred feet, clung four or five deep to the pontoon like so much scrap metal to a magnet and with about as much sense of order.

Between me and the pontoon, some fifty yards away, stood the most motley collection of wooden shacks and stalls ever to be erected in the service of providing quick snacks. Put together from broken-up crates and river salvage, these 'canteens' were selling pots of steaming rice and fish, or cold drinks and fruit for those whose business or pleasure was to be had along the river front. Through these stalls wound a narrow route that provided access to the pontoon for trucks and pedestrians alike. As I made my way along this track the ground underfoot became more and more muddy, since the continual throng of people and trucks had contrived to turn the latter part of the access into a pulp of river mud, rotting fish and spilled fruit and corn. In the end numerous large planks had had to be laid through this 'soup' in order to provide safe access as far as the gunwales of the pontoon. It was this pontoon which acted as a quay for all those boats bound for Santarem, the first and only port between us and Belem.

The riverboats, or 'river buses' as the locals called them (a fair enough name considering the purpose they served), are best described as looking like Mississippi paddle steamers without the paddle, and while many of the boats were dedicated to passenger transport the majority of the vessels tied to the quay were primarily for cargo. Loading and unloading their holds was a wholly manual task and consequently there was a constant stream of sweating Brazilians hurrying back and forth, heavy with sacks of corn or crates of beer – all carried on their heads. This balancing act was complicated by the bearers having to cross sagging planks and clear three or four sets of gunwales *en route*.

The scene was made complete by the isolated drama of a group of men trying to secure a cow which, having recently been driven across the planks and gunwales, was now stuck in the companionway of one of the smaller vessels.

With nobody apparently in charge of operations on the pontoon, I ended up enquiring after a suitable berth from an enterprising fellow who was running a small bar in the middle of the pontoon. 'Yes', there was a boat leaving for Santarem on Monday the 1st of October, and 'No', I couldn't buy a ticket because the boat wouldn't be in Manaus until the next day.

We had ascertained earlier that our trip would have to be done in two stages, since boats direct to Belem were too infrequent to meet our deadline of the 5th of October. A characteristic of travel in Brazil at that time was that you could never plan more than one stage ahead, nor could you easily get information about that next stage until you had arrived. With the name of the boat to Santarem carefully noted in my book, I left the pontoon and returned to the relative sanity of the city.

After returning to the hotel to pick up 'old club foot' it was time to find a beer and a bite to eat before starting some serious sightseeing. Manaus proved to be the most pleasant city we visited in Brazil. The atmosphere was gay and cheerful and the air was always full of music, and although we found Brazilians generally to be friendly and helpful, in Manaus they excelled themselves in their hospitality.

Of all the streets and alleys, nooks and crannies into which we poked our noses that afternoon, the Mercado Municipal was perhaps the most memorable. Situated close by the 'Santarem pontoon', it is an elegant steel structure; a relic of the rubber-boom days, and bearing more resemblance to a railway station of the art nouveau era than to a market place. Inside we found three separate halls dealing in meat, fruit and fish. The fish hall was particularly interesting since all the fish were from the local river and yet there was such diversity in type and size; indeed, some of the larger types easily weighed ten kilos. Later we visited Manaus's floating market where the fish were unloaded along with bananas and other forest produce from *peque peques* or native canoes.

The term 'floating market' derives from the fact that the produce is both unloaded, and to a large extent sold, on the pontoon which acts as a quay. Our evening meal that day was taken in a small cafe above the Mercado Municipal. We ate fish.

The following day, the 30th of September, was a Sunday and what better place to spend it than at the beach. We were beginning to realise that the Amazon has more in common with the sea than with one's normal concept of a river, for besides producing fish the size of sharks, it also has its share of sandy beaches capable of satisfying the requirements of a whole city population.

We had already learned that any high ideas we might have had about fishing trips, hunting trips or just plain jungle exploring trips, would have to wait until another visit when time and money were less critical. We therefore resigned ourselves to taking a local bus to the 'end of the line', a place called Ponta Negra, some twenty miles up the Rio Negro where we were told there was a pleasant beach. As we stood at the bus stop at nine o'clock in the morning we were surprised to discover that Ponta Negra was the destination of half of Manaus as well!

As it was so crowded, we didn't stay long at the beach and instead visited one of South America's most opulent jungle retreats, the Hotel Tropical, Manaus.

Cut out of the jungle on the banks of the Rio Negro, this gem of a hotel had, within its grounds, its own zoo and botanical garden as well as all the normal attractions offered by a five-star country hotel, such as a shopping arcade and tennis courts. We indulged ourselves for the day, breakfasting and wandering in the gardens. Being an area of the jungle within the hotel grounds (which the proprietors had simply not chopped down), the 'botanical garden' afforded a superb opportunity to get a first-hand feel for the jungle that we had seen around us since leaving Cuiaba.

Any romantic fantasies of thrashing through virgin jungle with our machetes were soon brought up short by the onslaught of a myriad of disturbed mosquitoes and a wide variety of other flying and crawling insects – reminiscent of an experience I once had trying to explore the Everglades in Florida. Ten minutes later and quite exhausted by our jungle expedition, we retired to the poolside for a quiet beer – costing more than our hotel room in Manaus. I say 'quiet' but in fact it was interrupted by the noise of the daily thunderstorm which decided to vent its fury on our pleasant little scene of opulence. With the storm over and after a quick browse through the shops, we made our way back to the bus and central Manaus.

Our route home took us through Manaus's shanty town or favela. The favela is a feature of most large population centres in Brazil, though the one in Manaus seemed particularly appalling and extensive. They typically consist of crude wooden dwellings almost always of single-storey construction, which may form an independent unit or part of a maze of interconnected shacks, raised on stilts that act both as a damp-proof course and foundation.

Brazil inherited a very well-defined class structure which, to its credit, was not based entirely on colour. Indeed, the more I observed, the more impressed I became with this nation's attitude to issues which, at the time, other nations were finding more difficult to accept; issues such as inter-marriage between 'white' and 'black'. It was more the exception than the rule to find someone whose skin colour was pure black or white, a point that probably contributed significantly to the racial harmony which we experienced in Brazil during our travels. In fairness to Brazil as a whole, I must point out that my experience was limited to the central and northern regions of the country, as I was led to believe that south of Sao Paulo such racial mixing was not as common.

However, the disparity between 'upper' and 'lower' was enormous, to a large extent polarised, and based almost wholly on wealth. In the seventies a pyramid of wealth for the Brazilian population showed 40 per cent 'poor', 45 per cent in the 'middle' and 15 per cent 'rich'. At the time of our visit, some ten years later, these figures had changed to 55 per cent, 29 per cent and 20 per cent respectively; an alarming polarisation which had become a political as well as social challenge for the Brazilian Government, as they prepared to face the prospect of a communist contender in the January 1985 elections for the first civilian president in twenty years.

Monday morning was busy with packing and shopping for the evening departure, along with a quick visit to the Indian Museum in Manaus – a fairly uninspiring affair. More memorable by far was the opportunity which both of us had to use a blowpipe. We came across it in a shop in Manaus that stocked a large selection of Indian artefacts; some genuine, the remainder for the tourist industry. The pipe itself was about six feet in length and an inch in diameter, and was constructed from a single piece of hollow timber similar to bamboo and of about the same weight. I learned later that in fact the 'bamboo' only acts as a sheathing for a much finer, hollow reed that gives the pipe its extremely true barrel. At one end of the pipe a wooden mouthpiece was fastened so that it covered the full mouth of the user when blowing. The neck of the mouthpiece appeared to be fashioned slightly narrower than the body of the pipe to facilitate loading and firing.

In this case the darts consisted of pieces of steel six inches in length, and an eighth of an inch in diameter and sharpened to a point. At the following end of the dart was a small wad of cotton fibre wound onto the dart in the same way as wool is wound on a bobbin for spinning. This wad appeared to give the dart the resistance needed to allow pressure to build up behind it in the mouthpiece before release.

Thus, the blowpipe relies on the user blowing hard but not sharply, contrasting with how one might use a peashooter for instance. The advantages that this mechanism affords over the peashooter, in terms of a more stable and controlled moment of release, are clear. Indeed, with only a single shot we both successfully hit a six-inch target at five yards.

Before leaving Manaus we said a final farewell to Angelo and Sandra – a most odd couple. During our stay in Manaus, Angelo had suggested I try some of his 'medicine', a noxious brew that he had concocted himself. Our many conversations had convinced me that Angelo was no fool. Indeed, he was quite obviously a very intelligent man and a deep thinker with a clear perception of people, if not things, around him. Yet here he was, fully persuaded that he had before him the solution to man's internal conflicts, in the form of a liquor of fermented creeper.

For centuries this potion has been found among the Indians of South America, from the Amazon basin to the Inca kingdoms of Peru, being used for every kind of complaint from toothache to arthritis. The Brazilian name for the potion is *ayahuasca* and it is made from the vine of the same name. Its scientific name is *banisteriopsis caapi*. In essence the drink is hallucinogenic, allowing the person access to the inner mind where the problem may be isolated and addressed.

This follows the familiar theme of a healthy body being like a song in which every note is required to be correct for true harmony to exist. This, and the total interdependence of the psycho and the soma. According to the 'science', once isolated in this manner, the offending evil or disease is driven physically from the body by induced vomiting or bowel movements. I listened to what Angelo told me of the liquor, and was subsequently able to check his facts against more level-headed opinion. Interestingly, the two accounts appeared to agree!

By five o'clock on the afternoon of the 1st of October, we were settled into our hammocks on the *Rio Guama*, along with around thirty other passengers, ready for an imminent departure for Santarem. A fairly careful check was being kept on numbers where passengers were involved, following a run of over-loadings which had resulted in vessels sinking with loss of life. Where passengers were not involved, no such checks were in evidence and we saw many vessels leaving the pontoon with water lapping over the gunwales in a most precarious state of equilibrium.

As it happened, our 'imminent' departure didn't take place until ten o'clock due to engine problems and so, having met up with a Brazilian lawyer who spoke English and who was also making the passage down river, we decided to take up his offer to buy us a fish dinner and set off back into town. The meal was splendid and the conversation most informative. Besides discussing the problems of the Brazilian economy (always guaranteed to raise a grimace as the inflation rate was well above 200 per cent), we took the opportunity to ask about the names of some of the foods we had been eating.

The case of farinha is a good instance. Farinha is grated manioc (also known as cassava), a root which is native to Amazonia and which I had not encountered outside of Brazil. The gratings were dry and golden in colour and looked something like toasted breadcrumbs. The use of farinha was so widespread that it appeared at every meal either in a dish or in a large salt shaker and was sprinkled lavishly over everything. 'Why?', is another question, as the root in this form is virtually tasteless.

Occasionally, the juice of the manioc would appear on the table as well as the farinha. In this form, however, it has a definite spicy flavour to it.

By eleven o'clock the *Rio Guama* had cleared the pontoon and we prepared to spend our first night in a hammock, swinging in the night air alongside the other passengers. We were the only non-Brazilians onboard.

The river trip turned out to be an ideal opportunity to observe the Brazilian in his natural habitat, dozing in his hammock! Having bought my hammock in Fortaleza some two weeks previously, I was already well aware of the extremely comfortable nature of a large, well-made hammock, though I was delighted to discover that it remained so even if one barely moved from it for twenty-four hours at a stretch. I think that drifting down river in a hammock must be one of the pleasantest ways of crossing any continent. Either side of us, sometimes only a few yards distant, other times up to half a mile away, the Amazon jungle towered right up to the very riverbanks. Occasionally one would see smallholdings consisting of palm-thatched wood cabins surrounded by a few yards of cleared jungle and now and again the riverboat would pull alongside at these places to let a passenger off who was returning home after a monthly shop in Manaus.

During the day a bar was kept permanently open for drinks and snacks and at lunch and dinner hot meals were served. These were typically rice, spaghetti, meat (usually beef) and farinha. Between meals we read, wrote, chatted and generally relaxed. The hammock is such an adaptable piece of furniture for relaxation. You can sit in it, stretch out in it, curl up in it or simply just slump and it will accommodate each movement you make as if it were built specifically for just that position.

About twice a day the boat would make a scheduled stop at a little village along the route. For the villages as well as the farms, the river provides the only means of communication and so our arrival usually became the focus of a great deal of activity. At one of these stops early in the morning of our second day, an American couple came onboard and set up hammocks close to ours. We soon discovered, and not to our surprise, that they were missionaries. Spreading the gospel through actions as well as words, they had just spent the last three weeks, ninety miles inland from where we picked them up, establishing a sawmill in an Indian village. 'Oh, for the opportunity', I thought! There we were just scratching the surface whilst the real South America was out there behind that seemingly impenetrable wall of jungle.

We arrived in Santarem a little earlier than expected – around midday on the Wednesday. Not a great time to arrive anywhere in these parts as the heat was intense. Finding a boat to Belem was the worst task we experienced in Brazil; no one was prepared to say simply that they didn't know, even when we asked in our best Portuguese! Consequently, the whole day was spent in one long trek from point A to B and back to A again. At one stage we almost resorted to catching a plane on to Belem, but balked at the price. The problem was not just that the promised daily stream of boats travelling from Santarem to Belem did not exist but that, having accepted that we would have to wait a while, the port authorities and the Captains differed in their estimation of when a particular boat was leaving, or even if it was to leave at all. In the end we concluded that the first boat out was to be the very boat we had arrived on and that that was not to leave until the Saturday, three days hence.

Tired and feeling somewhat let down, we went first to the Post Office to telegraph Tom that we would be late arriving in Belem and then secured for ourselves a cheap hotel located above the town's fruit and vegetable market, looking out on the town square. No air conditioning was available in any of the rooms, save for a ceiling fan which churned up the hot damp air. The effect was similar to that experienced when sticking your head in a tumble drier to unload a pile of not quite dry clothes. However, it did provide sufficient force to keep the mosquitoes off and for that I was grateful. The cockroaches I just accepted – it was simply too hot to do otherwise.

In the evening we met up with three South Americans whom we had met earlier in the day, two Brazilians and one Argentinian. Santarem is only a small town and not geared to mass catering in the evenings, so we were pleased to have the benefit of local guidance in finding somewhere to eat. We then passed a most pleasant evening, if an expensive one, eating steak and making what conversation we could with our few words of Portuguese. Perhaps I am being over-modest concerning our linguistic achievements, for by necessity our Portuguese had come on in leaps and bounds since leaving Fortaleza, almost three weeks previously.

The Argentinian, it turned out from the papers he showed us, was engaged in the Falklands scrap. His attitude was very anti-Galtieri and the stance that he had taken over the islands. His attitude to us couldn't have been pleasanter or more genuine.

For Karin the evening was memorable but for other reasons. She had developed a fever and so while I sat, sweating in shorts and tee shirt, Karin shivered in every ounce of clothing the five of us could muster. As is the nature of some fevers, it went as fast as it came so that by the morning the worst of it was over. However, convincing our South American friends that it was not malaria was another thing altogether!

Hollywood has managed to construe the situation of sitting in a sweltering bar in some tropical backwater, waiting for a boat out, as intrinsically romantic. The concept might be, the reality is not! Most of our first full day in Santarem was spent sitting out of the heat in dingy bars drinking guarana in an effort to keep cool. Santarem was every bit as hot as Porto Velho, but for all this it was not entirely without its own particular charm.

On our second day we were determined to make more of an effort and so, accompanied by a young Brazilian student who was keen to improve his English, we set out for Alter do Chao, a most charming little riverside village some twenty miles from Santarem.

The bus ride was an experience in itself as the two-hour-long journey took us along narrow dirt roads and over crude wooden bridges which crossed the innumerable creeks. The dirt road was nothing but an access track linking the little clearings in the jungle where families had chosen to carve a living for themselves. At these points people would get on or off with branches of bananas or sacks of meal. Eventually we came upon the river Tapajos. This is the tributary which joins the main stream of the Amazon at Santarem.

At Alter do Chao (which is where we had now arrived), a large lake had formed adjacent to, but still fed by, the river. Dividing the bulk of the lake and the river was the most idyllic sand spit I've seen outside Mozambique. The golden yellow sand was shaded by coconut palms and cashew trees; and the water, in sharp contrast to the muddy waters of the Amazon, was a deep clear blue. In order to reach the spit we had first to cross the channel of water which connected the lake with the river and so, after a beer and a bite to eat, we solicited the services of a local fisherman to paddle us across the fifty yard gap in his canoe. Swimming, sunbathing and collecting cashew fruits filled the remainder of the afternoon.

Our journey back to Santarem was completed in the dark, winding our way through a totally black and imposing jungle, full of exotic noises from the unseen world which inhabited this land.

After a third night under ceiling fans, we packed, shopped for a little fruit and headed back to the good ship *Rio Guama* in time for a twelve o'clock departure for Belem. Among our fellow passengers we found one of the Brazilians with whom we had eaten on our first night in Santarem, and the proprietor of our hotel in Manaus – the sort of coincidence that we found time and time again during our travels in Brazil.

If anything, this leg of our Amazonian journey proved even more beautiful than the first. As the river approaches the sea (that is to say, when it is within the region of two hundred miles from the sea) it begins to fan out and the water divides between innumerable islands. This region, known – and justly so – as 'the narrows', afforded the most splendid opportunity for observing the jungle that had presented itself thus far.

One moment we would be following a channel over five hundred yards in width, the next the boat would sheer off to pursue what appeared to be little more than a creek, sometimes as little as thirty yards across. Here, we could almost reach out and touch the jungle. Parakeets and other colourful birds disturbed by the noise of the boat, occasionally broke cover and flew squawking across our path, whilst at every native hut we passed, a young indian boy would invariably be seen paddling furiously to put his canoe alongside our boat to receive pieces of fruit or biscuits from obliging passengers. No photograph or painting could quite do justice to these modest abodes, fashioned from the very wood which surrounds them and which threatens at any time to engulf them.

At each turn or junction of this maze of waterways, I found myself more and more astonished at the means of navigation for, despite questioning the crew and even a personal search of the bridge, I was unable to discover a single chart onboard. Their sole source of information being a wiry old man who sat on the foredeck all day, and for all I know, all night, indicating our route to the bridge whenever a change of course was deemed necessary. Yet there were no obvious landmarks; one lot of jungle looking very much like the next. That this method of navigation should have proved reliable through the many hundreds of junctions that we passed during our two-day passage from Santarem to Belem was remarkable enough, but when one considered that the same method was employed with the same apparent success at night, when overcast skies often rendered the scene pitch black, was to me beyond comprehension.

On our second day out from Santarem, we were woken early by an unfamiliar pitching and rolling. On closer inspection we found that we were at a point along the river where there were no islands to restrict our passage. Although still some one hundred miles from the sea, it was barely possible to see either bank of the river. With the advantage of observation from the top deck and the good visibility, this would have put the width of the river at that point as being over twenty miles (that is to say, wider than the English Channel at Dover). However, reference to the map showed us the error of our assumption. The bank off to our port side was in fact the island of Marajo, an island almost the size of East Anglia. The true width of the delta at this point being one hundred and eighty miles. Later that morning we docked in Belem.

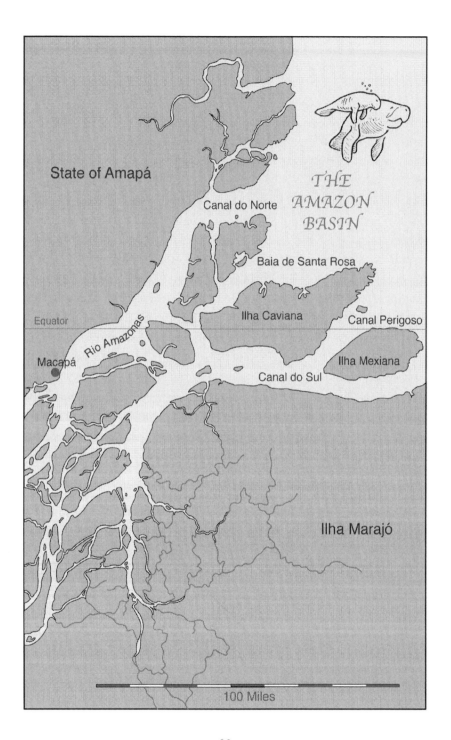

State of Amapá

Canal do Norte

THE AMAZON BASIN

Baia de Santa Rosa

Ilha Caviana

Canal Perigoso

Equator

Rio Amazonas

Macapá

Ilha Mexiana

Canal do Sul

Ilha Marajó

100 Miles

CHAPTER FIVE

The Amazon Delta

Our trip into the interior had been a great success and had over-delivered in terms of memorable experiences and learning about the country. But it had been hard work and at times extremely frustrating. It was therefore with an odd sense of 'home coming' that we rejoined *Morvran* and, for me, a welcome opportunity to catch up with Barry who had stayed onboard to help bring the boat up from Fortaleza.

Our stay in Belem was brief, as both Tom and Pat were both keen to set sail the morning after our arrival. However, from our short experience, Belem appeared quite a conventional city; a few nice buildings, too many skyscrapers, a large dockland and an impossibly complicated bus system – but perhaps I'm being overly harsh and a more thorough visit might have uncovered hidden treasures.

As the guidebook had suggested, the rains along this part of the Atlantic coast were almost as regular as clockwork; one strong blast once a day around four in the afternoon – this area of Brazil being unaffected by the rainy season which we found dominated the lives of those living in the interior. Working around this downpour, our last job on the afternoon before departure was to visit the customs office to officially clear out of Brazil, despite the fact that we were planning to spend the next three weeks sailing in Brazilian waters! Such is bureaucracy!

On the morning of the 9th of October, we set sail for the interior, retracing much of the route that we had taken on our journey to Belem in the *Rio Guama*. This time however, there was time to explore our new environment in more detail.

In order to gain maximum advantage as a sailing boat we would work the tides. The Amazon remains tidal for almost six hundred miles and so in the region of the delta these were still quite pronounced. Rarely, unfortunately, did the tides fall at convenient times and a typical day might run as follows:

We would rise at first light. That is to say, around five o'clock. At this time of day the air was cool but still not cool enough to demand more than a sarong in the way of clothing. It would usually take about an hour to clear our anchorage of the mass of vegetation that had attached itself to the boat during the night. The debris consisted in the main of 'floating islands', plants rather like lilies that varied in size from a single plant no more than three feet wide to a collection of plants which floated down river as a single body of up to sixty feet across. Thrown in for good measure would be half a dozen logs and occasionally whole palm trees. Once away, we would motor or occasionally sail until the tide turned foul, at which point we would anchor or tie up to a tree until it slackened sufficiently for us to continue. At these times the heat would become intolerable.

The temperature inside *Morvran* would be just under 100 degrees Fahrenheit (38 degrees Centigrade) and in typing out my log on the ship's portable typewriter I regularly resorted to a head band to stop the continual stream of sweat from dripping onto the keyboard. Beside me would be two glasses, the first containing rain water that we collected each evening and which provided us with our drinking water, and the second containing wine vinegar which I used to apply to the flea bites and mosquito bites that peppered my legs and arms and which at the time numbered between twenty and thirty. Outside, the deck was too hot to stand on and there would invariably be no wind, save the slight breeze caused when the boat was in motion. The solution to the heat was to swim.

The waters of the Amazon are deep and muddy to the point of opaqueness and beneath the surface there lives one of the most diverse ecosystems to be found in any river in the world. The guidebooks are quick to tell you about its piranha fish, caiman (or South American alligator) and river serpents, but the Amazon is also home to the pink dolphin or 'boutu' and the threatened manatee or sea cow. However, of most interest to us at these times was the fact that its temperature was a steady 90 degrees Fahrenheit (30 degrees Centigrade). Hardly refreshing but wet and very welcome! Indeed, at five o'clock in the morning the difference in temperature between the air and the river would cause a very fine mist to form on the surface – rather like the memories I have of dawn on the Ganges.

I have to admit that our first swim was taken with a degree of trepidation, as all of these creatures had at one stage or another been spotted as we sailed along or, in the case of the piranha, seen on a fishmonger's slab! But in terms of numbers these sightings were so few and far between that caution was soon – and I think justifiably – thrown to the wind.

Most prolific of all the river creatures we saw were the dolphins, 'boutus'. Pink in colour and with a less pronounced fin than those on the dolphins we had seen at sea, these creatures would often be found playing around the boat. In shallower anchorages the Amazonian manatee could be seen coming up for air between periods of feeding on the river bottom. About six feet in length, it looks from the surface a bit like an overgrown otter. It has a mermaid's tail and a very distinctive pig-like snout with whiskers and large flaring nostrils. Although both these creatures were present on many occasions when we were swimming, they never ventured closer than about twenty yards while we were in the water.

Besides swimming, these forced breaks were a good opportunity to explore inland a little further. Here at last we had the chance to do what we had been longing for ever since we began our travels in the Amazon basin. Our forays into the jungle normally took the form of a short row to a suitable landing spot, either up a creek or under the branches of an overhanging tree. Having secured the dinghy we would then head inland with compass and machete in hand, and clothed from head to toe in an effort to reduce loss of blood to the ever-active insect community. Even when we made these trips at night we found ourselves amazed at the lack of visible life. There was some evidence of four-legged life in the form of fresh tracks in tidal mud, but not once did we ever see anything – though I'm not quite sure what we would have done had we come face to face with the infamous jaguar!

Similarly, monkeys could be heard but were rarely seen – their howling calls penetrating the still nights. However, birds, and bats at night, were in abundance. Parrots, parakeets and toucans being among the easiest to identify. But perhaps among the most beautiful of all the creatures we saw were the butterflies, and of the scores of colours and sizes, none surpassed the magnificent turquoise, Morpho butterfly. With its four-to-six-inch wingspan it would glide effortlessly along the riverbank, bringing a splash of vibrant colour to the otherwise green montage of the jungle foreshore.

When neither swimming nor trips inland sufficed to fill the time, then the Monopoly board would be set up under the shade of the cockpit canopy. Looking back, it now seems a little odd that we should be trading Park Lane or Old Kent Road in the middle of the Amazon jungle, but then again, there was little about this trip that could be described as 'normal'! Eventually the tide would turn and we would be once more on our way.

Because of the complexity of the channels that make up the delta, it was not always possible to predict the direction of water flow. A number of arbitrary watersheds exist within the delta which can lead to unexpected tides. One minute, for example, a flood tide would be with you but then the next you might find that the river is flooding from the opposite direction and you are motoring against it. Once we had got the hang of this it became possible to predict these points more accurately and therefore time our journey to take advantage of the flood from one direction followed by the ebb from the other. In this way we managed to average around twenty miles a day during the two weeks that it took us to reach the open sea again.

At around six o'clock, or earlier if the tides dictated, we would search for a place to stop for the night. Mostly these places were of our own choosing, being little side creeks with overhanging trees or places where the water was shallow enough for anchoring, but occasionally our night halt would be forced upon us.

One such time occurred on our second night out from Belem. The chart we were using for navigation was a small-scale Admiralty chart which was clearly marked 'for planning purposes only'. It had proved impossible to obtain detailed Brazilian charts in Belem and so we were left with no other choice, despite the fact that our Admiralty chart did not show anywhere near all the channels. It was precisely this fact which led us, on that second night, to take a wrong turn. The channel in which we found ourselves was particularly beautiful and, in retrospect, it would have been extremely sad if we had avoided our mistake. But at the time we saw our situation from a very different perspective.

The tide was ebbing against us as we entered the channel and the sun had just passed its zenith. Although some thirty yards wide at its mouth the channel soon began to reduce as the route became more tortuous. Branches from overhanging trees were starting to become tangled with the cross-trees at the top of the mast. As we pressed on, this problem was compounded by fallen trees which restricted the channel even further, forcing the yachts closer into the bank. Foliage and broken branches came crashing onto the deck as the mast sliced through the undergrowth. This was dispatched with equal speed over the side to prevent the numerous ants and spiders which accompanied them from gaining access to the boat.

As it happened, this proved to be a good way to observe nature at close quarters, as quite a wide variety of insect life would be shaken down onto the decks in this manner. Most memorable of these occasions was when a small tarantula landed in the company of a dozen or so large ants. As luck would have it the creature landed only a foot or so from where I was standing and so I was able to get a good look at it before sweeping it off the deck with my hat. Although I can relate the incident in a casual manner now, it didn't feel 'casual' at the time, with the prospect of another one landing on my back as foliage came crashing down around us on all sides.

In the end it was a matter of depth and the ebbing tide which brought us to a halt. An hour later we sat high and dry in a channel barely wider than the length of the boat. After a customary row upstream in the dinghy in what little water remained, we returned to the yachts, slung our hammocks, poured a drink and settled down to listen to and observe the jungle at its best – the time of the evening sun.

The toucan invariably dominated the chorus of birdsong (though we rarely saw the actual bird – and only twice in flight) while the turquoise Morpho butterfly would glide from branch to branch along the shore. As the evening sun set, the birdsong was drowned by the noise of the bullfrogs and the insects, and in the trees and along the bank fireflies, like so many glowing match heads, darted about entertaining the patient observer. Even before the darkness is complete the jungle's many species of bat have taken to the wing and now wheel and dart in amongst the rigging.

Charles Waterton, a nineteenth-century Amazonian explorer, writes at great length about bats, and in particular vampire bats, in his thoroughly enjoyable book *Wanderings in South America*. From his clear descriptions of the vampire bat, and from other sources of reference, it soon became clear that we were, that night, in 'his' territory. At least two of the creatures had flown past the yacht as we sat in our hammocks.

According to Waterton, the vampire, when sucking a human, always goes for the big toe – not the neck as is customarily assumed – and that such is the skill of this nocturnal surgeon that the victim invariably never wakes up while the creature is at work. Many times, so Waterton relates, he would sleep with his foot out of his hammock as an invitation to the creatures, but despite all his efforts he was never once 'sucked', though he often witnessed 'the surgeon's' work on a colleague who had been sleeping in a hammock beside him. Perhaps it was the euphoria which the closeness of the jungle had produced in all of us that evening, or perhaps it was the spirit of adventure that Waterton had aroused in us, either way Barry and I both knew without a word where and how we would be sleeping that night!

With Barry's hammock slung in the aft rigging and mine up for'd we settled down to sleep, a foot protruding from each hammock. On one side of us the jungle overhung the deck while on the other the moonlight shimmered on the waters of the creek, now at full tide again, with the jungle appearing as a black wall ten yards off. Neither one of us was visited during the night and though we saw many other bats in the nights that followed we never once saw another vampire.

So passed our days in the Amazon delta. Occasionally we would pass settlements of a dozen or so houses, and twice these were large enough to warrant stopping to buy fresh fruit and vegetables, or to search out a cold beer. On the river we were in constant company with other small river craft such as diesel-powered cargo boats, similar in size and shape to the old Norfolk wherry, or dug-out canoes which would paddle past us transporting individuals or families to and from villages. Occasionally we would offer these folk a tow, a custom that seemed well established in the backwaters of the delta and one which reflected the atmosphere of friendliness we encountered throughout the two weeks that we spent in this paradise of a cruising ground.

On our fourteenth day out of Belem we emerged from the tranquil waters of the 'narrows' into the choppy waters of the estuary. We were out, our objective accomplished, or so we thought. In the event, it took us a further six long hard days of sailing to cover the ninety miles from the point where we emerged into the delta to the open sea. All the time there was a force-three to -four headwind, so that while the ebb was with us the sea conditions were abysmal – being wind over tide – and during the flood we simply went backwards. There proved to be very few sheltered anchorages available on our way out, most of the creeks which were marked on the chart being silted up well out into the channel. Only one proved passable and therein lies a tale.

Although quite a sizable river by UK standards, something similar in size to the Dart or the Ouse, and opening out to over one hundred yards at the point where it joined the Canal do Sul, the Rio Cajueiro was restricted at its mouth by the same line of sand bars that we had experienced at all the other creeks we had tried to enter. This time, however, we persevered. For the previous two nights we had anchored in the main channel in a chop similar to that which one might experience during a force four in the Bristol Channel. To add to the anxiety of a main channel anchorage we were all too aware of the 'dead heads' or part-submerged tree trunks that drifted up and down with the tide and which were partially responsible for our decision not to sail at night. Thus, when no obvious channel could be found into the Rio Cajueiro we braved the surf and edged our way straight over the bar with three foot to spare. This is no country for a fin-keeled boat!

Before us lay the most ideal anchorage we could have wished for, sheltered from wind and swell and with the jungle all around us once more. The howler monkeys were in full chorus as we dropped our anchors and prepared for a relaxed evening. Supper was served at seven. At half past seven it began.

At first we thought it had started to rain and quips were made about whose turn it was to set up the water collecting gear. Outside however, all was dry. Then we started to notice twigs and branches caught by the moonlight for fleeting moments racing past the boats. In the delta region the flood tide is held back by the sheer volume of the Amazon waters until the very last minute and then the sea overcomes and the flood waters rush in. Out in the main channel this effect had been lost but here, up a narrow creek, we were about to witness the process at its worst.

Before the flood began the two yachts were rafted together and sitting high and dry on a shoal patch. Now as the waters rose visibly around us the yachts began to rock. The tide was coming in at a rate of ten knots. Debris was flashing past and the roar of the water even drowned out the howler monkeys who sat laughing at our plight. Suddenly *Morvran* began to float. The horror of the situation broke in upon us. *Morvran* had no anchor down since both yachts had been lying to Pat's anchor and Pat was at this moment still aground.

The mooring ropes which fastened us to *Ocean Winds* fore and aft strained against the force of the bore. In a frantic effort we began casting off. Things happened faster than we could work and first the aft and then the for'd fairleads tore themselves loose from the deck and were catapulted into the foaming waters around us. (A fairlead is a metal guide, fixed to the deck, through which mooring warps or anchor chain are passed to prevent them from sheering along the side of the boat.) As soon as the last warp twanged free we began speeding upstream. At the same moment we released our anchor which dragged at first and then bit, bringing us up short. We at least were safe.

However, when *Ocean Winds* came free from the sand she was not so lucky. The ten-knot tide tore at her anchor until it succeeded in pulling both boat and anchor upstream with it. They sped past us, Pat furiously pulling at their dragging anchor. A second anchor was cast overboard into the torrent. At first it appeared to dig in and the bows of *Ocean Winds* plunged as the chain took the strain, then 'crack', the bows lunged back out of the water and the boat continued upstream leaving the anchor and chain (worth £100) sitting on the bottom. Eventually, some five hundred yards further upstream the original anchor re-bit and *Ocean Winds* came to rest. Within half an hour of it starting, the flood tide was complete and the ebb had begun again.

At six o'clock the following morning, after a quick sortie into the jungle in an effort to catch a glimpse of some early risers, we began a search for the anchor. Up to our waists and feeling with our toes – with the dinghy in tow since some of the sand was quick – we wandered up and down the river but in vain, either the waters or the quicksand had already claimed it. By eight o'clock we were back onboard our respective vessels, preparing for the next flood tide. Securely anchored and facing the right way this time we outrode that morning's onslaught without incident. By twelve o'clock we had cleared the bar once more and were back into the pitch and toss of the main channel.

It took a further two days of tacking back and forth before we finally left the main channel behind us, and with it the Amazon Delta. Eventually, having felt our way clear of the last lot of sand bars with help of the echo sounder, we altered course and began the long journey north to Cayenne – capital of French Guiana.

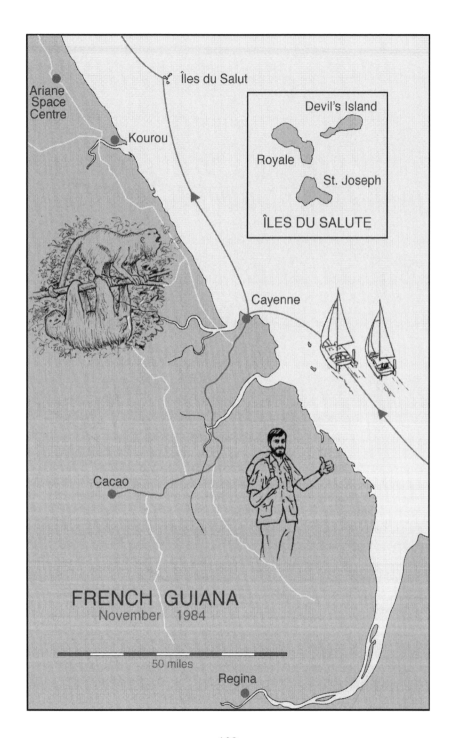

Ariane
Space
Centre

Îles du Salut

Kourou

Devil's Island

Royale

St. Joseph

ÎLES DU SALUTE

Cayenne

Cacao

FRENCH GUIANA
November 1984

50 miles

Regina

CHAPTER SIX

French Guiana

French Guiana is an overseas *Departement* of France inhabited by French
expatriates, black African descendants of the slave trade and Guianan
Indians. At the time of our visit the total population was only 80,000, of
which 38,000 lived in the capital, Cayenne. These were mostly all
French and Africans, since the Indians seemed content (or destined) to
remain in the jungle (which still covers over ninety per cent of the
country) living a lifestyle that has remained unchanged for centuries and
which the French, to their credit, seemed happy to respect and leave well
alone.

We found Cayenne itself to be a curious place. Being great believers in
the concept of 'Metropolitan France', the French way of life had been
super-imposed in amazing detail on a Creole community which was just
as happy sitting down to monkey stew as they were to croissant and fresh
ground coffee. Thus, the currency was (and perhaps still is) the then
familiar French franc; the road signs were unmistakably French; and
that ludicrous system of *priorite a droite* was religiously maintained. Many

of the old buildings were still standing, albeit in a somewhat dilapidated state of repair, giving the place an air of 'times past', not unlike the effect created in the French quarter of New Orleans, which in my view is one of the very few North American cities of aesthetic quality. Cayenne's biggest downfall was its complete lack of public transport, making the three-mile trek out to the post office and back a most laborious affair. Overall, however, my impressions of Cayenne were favourable.

Arriving mid-afternoon on the 30th of October and leaving again on the 6th of November we had only six days in which to mend sails, re-water and re-stock the boat – as well as seeing something of French Guiana. Keen to continue our exploration of 'the real South America', Karin and I were soon pouring over a sketch map of Guiana, but it quickly became clear that seeing something of the interior was going to be no simple matter. For instance, how do you get 'in' to a country which has one coastal road going north and one going south, and nothing but rivers and jungle tracks going into the interior – and not a single bus to be found for love nor money. In the end the answer proved simple enough: you take rivers and jungle tracks and you hitch – or fly.

So, bright and early on the Saturday morning, we set ourselves up on the roadside with a placard reading 'Regina', a settlement we had seen marked on the map some seventy miles from Cayenne. A French car soon stopped and delivered the good news. In well-controlled French the lady driver politely informed us that if we really wanted to go to Regina we should be aware that the route was four-wheel drive only for most of the way, with no road at all for the last twenty miles. And besides, there were only five houses and a Foreign Legion camp there anyway. So much for the placard.

In the end we agreed to take her offer to go inland as far as she was going and to amend our destination to Cacoa, a little Vietnamese refugee settlement, about forty miles inland and on a road which was at least passable for most sturdy vehicles outside the rainy season. After about an hour, the French woman pulled off the road with the half apologetic statement, 'Well, that's about it I'm afraid, this is as far as I'm going.'

Ahead of us was a single-track wooden bridge which spanned a slow-moving river some forty yards wide. Beyond the bridge the dirt track road continued as before, penned in tightly on both sides by dense jungle. The last car we had seen had passed us about ten miles back, going the other way. As we disembarked we could hear the noise of an outboard engine approaching from up the river. Our driver had come to this point to meet up with some friends who had a cabin some twenty minutes upriver from the bridge and where they were all planning to spend the weekend. Five minutes later the boat was speeding away round the bend with our friend as passenger. We were on our own again. It began to rain.

Our time in Brazil had not been without its lessons and so we had come suitably prepared for this sort of predicament. I had made sure that our rucksack had included hammocks and waterproof canopies, not to mention gallons of mosquito repellent, and so while Karin stood by the bridge watching for cars, I did a quick reconnoitre of the immediate area in case we were forced to stop there for the night.

As luck would have it, there appeared to be the remains of some sort of night shelter built as a weekend cabin close by the bridge, and although it had no walls and very little roof remaining, its timbers were still substantial enough to carry the weight of our hammocks. With this observed, I headed back to Karin.

Half an hour later we saw a pick-up van approaching. We stuck out a thumb and looked hopeful. It stopped. The window was wound down and a shotgun and a black face protruded out into the rain. 'Cacoa?', I said, trying not to notice the gun. 'Sorry my friend, I turn off long before then, but the Vietnamese will be returning from Cayenne market soon, so hang about awhile and you're bound to get a lift.' With that, the black face disappeared along with the gun, and the van sped away.

As the noise of the van's engine faded away and the incessant racket put out by the jungle asserted itself once more, I began to wish I knew a little more about the political stability of Guiana. After a further half hour wait, another van appeared, slowly the bridge and travelling in our direction. This time the occupants were Vietnamese. Full of smiles, they hustled us into the back of the van amongst the market produce and we all drove off towards Cacoa.

Propped up between the French bread and the potatoes was a shotgun. By now, the rain had slackened off to a steady drizzle, but the van still slithered about on the familiar red clay. Then, without warning, and with no apparent explanation, the van slowed to a stop. All around was dense jungle. We were quite alone and felt suddenly very vulnerable. The driver and his associate got out of the vehicle, opened the back door, and indicated for us to step down onto the road. With a nervous glance at the shotgun we reluctantly complied and now found ourselves standing in the drizzle by the side of the van. But instead of showing any particular interest in us, our 'new friends' started pointing into the trees and encouraged us to follow their gaze. To our amazement they were not about to commit some sort of act of piracy but had spotted a three-toed sloth and had rightly judged that this would be very much of interest to us. Charles Waterton speaks at great length about these sleepy, monkey-like creatures which hang upside down in trees in defiance of normal convention, and so we were indeed curious to see one for ourselves. After ten minutes or so, and feeling rather foolish, we all piled back into the van and continued our journey. An hour later we arrived in Cacoa. We could just as easily have been somewhere in South East Asia.

During the seventies when most European countries were taking in Vietnamese refugees, the French decided that the old penal colony of Guiana would be an ideal second home for a few hundred of these wretched people. So, wishing not to risk racial disapproval from the expatriates in Cayenne, the French government built Cacoa, a village on stilts deep in the Guianan jungle. Here, these folk lived out their lives of poverty growing vegetables and catching a few fish from the river which they then sold at the market in Cayenne. We wandered around for about half an hour and then settled to have a coke at the only bar in the village, overlooking the river.

The dividing line between jungle and village was drawn very suddenly at the edge of the village, and so we felt that here was a good opportunity to take a last quiet look at the environment we had come to love and admire. We had noticed a French couple in the bar when we had been drinking our cokes, and had concluded that they had, at some stage, to return along the only road out of the village.

Failing that, there was an open barn at the entrance to the village that would make an ideal place to sling our hammocks should we be forced to return to the village at nightfall. Therefore, with all eventualities covered, we set off on foot back down the road we had come in on, with our senses alert to the sounds and smells which bombarded us. Half an hour out of Cacoa the rain began again.

From what little we saw of the jungle in Guiana, there appeared to be three differences from that further south in the Amazon basin. Firstly, the trees tended to be taller here, towering above us as we walked along the narrow red track which served as a road. Secondly, the terrain was less flat, indeed the approach to Cacoa had been quite steep and hilly, giving an added dimension to the outline of the jungle and making the trees appear even taller. Thirdly, it was wetter. Not just because of the rain which we were experiencing at that moment, but by the general appearance of the vegetation it was clear that this was a rain forest. Actually, I suppose there was a fourth difference insofar as we saw more wildlife during that quick walk than we did for days at a time in the Amazon; not only birds and butterflies but monkeys as well.

Standing in the middle of the track now some two hours' walk out of Cacoa we realised that the time had come to make a decision. The rain had once again settled down to a steady drizzle. It was a cooling rain – mildly refreshing, but still not cool enough to keep us from sweating buckets through the simple labour of walking, despite wearing only a thin shirt and a pair of shorts. Not a single vehicle had passed us heading towards Cayenne since we had left Cacoa.

We knew we could find shelter by the bridge where we had been dropped earlier that morning but that was a good five hours' walk away. Alternatively, we could turn back and sling our hammocks in the barn on the outskirts of Cacoa. Also relevant to the decision was the fact that there were only three hours of daylight remaining.

I had to admit that the prospect of completing the journey in the dark with a totally overcast sky, leaving our imaginations to contend with the noises of an unseen jungle at night, was not one which I readily relished. On the other hand, as long as we kept to the track we couldn't go far wrong, and the thought of turning back did seem a bit defeatist. And besides, there was always the chance that the couple in the bar in Cacoa were still planning to return along this route tonight. A beautiful Morpho butterfly fluttered its way across our path as we stood there deliberating on our problem and the decision was made. We would go on.

As with so many of these situations, the worst never happens and good fortune invariably lends a hand in the end. In this instance, it turned up in the form of a car which trundled past an hour before dusk. Our friends in the bar had decided to return to Cayenne after all.

It had always been my intention to be just that little bit more adventurous with my eating habits in French Guiana than I had been in Brazil. Therefore, on our final night in Cayenne, we went in search of a local restaurant that would satisfy our tastes, budget and curiosity. Down by the creek, which runs through the black quarter of Cayenne, we found just the place. The restaurant was pleasant enough, but the waitress had the attitude and demeanour of a typical British transport cafe waitress. You could almost hear those immortal words: 'Two eggs, chips and beans, and two coffees', being shouted through to the kitchen. In this little restaurant in Cayenne, the system was the same, only here the cry was: 'Monkey and chips twice, and two beers', I almost had her repeat it just for the fun of it!

In the end we ordered some snake and alligator too, in order to make some sort of comparison. These were our conclusions: The snake was an anaconda, one of South America's largest and most notorious snakes, being not unlike a boa-constrictor. The meat when cooked tastes something like belly pork and has very thin needle-like bones which run parallel through the meat, rather like the strips of cartilage which you find in a piece of spare rib.

The monkey was an interesting one. Somehow it is difficult to eat it without just a twinge of squeamishness – the 'boiled baby' syndrome, as

Barry called it. Still, when you end up with a ball and socket joint from a shoulder on your plate, it is difficult not to make the comparison! The meat, however, was very enjoyable. It is a strong red meat, quite dry and fibrous, and very much like venison to look at. To taste, it is a cross between venison and biltong.

The alligator, or caiman as it is called in South America, was the nicest of all. It is a white meat very similar to turkey and just as succulent. Although the meat itself is fibrous like poultry or beef, the bone structure is scaly causing the meat to initially fall away from the scales in flakes, in the same manner as tuna for instance.

The subject of food is perhaps as good a point as any to turn to domestic matters onboard the two boats. Since our arrival in South America there had been a number of crew changes. Ann had left *Ocean Winds* to return to America whilst Jeanette had left *Morvran* in Fortaleza to continue north to the Caribbean overland. In Belem, *Morvran*'s full complement of five was restored by the arrival of Polly.

Polly, a slim, cheerful woman in her early fifties, not only eased further the already easy watch rota, but stepped in as fulltime cook as well – a post I was always pleased to see filled by someone other than myself, especially when they were as competent at the job as Polly. However, in Cayenne the time had come to say farewell to Barry who had to return to Switzerland for the winter season and work. Barry had turned out to be a good friend and confidant over the months we had spent at sea and his spirited company and diplomatic manner onboard were to be sorely missed. With all these changes the two crews now consisted of Pat and Brenda, who with Ann had been on *Ocean Winds* from the start, and Tom, Polly, Karin and myself on *Morvran*.

On Tuesday the 6th of November we hauled up the anchor, this time without the assistance of Barry who, as we cleared the harbour wall, stood on the quayside like some deportee of old, waving a final farewell before heading back into town and the Air France office.

Our next destination were the Iles du Salut, lying about twenty miles off the coast of French Guiana and some four or five hours' sailing north from Cayenne. With the wind on our quarter and the current running in our favour, we were at anchor again under the lee of Royale by nightfall.

There are three islands in this notorious group; Royale, St Joseph's and the famous Devil's Island, but the biggest of the three is Royale. In the days when the mention of French Guiana struck terror into any self-respecting criminal, the Iles du Salut represented the final threat in a land which was peppered with prisons and labour camps. Here, the victim of France's infamous miscarriage of justice, Alfred Derfuss, was imprisoned for five years. It was also here that Henri Charriere was eventually sent and from where he claimed to have escaped in order to publish his book *Papillon*.

Charriere was one of the fortunate few. Of the 60,000 men who were incarcerated on the Iles du Salut, only 2,000 survived, the majority dying from the brutality of confinement or as 'fish food' for the sharks which encircled the islands in anticipation of escapees.

As we lay at anchor on our first night, history shouted at us over the noise of the jungle and peered at us from behind the island's craggy foreshore. In the morning we launched the dinghy and went to see it for ourselves.

The last of the prisoners was moved out of the islands at the end of the second world war and since then the buildings have been left to decay. However, sufficient remains to grasp a good impression of what the place must have looked like in Papillon's day.

The weather was hot and sunny as we strolled up the flagstone path which connected the landing quay with the main prison complex on the top of the island. It seemed incongruous that such a beautiful island should have been associated with such an ugly history. None of the islands were more than three-quarters of a mile long and all were covered with coconut palms and jungle bursting with life. As we reached the one-hundred-and-fifty-foot summit, the jungle gave way to a grassy clearing around which were scattered the remains of a large number of different-sized buildings.

The chapel was still in perfect condition and the hospital too had most of its walls and floors intact. These two buildings formed two sides of a very rough rectangle some three hundred yards by six hundred yards. Opposite the hospital stood the guards' quarters, while along the remaining side were the prison cells themselves. Sadly, these were the buildings which had suffered most from the deprivations of thirty years.

Creepers and vines had worked their way into all the corridors and cells, and much of the ironwork had completely rusted away, but what remained sufficed as evidence of what kind of place this had been. Row upon row of solitary cells no wider than five foot and no longer than seven, with the rusted remains of a narrow bed and iron rings set into the wall at the foot of the bed to receive leg-iron chains. On St Joseph's the following morning we saw hundreds more of these cells.

St Joseph's island had the added advantage that it had remained completely untouched since it had ceased to be a prison, whereas Royale had developed a bit of a 'tourist air' about it, with corrugated roofs to some of the old prison buildings and a small hotel which had been established in the old prison warders' complex. It was in this hotel that we made a couple of interesting chance meetings over a beer.

The first was a BBC film crew who had come over by boat that morning to do a feature on the island's past, while at the same time covering the Ariane rocket launch that was due to take place on the mainland the following day. This, by the way, was French Guiana's whole *raison d'etre* at the time – the European version of Cape Canaveral. It was John Craven of *John Craven's Newsround* who wandered up to me having heard my English accent at the bar and started chatting. He seemed an appropriate fellow to ask about news from England, and so I had an enlightening quarter of an hour, catching up on current affairs at home. Of more consequence, however, was my second meeting. On this occasion I was with Karin, the two of us having returned to the island a second time after changing the film in our cameras.

There can't have been more than around a dozen people on the whole island and the film crew accounted for a good number of those, so to hear two further English voices was extraordinary. Their dress was more extraordinary still. They wore identical shorts and running shirts and their hair was a familiar army crew-cut. 'The British Army in French

Guiana?' I thought aloud. It didn't seem very likely, then I remembered Regina with its Foreign Legion camp buried deep in the Guianan jungle. My curiosity got the better of me and I wandered over to enquire. This is what we learnt of that legendary fighting force, the French Foreign Legion.

There were seven regiments spread around the world, representing about 9,000 full-time soldiers. In terms of nationality it was difficult to be precise, but the majority were French-speaking; the remainder were chiefly English or German, though just about every other nation on earth was represented to some degree. Generally, the numbers would increase after a 'scrap'. After the Falklands for instance, a lot of British joined the Legion, and after Vietnam a lot of Americans. It is a mercenary outfit and your pay is reflected by the degree of action in which you are involved and the length of service that you have done. Thus, a private may be earning more than a corporal if he had been in the Legion for a longer period of time. Starting pay for a private was about £250 per month (1984), but he was provided with all food and accommodation on top of that. The minimum service period was five years and, unlike in the regular army, you could not buy your way out – you could only desert. As in the days of Beau Geste, the Legion still respected the privacy of the individual. Thus, you could enter under any identification you cared to give and this would be accepted and protected from any outside inquiry.

Our 'friends' maintained that they were even eligible for a French passport, on the same basis, once they left – though frankly I would like to have questioned that piece of information further! More intriguing still, they went on to explain that included in their regiment were a number of Nazi SS officers who had joined up at the end of the Second World War to take advantage of the anonymity which the Legion offers and who, now in their late fifties, were still on active service.

As for themselves, one had joined up after the Falklands because having seen real action he had no desire to return to an endless programme of exercises on Salisbury Plain, while the other had used the Legion as a way of getting out of problems he'd faced in Northern

Ireland. It appeared that from the point of view of getting to see more action, the regiment based in French Guiana had 'drawn the short straw' as it seemed to spend most of its time building roads. All the jungle roads were constructed by the Legion, though of course its primary political role was the defence of Ariane.

Their presence on the Iles du Salut was explained by the fact that the Legion owned the island of St Joseph and they were spending a few days leave with the lighthouse keeper. With their obvious knowledge of the interior we then asked them about living in the jungle and, in particular, what they considered to be the most dangerous aspect of such an existence. Here, their verdict was unanimous.

If you were unfortunate enough to be bitten by a tarantula or attacked by a jaguar then the effects could be pretty terminal but really such attacks were rare. The insects, however, never stopped. Ants were particularly bad as they always acted as a group. They were tacticians. A group of half-inch-long soldier ants for instance would surround a three-inch black scorpion and systematically attack it, one at a time from all sides. The scorpion never stood a chance and would be dead within minutes. Yet during a rainy night when sleeping out in the jungle on an exercise one would often wake to find thousands of the creatures sheltering under the hammocks, keeping their feet dry. Flies too were more than just a pest. In South America they could be killers, and both Legionnaires said that on one occasion they had seen a whole company of men drop their weapons and run when a particular fly's nest had been upset.

The morning after this little encounter, we up-anchored and moved the boats round to re-anchor off Devil's Island. Open to the Atlantic swell on its only approachable side, the island offered little protection and so getting ashore with the dinghy proved a somewhat treacherous operation, but one we were determined to achieve.

The whole island, which is no more than half a mile long by a few hundred yards wide, was covered almost entirely by coconut palms from which we collected a moderate supply. However, in the centre of the island stood the remains of a number of small brick dwellings which had been used to house the prisoners who had had the misfortune to be sent there. These were the 'politicals' such as the aforementioned Captain Alfred Dreyfus, a French military officer who was accused of spying for the Germans in 1894 and sentenced to life imprisonment in this hellhole. The Dreyfus case gained notoriety by virtue of it being eventually overturned – he was a Jew and the trumped-up charges against him were anti-Semitic. Others, however, were less fortunate and often fell prey to rats, army ants and vampire bats as they lay shackled, day and night, in their cells.

To this day Devil's Island is 'off limits' to tourists and it therefore felt significant to have at last achieved what we had for a long while doubted would be possible – to stand on the famous Devil's Island and gaze out on the wide Atlantic as some of the most notorious political prisoners in Europe had once done.

On Thursday the 8th of November, with the sun just passed its zenith, we turned our backs on the ghosts of Devil's Island and set sail for the Caribbean islands of Trinidad and Tobago.

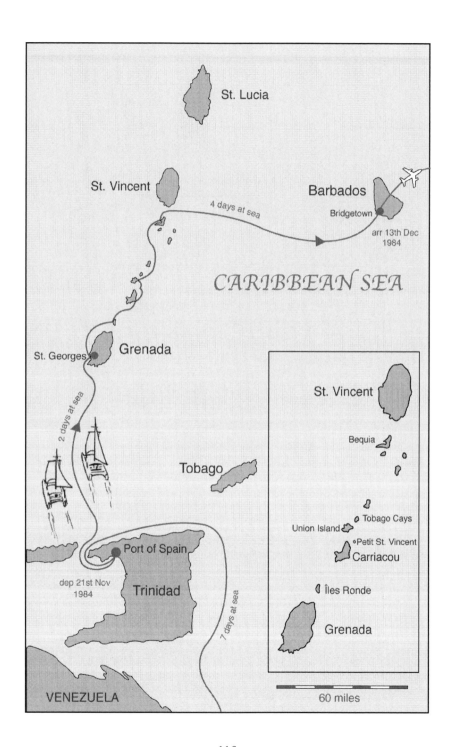

St. Lucia

St. Vincent

Barbados

4 days at sea

Bridgetown

arr 13th Dec
1984

CARIBBEAN SEA

St. Georges

Grenada

2 days at sea

St. Vincent

Bequia

Tobago

Tobago Cays

Union Island

Petit St. Vincent

Carriacou

Port of Spain

dep 21st Nov
1984

Trinidad

Îles Ronde

Grenada

7 days at sea

VENEZUELA

60 miles

CHAPTER SEVEN

The Caribbean

Trinidad lies some six hundred miles north of the Iles du Salut and for the whole of the passage we had nothing but the very best sailing weather, a steady force-three following wind, allowing us to rig the square-sail for the first time since the Atlantic crossing.

As crew, we had settled into the roles of an old-style, traditional family unit, adhering to all the gender stereotypes of the time. There was Polly, or 'mum', who did all the cooking and cleaning; Tom, or 'dad', who made all the decisions and shouldered the ultimate responsibility; and Karin and I, the 'kids', who (like a brother and sister) were simultaneously nagged at and doted upon by 'mum' and whose constant topic of debate was whether it was 'his' or 'her' turn to wash up.

With Polly working the galley, the three of us, Tom, Karin and myself, took all the watches. This worked out at three hours on and six hours off – a very workable arrangement.

At two o'clock in the morning however, things didn't always appear that way. It had hardly seemed moments since I had fallen asleep on our second night out from the islands, when a hand reached in through the curtains to my berth and gave me a not-too-gentle shake. 'You're on in five minutes Chris. Steering's up the creek.' That was all I needed; three hours of fighting the square-sail.

It was five to two in the morning and I had the two o'clock to five o'clock watch. Karin's voice had reflected the frustration that I knew now lay in store for me and I didn't relish it one little bit. Earlier that day, Tom had just about managed to get the autohelm (an electronic self-steering device which works by following a pre-set magnetic guidance compass) working well for the first time in 5,000 miles and now, as I stumbled into the saloon, I vaguely wondered what could possibly have gone wrong with it this time. On reaching the cockpit all became clear. There, being enacted before me, was the timeless struggle which has existed ever since the invention of the wheel; human versus machine.

Karin, it appeared, had inadvertently plonked her cushion and herself right up against the autohelm's guidance compass, cunningly placed in the cosiest spot in the cockpit. It had objected to this effrontery and had set about showing its disapproval. Sitting on her cushion with a face like thunder was Karin, fitfully fighting the main rudder to port, while behind her back the autohelm was going 'whir, whir, click, click', stubbornly fighting the separate autohelm rudder to starboard. The yacht was doing its best to appease both masters.

A few soothing words to both parties and a minor readjustment of the guidance compass soon redressed the balance and I pottered off to the galley to make some cocoa. In fairness, I suppose I shouldn't sound so smug, as later that night I was called out of bed to help lower the square-sail because one of the sheets had parted and the thing was flogging wildly in the night air with the boat going nowhere. It was during this operation that I contrived to send the starboard foresail halliard up to the top of the mast – an embarrassing mistake, for which I deserved more jip than I got!

Apart from the near-perfect sailing conditions, the journey from the Iles du Salut to Trinidad was notable for one other reason. We caught our first fish in nearly 6,000 miles of sailing! It has to be admitted that no one, bar Karin, had taken much of an interest in the fishing since Cape Verde, and therefore it had not been without a good deal of perseverance and effort that we still had lines to trail at this stage of the expedition. But at last here was her reward, a three-foot-long, three-kilo 'thing' – we never did get around to identifying it – from which we made two good meals. A quarter of an hour after the same line had been recommitted to the foamy wake, it went suddenly tight and then slack. It had gone the way of all the other lines and equipment – which by then had amounted to a considerable investment – bitten off by some larger predator.

On the 14th of November we arrived in Trinidad. The approach was quite remarkable with steep, thickly-wooded islands breaking up an equally wooded mainland. On the whole however, Trinidad proved a disappointing island. Bureaucracy was rife, and a declaration that we had firearms onboard did nothing to speed up the already painfully slow process of gaining customs clearance. It came as a surprise to all of us that there was not a single other foreign yacht in Port of Spain – we had somehow expected this to be the start of the Caribbean yachting scene but that, it appeared, didn't start until Grenada.

The island – in common with most, if not all, of the Caribbean islands we visited – was completely devoid of an indigenous population, its inhabitants comprising an ethnic mixture of African, Indian and Oriental which formed quite distinct groups within the community. That said, we found Trinidad to be a very 'modern' island with twenty-four-hour radio stations running on an all-American system of perpetual advertisements and Christmas jingles months before Christmas. The attitude of the locals to us was friendly and hospitable, though there was an anti-white feel to the place, which occasionally voiced itself.

From necessity we spent most of our days in Trinidad tied up to the quayside in the central dock area which had the one redeeming feature of being bang in the centre of town and therefore perfectly located for banks, shopping, etc. The town of Port of Spain had little to recommend it, except for a small collection of rather spectacular houses located on a single street, opposite the town's 'central park'. The ostentatiousness of their design, which ranged from French chateau to Spanish colonial mansion, reminding me of St Charles Avenue in New Orleans.

We made two sets of friends in Trinidad that proved the salvation of the visit. The first were three Dutch guys who were working on a dredger tied up alongside us in the docks. Their genuine friendliness made an immediate impact on us but not quite in the same way as it had almost done earlier, on the day of our arrival.

At that time, I had been piloting the yacht into Port of Spain while the rest of the crew, including Tom, were clearing away after lunch below deck. Intent on negotiating our passage around the back of a ferry which was making its way out of the port, I completely missed seeing the dredger that was bearing down on us at fifteen knots on its way into the port. A long loud blast on its whistle and a few words of sporting encouragement from Karin, who had suddenly spotted the vessel from the galley window, sent me diving across the cockpit, tiller hard over, to put the yacht about. In a quieter moment, later that evening, we learnt that the Dutch crew of this vessel had only three weeks left to go on a thirteen-week dredging contract and were, therefore, quite pleased to have other European company.

The other contact we made was on the advice of Jeanette who, having visited Trinidad a few weeks earlier, had left a note in Poste Restante saying that we should contact this fellow on arrival. His name was Karl King, a young oriental guy who owned a bar with his brother in a rather exclusive quarter of town. A better friend we could not have wished for. On identifying ourselves as friends of Jeanette, the hospitality he showed us was overwhelming to the point of being embarrassing. The morning after we had made contact with him in his bar, he arrived at the boat in a four-wheel-drive jeep to pick up Polly, Karin and myself for a tour of the island. Without this insight into the real Trinidad I should have come away thoroughly disenchanted with the place.

If one word was required to describe Trinidad, urban and rural, then I should choose 'cosmopolitan' to describe urban Trinidad, and 'lush' to describe the countryside. The topography of the island consists of a range of mountains which run roughly north–south, leaving the western side of the island as a verdant plain where sugarcane forms the primary crop. The mountains are at their most impressive in the north, and it was here that we went with Karl. His local knowledge was invaluable. Here we saw cacoa (or coco), coffee, guava, mango, paw-paw, pineapple, golden apple, grapefruit and banana, all growing in abundance but with little effort being made to grow the fruit on a commercial basis.

It seemed a terrible waste of opportunity, to have a perfect climate and soil, and then choose to import from overseas rather than grow things locally and so I questioned Karl on the point. In his opinion the problems facing Trinidad had much in common with those facing other oil-rich countries. In Trinidad, when the oil was at its peak, it paid people to leave their farms and get a job, any sort of job, in the oil business. There was so much money 'swilling around' that the country didn't need to have any form of agriculture, it could afford to import from the other islands. However, with the oil boom in Trinidad clearly over, the country was left having to continue importing all its goods but without the economy to support it.

As we meandered through Trinidad's abandoned 'gardens', we passed through delightful little villages and stopped at one or two of the many palm-strewn beaches that line the northern coast, to buy cold drinks and shark-meat fritters. It proved a thoroughly enjoyable day out and I was in a way sad that it was our only opportunity to do justice to what must be quite a beautiful island.

It was strange being in a country with a predominantly black population and yet hearing English spoken all about you; and English with such a fascinating accent at that. It was even stranger still to find ourselves in a 'black culture' where we were the paupers, for in Trinidad the cost of living, boosted by the recent oil boom, stood high above that in the UK. Another unavoidable feature of Trinidad was the noise. Trinidadians love noise!

In general, this comes in the form of the 'calypso', a very rhythmic beat which has its origin in Trinidad. Everything you hear is played in this rhythm, even Christmas carols! Christmas is an extremely popular institution in Trinidad. When you're in the mood, the atmosphere is relaxed and inviting but for us, in Port of Spain, there never seemed to be the time to relax. Banks, customs and telephone calls seemed to dominate our brief stay.

On the 21st of November we cast off and headed out of the port for a pretty little bay in the Dragon's Mouth, the narrow strip of water that separates Trinidad from the mainland of Venezuela. As we set sail, we had two additional crew – Anne and Karl.

Anne was a farmer's wife from Cornwall, and was nearer Tom's age group than that of Karin and myself – so now we had two mothers! For Anne, the six weeks she was to spend with us was by way of a winter holiday and preparation for the rigours of the lambing season back home. The other addition to our crew was Karl who was joining us on a temporary basis for the Trinidad–Grenada stretch.

The little bay where we stayed for our first night out of Port of Spain was called Scotland Bay, and the narrow, twisting, steep-sided recesses into the coast which it formed, offered a refreshing change to the hustle and bustle of Port of Spain. The following morning we negotiated the steep chop and alarming eddies of the Dragon's Mouth itself, and set a course for St George's in Grenada.

The ninety-five-mile passage was all close hauled and the weather was abysmal – rain, squalls and calms. All the regulars were sick, including me – my first time since the Canaries four months previously. Still, eventually we arrived, and the view that greeted us was fair recompense for all our trials.

St George's is nestled in an old volcanic crater which has been breached by the sea for about a third of its circumference. The whitewashed houses that crowd its foreshore and spread up the slopes of the barely-definable crater, give the town the appearance of a picture-postcard English fishing village, while the large gaff-rigged fishing schooners which are anchored in the bay, lend the scene its Caribbean flavour.

The atmosphere in the town itself was far more relaxed than in Trinidad. The girls at least felt more inclined to wander about at night than they ever would have in Port of Spain, and the condensed nature of the layout made shopping and sightseeing a far more pleasurable pursuit. The damper on the whole affair, however, was the rain. It rained almost non-stop from the time we arrived until the day we left the bay, three days later.

In that time we made a couple of trips inland, one on foot and one by taxi, in order to get an impression of the island. In many ways it was very similar to the nicer parts of Trinidad. The whole island, some fifteen miles by seven miles, consisted of well-wooded hills and valleys. Everywhere appeared very lush and green, which I suppose was hardly surprising considering the deluge we were experiencing. Fruit trees were in abundance (coconuts and cacoa being predominant) and with fishing as the only other major industry, apart from tourism, the island's beauty was unspoiled by the trappings of modern industrialisation.

Superimposed on this village atmosphere was an unaccustomed tension that dominated every conversation we eavesdropped upon. Election fever had Grenada in its grip. For Grenada this was no ordinary election. Ever since the assassination of Maurice Bishop the previous year, Grenada had been governed by an interim government and there was a strong American presence on the island, which seemed in general to be accepted rather than welcomed.

On the afternoon following our arrival we tried to enter a hotel that we knew to have a particularly pleasant beach, and were surprised to find our path obstructed by a barbed wire barricade and an army control post manned by a black Grenadian soldier and a white US soldier. On enquiring, I was told that the hotel had been taken over at the time of the invasion for use as a headquarters. I explained that I was new to the island and was simply hoping to get to the beach for a swim. 'You'll have to head back along the road, and then turn left when you get to the tennis courts, old chap', the US soldier said, with a grin on his face as he mimicked my English accent and pointed back the way we'd come with his gun. 'Thanks Mac', I replied, as we took a last glimpse over the barbed wire before turning back on our tracks.

As we walked away from the hotel, I tried hard to remember whether, in that triumphant statement issued only a few days after their invasion of Grenada following Bishop's execution by firing squad, the Americans had said that they were moving the remainder of their troops *off* the island or whether they had said that they were preparing to move the remainder of their troops *on* to the island. Either way, they certainly hadn't gone yet and were not likely to, until the forthcoming election provided a satisfactory outcome.

On the 26th of November, we weighed anchor in St George's Bay and headed slowly round to the south side of the island to do some exploring. Our first stop was Prickly Bay. This was more like it! The sun shone for us all day, the sea was refreshingly cool and clear(ish), and the scenery was just as all the brochures describe – green wooded coastlines, palm-lined beaches and a companionable spread of stylish yachts. We spent three days sailing from one bay to the next, swimming, snorkelling and making full use of the windsurfer – the first real use it had had since we left England. Then, on our third day we headed back around the end of the island to St George's in order to re-stock with food, beer and water and to attempt to purchase bonded stores.

Returning to St George's with us was the rain, although this time it was less persistent, and we enjoyed sunshine for most of the two days which we spent provisioning and sorting out clearance for our bonded stores.

During those two days we said goodbye to Polly who had decided to return home for Christmas with the aim of re-joining the boat in the New Year after the birth of her grandchild. Also returning home was Karl, back to Trinidad, having spent most of the passage with his head in a bucket and now feeling convinced that sailing wasn't perhaps always all that it was cracked up to be! Quite what his original motivation had been for joining us on that passage from Trinidad to Grenada, became a topic of intrigue and speculation, never to be resolved!

From the island of Grenada we bashed our way north against a strong head wind towards the island of Carriacou, stopping overnight in the lee of Ile Ronde, just across the way from the north tip of Grenada. It was sunshine all the way again now and if it hadn't been for the wind, which was bang on the nose, the sailing conditions would have been perfect. No arduous navigation was required, as we could always see at least three islands ahead of our course. It was just like sailing your way through a giant chart!

Most of the islands presented a similar backcloth as we sailed through the turquoise blue waters of the Grenadines. Covered in scrub or woodland and with thin white sandy beaches which extended far down into the crystal-clear waters, each island sat secure and sheltered from the Atlantic swell within its own collection of coral reefs protecting it like the defences of some medieval fortress. Occasionally we would pass isolated sandbars where a few palm trees had established themselves – genuine desert islands.

Carriacou lies only twenty miles north of Grenada, but the trip took us two days to complete. At Carriacou we anchored in Tyrell Bay (in the southwest corner of the island) and walked over to the main village, situated further up the west coast, to do the odd bit of shopping and to clear customs. In the Grenadines, half the islands are governed by Grenada and half by St Vincent, but despite this, you are still expected to clear in at each island you visit. After a while, we gave this up as a bad joke and just cleared ourselves right through to Bequia (pronounced beck-wee) just south of St Vincent, steering clear of customs on all the minor islands we visited in between.

None of the islands were more than five miles in length and so an atmosphere of easy living and an unhurried life prevailed whenever we stepped ashore. Tourism with a small 't' was the major concern throughout the Grenadines, not the high-flying tourism of night clubs and hotels we found in Port of Spain, but a more subtle blend of the trade, geared chiefly to the yachting crowd that made up the largest proportion of visitors. Thus, wherever we went ashore, we would be sure to find a quiet little bar or beach-side restaurant to tempt us into parting with our dollars. Nowhere more so than on the island of Petit St Vincent.

Petit St Vincent was our next port of call after Carriacou. This privately-owned little island, no more than one mile long, provided a first-class hideaway for those looking for the Caribbean holiday with a difference – the difference being US$465 for a double room per night, which in 1984 was astronomic! For that, the guest had complete privacy in little cottages, carefully located on the windward side of the island, while the excellent bar and restaurant – open to visiting yachts as well as hotel guests – was located on the leeward side. This idyllic spot was enhanced by a careful conversion of the scrub land, which must once have covered the island, into a botanical garden with well laid out paths across luxuriant lawns.

From Petit St Vincent, we had a most pleasant broad reach for the five miles to Union Island, where an enclosure full of nurse sharks remains with me as the most memorable impression of the visit. This 'fishpond' was situated in front of one of the island's two restaurants, looking out into the little bay in which all the visiting yachts were moored.

The following morning, after a quick snorkel around the reef, we bashed our way to windward again for a couple of hours in order to fetch Tobago Cays, an extensive coral reef which lay some five miles north of Union Island. Here we saw the greatest variety of fish and coral to date. And it was here that I saw my first fan coral. Up to three feet in diameter, this most magnificent specimen of living rock, only millimetres thick, wafts back and forth in the current with its attendant shoals of brilliantly coloured fish.

Snorkelling around these reefs was like gazing into an enormous tropical fish tank stocked to the point of gaudiness with colour and variety of life.

We spent the whole of the next day anchored off the reefs of Tobago Cays, swimming, windsurfing, and of course, snorkelling. Then at dawn the following day we set sail for Bequia, only twenty miles away, but dead to windward again. It was a shame in many ways that we did not have more time on our hands to spend in Bequia, as it appeared a most attractive little island and well deserving of the decision by Pat and Tom to return there for Christmas. However, it was now the 9th of December and my time onboard *Morvran* was drawing to a close.

My decision to leave the yacht was not made lightly. I was determined to return home from the East (consistent with a circumnavigation) and was now faced with two attractive options. On the one hand I could remain onboard *Morvran* with Tom, who now hoped to continue into the

Pacific. But this would not be possible until March due to weather patterns, putting me seriously behind schedule for a September start at business school. The other option was to continue overland. Whilst mulling my decision I was contacted by an old friend, Laurence, who was planning some travel and looking for a companion. Best use of time and the prospect of a new adventure soon sealed the decision – but where to start!

I still have very vivid memories of sitting in a public telephone booth in the post office at Cayenne, studying a tiny two-inch by three-inch map of the world, which was printed on the inside cover of my Letts diary, arguing with Laurence over the logic of visiting Africa, Australia or Asia. In the end Asia won and we agreed to meet in Hong Kong on New Year's Eve. My plan, initially, was to fly from Barbados to the US and then on to Hong Kong, which we would simply use as a base for exploring China. Although the US route was the shortest, such logic doesn't always prevail when it comes to deciding airfares, and so it was that I ended up buying a flight back to the UK and then out to Hong Kong, flying east rather than west. My flight to the UK was booked for the 16th of December, and so with due consideration to the prevailing winds and currents, we decided to leave Bequia the following morning and begin our passage for Barbados. As it turned out this was a wise decision.

Barbados lies ninety-six miles due east from Bequia. But for the yachtsman this is of little consolation, as the currents run to the northwest at about one knot and the wind is prevailing northeast. Unfortunately, in the week that we had chosen to make our passage, the wind had veered to a very steady ESE, a wind that was not only bang on the nose but which acted to enhance an already adverse current. In the end it took us four days to complete a passage which as a run would have taken us less than twenty-four hours. Some of the time we would be putting in three-hour tacks, only to find that after six hours of sailing, having covered almost eighteen miles over the ground, we were only two or perhaps three miles further along our course line. On some occasions we would even find ourselves moving backwards, being driven by wind and tide in the direction from where we had come. At such times I was company for no man. I had, before we left Bequia, considered flying the final leg to Barbados as I could see that it was not going to be a straightforward trip, but the sheer expense of such a precaution had eventually persuaded me to take the risk and sail. However, as we tacked back and forth with only two days to go before the flight, I was beginning to regret my decision. I suddenly saw my parents standing at Heathrow with no one to meet, and with no way of knowing what had happened, not to mention the loss of my non-refundable air ticket – worth £460. The whole episode made me feel very frustrated and homesick and I would never want another journey like it.

In the end we got a slant twenty miles out from Barbados and completed the trip during late afternoon on the 13th of December – giving me a full day and a half to spare. Approaching Barbados from the west, the island appeared very different from the Caribbean islands we had visited on the trip to date. Far from appearing hilly and wooded, the island seemed quite flat and featureless with cultivated fields and pastures in place of wild and rugged woodland. I felt I was being broken in gently for my return to England!

However, the weather was still going to remain a big shock to the system. Since arriving in Trinidad, the temperatures had continued to moderate to a more comfortable level. The days being hot, but not exhaustingly so, and the nights cool enough for sleep to come easily. While we had been in South America the sun had simply been too hot for sunbathing and indeed most of us lost a great deal of our trans-Atlantic tan as we covered up to avoid the harshness of the sun. Now in the Caribbean we could afford to relax a bit, and as we sailed from one island to the next, we all took advantage of the catamaran's wide decks, basting and bronzing ourselves in the warm sun.

In all, I spent two days in Barbados before returning to England. The first day was split between stitching up the official side of the visit; obtaining immigration clearance to leave the yacht, squaring up financially (which meant lengthy visits to the bank), posting parcels of excess baggage back to the UK and confirming air tickets – as well as doing some last-minute souvenir shopping in Bridgetown. By the end of the day everything was complete, including a last-minute purchase on Karin's behalf of an air ticket home. She had decided to invest her few remaining dollars in driving lessons in Norway rather than gambling on a very swift tour of the States, which had been her other option.

Bridgetown is blessed with a picturesque 'careenage' (previously used for beaching ships during repair) which winds its way up into the town centre, flanked on either side by cafes and with quaysides lined with yachts and local fishing vessels. It was all in all a much pleasanter surprise than we had bargained for. In the centre of town, bordering the careenage, is Trafalgar Square with its own rather diminutive statue of Nelson and an impressive stone building which houses many of the government offices. The shops in the town were modern and far better stocked than we had found anywhere else in the Caribbean. Its nearest comparison was Trinidad, but in Barbados we found the atmosphere to be much more friendly and relaxed. There were also a far greater number of resident Europeans in evidence, which I interpreted as being a favourable indication of good relations between the now self-governed Barbadians or 'Bajans', and the previous British presence. Barbados gained independence in 1966 after three hundred and fifty years of uninterrupted colonialism.

The end of our first busy day was marked by a farewell meal at a charming seafront bar which overlooked our anchorage. With all the tasks complete, Saturday was delightfully free and so I took one of the cheap local buses across the island to see a little of the interior and to get a glimpse of its windward side.

Barbados is only about twenty miles by ten miles and so a single one-hour bus ride was enough to get a pretty good feel for the place. As I had noticed when we were coming in, this was very different from the other islands we had visited.

The 'pastures' that I had seen from the boat turned out to be acre upon acre of sugar cane, swaying gently in the almost constant breeze, though there were also genuine grazing pastures which lent the island an air of rural England in the summertime. As I travelled east across the island, with the bus winding its way through narrow country lanes that traversed the cane plantations, the ground gradually gained elevation until half a mile from the Atlantic where it suddenly began to fall again, losing almost 1,000 feet in under a mile. Here the ground was not suitable for cane to be grown, and so the land gave way to other crops and an abundance of tropical vegetation, bread-fruit trees being predominant. On the whole, I could find no sympathy with those who had written that of all the Caribbean islands, Trinidad and Barbados were not worth the visit – Barbados certainly was.

Sitting on the beach on the windward side of Barbados, looking out over the wide Atlantic towards home, I had time to reflect on the journey thus far. I had learnt so much. Not just about South America and the Caribbean, or how to sail a boat halfway round the world, but also about myself and my ability to cope with a constantly changing environment. I had learnt a great deal about containing my feelings and emotions, and managing to live in a confined community where I did not always have the final word, and where I often found decisions hard to accept. Decisions that, from time to time, bound me to a course of action I would not have chosen to take. However, I would only remember the good times, and rightly so, as these far outweighed the bad.

As Tom prepared to head up through the remainder of the chain and then finally out into the Pacific, my sights were already focused on the Far East and the next leg of my voyage, for which there was still much preparation to be done. First though, I was looking forward to Christmas at home and all the reunions which that implied.

PART TWO

Over Land

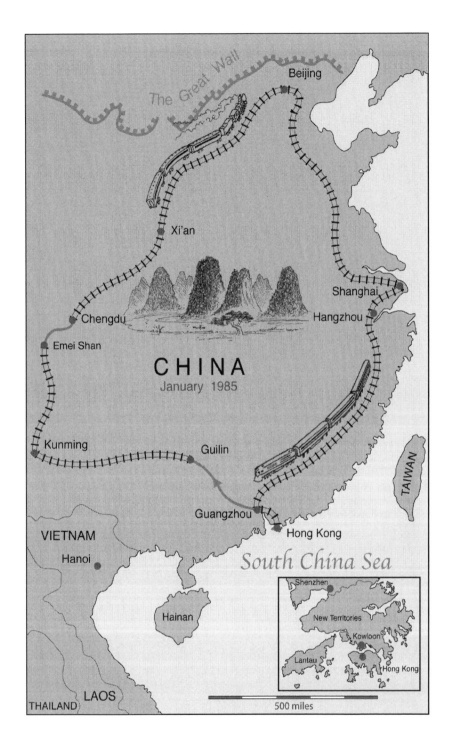

CHAPTER EIGHT

China

China! How to begin? Firstly, it was cold. Bitterly cold, and we were basically unprepared. It was January 1985 and Christmas in England had done little to reacclimatise me to sub-zero temperatures. Even in Hong Kong, where Laurence and I spent three days equipping ourselves for our expedition into China, we had never really appreciated how rapidly the temperature would drop as we travelled north.

It was soon clear that this was to be a tough trip and I felt really fortunate to have Laurence as my travelling companion. He was my longest and closest friend and together we had undertaken a number of road trips since meeting in the first year of university. As two people, we shared a lot of common ground, but also significant differences. We both had a habit of saying 'yes' to opportunity and were prepared to take some risk in our adventures. But Laurence's view and my own view, on what constituted risk, differed by several degrees! Consequently, when faced with a decision Laurence would be keen to push the boundaries of what was arguably possible, whilst I would play the part of 'Mr Cautious', quick to point out what might go wrong with the plan, often couching my concerns in the more acceptable language of a 'reality check'.

This worked well in the main, keeping our shared endeavours 'adventurous' but 'safe'. That said, the process of reaching decisions often seemed to involve an element of me being pulled beyond my comfort zone whilst Laurence was being pulled back from his more audacious plans. It was (and remains to this day) a very complementary and satisfying relationship!

Our visit to China was to properly test this balance – our very own 'yin and yang' – as the country was very unused to tourism and, particularly, tourists who were keen to explore off the beaten track. Politically, China was emerging from a recent past, dominated by Mao Zedong and now beginning to engage with the rest of the world under the more liberal guidance of Deng Xiaoping. But it was still a China of bicycles and blue workers' uniforms – very different from the China of today.

My most striking first impression of China, apart from the cold, was the sheer number of people. The streets were full of bicycles and the pavements provided a microcosm of life. Whether buying a coat or eating breakfast, it all seemed to happen out-of-doors.

Yet for such a densely-packed community everywhere seemed incredibly litter-free and, as far as possible, clean. The smells too made an immediate impression. The tantalising smells of Chinese cooking sensitising our nostrils as we strolled past the street stalls in Guangzhou (Canton), our first night-halt out of Hong Kong.

Language posed the biggest obstacle to the inquisitive, independent traveller in China in 1985. Numbers were commonly written in our script, which made catching buses and trains on time somewhat easier, but fundamentals such as where we were going, and knowing when we had arrived, foxed us on more than one occasion. For instance, early in the morning on our second day in China we caught an overnight bus out of Guangzhou for the picturesque city of Guilin. From information we had gleaned from a friendly, English-speaking Chinese girl, the bus was due to arrive in Guilin at ten o'clock the following morning. However, at four o'clock we ground to a halt in a largish town and everyone bailed out. It is difficult to appreciate, unless you have tried it, just how problematic it is getting a single word of Chinese across in an understandable fashion.

Nine times out of ten, our pronunciation of 'Guilin' was met with blank expressions. In any other country one could back up this sort of failure with a search above shop windows for a clue to the name of the place, but here, with everything written in an unintelligible script, this ploy was simply not possible. So, as we headed off down the main street at four in the morning, with our rucksacks on our backs, we had no real confidence that we were where we thought we were, or hoped we were, or even that we had caught the right bus in the first place! On this occasion we were in luck; we had arrived in Guilin, though why our journey had suddenly ended at four in the morning we had no idea. With a few hours' sleep behind us our first tasks in Guilin were to buy clothes and eat.

Thankfully we found the necessities of life to be quite cheap in China and so both Laurence and I were able to equip ourselves with one of the ubiquitous green trench coats and a fur hat, which was the Chinese winter dress. Though to my mind Laurence looked more like Omar Sharif in the film *Dr Zhivago* than a Chinaman, since he towered a clear foot above the rest of the population!

It is easy to understand why there are so many Chinese restaurants abroad as the whole Chinese *raison d'etre* is food and cooking. One can't afford to be too squeamish though. On our first evening in Guilin, we ate in a street restaurant huddled around a small brazier on which we were to cook our meal. Around us were many other tables, all with their own braziers giving warmth to small groups of Chinese folk dressed either in green trench coats like ourselves or in the crude blue jacket and trousers of the Chinese worker, which were to be seen everywhere in fields and factories alike.

The meal itself consisted of a pot of watery vegetable soup which remained boiling over the brazier and into which we dipped pieces of dog and goat meat, together with curd and lettuce, cooking these raw foods fondue style. It paid not to look too closely at the food as there was little alternative and the cold demanded that we ate. Bowls of rice padded out the meal, and we washed the whole thing down with Chinese beer.

The following morning we hired bicycles and took off into the countryside.

Geologically speaking, the region around Guilin is limestone karst and has produced the dramatic sort of scenery that is immortalised in so many Chinese paintings and ceramics. The mountains actually do rise vertically out of the mists and have blunt summits, making them look like baskets of up-ended French loaves.

During our cycle ride we accomplished many of our 'meet the people' aims. By getting out of the city and then cycling off the beaten track, we found ourselves passing through paddy fields with the towering 'Tolkien like' scenery of Guilin affording some splendid views. That is to say, on the few occasions when it stopped raining long enough for us to enjoy them!

It was market day that day in Guilin, and everywhere we passed folk taking their wares along the country lanes heading for the city. There were many heavily-laden mule carts carrying vegetables and sugar cane, being pulled not by mules but by men, straining against their loads. There were others who carried their wares in little wicker baskets which would be swung from either end of a bamboo pole, rather like a pair of scales, with the carrier's shoulder providing the pivot. Many times these baskets would carry live chickens or piglets, while larger animals, such as dogs, would be carried trussed up and hanging by their back legs from the seat of a bicycle.

I'm aware that the idea of hanging a dog by its back legs to be transported in this manner is, to say the least, an uncomfortable thought for many people, and I'm keen not to normalise or gloss over these practices. However, I'm equally keen not to reproach, as 'cultural norms' are not the same for everyone in this world – thank goodness! It has therefore been a fundamental tenet of my travels, past and present, to accept and experience life as I find it, and to try not to judge what I see by my own values and through my own cultural lens. That said, we were not unaffected by some of the treatment of animals and abject poverty that we were to witness on this trip, but it was nonetheless fascinating to see how people adapt and live out their lives in the face of what I would describe as intolerable conditions.

Each little village that we travelled through on our bikes appeared to possess its own small factory, and where the village was a new development, these were often grim-looking affairs – low buildings, with towering chimneys billowing black smoke like something from a Lowry painting.

We took the liberty of wandering into one of these little factories during our exploration and were allowed to take a good look around. This particular factory was not of the 'smoke-stack' variety and only employed about fifty people who were busy monitoring ancient machines, unwinding cotton from large reels and putting it onto small cotton reels. We were obviously a novelty as tourism, even in the cities, had only begun to open up during the previous three or four years, yet beyond looking up and smiling coyly, they were quite happy to accept us being there and nowhere were we mobbed as one might be in India, for instance.

On another occasion we wandered into a small village of no more than a dozen houses which was reached by crossing quite a long stone slab bridge onto a little island in the River Li. We had picked the village out from afar as being suitably off the beaten track and were keen to experiment with the effect we would have.

As with so many of these 'plunges' into the unknown, the results made the effort most worthwhile. A vivacious woman in her forties soon attached herself to us and invited us into the family house, a two-room affair with an open fire in one room and a front and back door which allowed all the family's animals free access into the proceedings. Children are so often good icebreakers and in this case the woman prompted her four-year-old son to offer us some water chestnuts. We were able to return the favour with the offer of some miniature bananas that we had picked up to supplement our rather meagre diet.

Sign language was our only form of communication but this sufficed to introduce all her sisters, mother and more distant relatives who made up the family unit. The almost medieval nature of our surroundings cannot be over emphasised and so it was to our embarrassment and surprise that we discovered the woman to be literate, as we showed her a pre-printed statement explaining that we were English and recognised her sing-song response as she read back our message – a feat that I had yet to master. The brief meeting ended with a family photograph, and then a portrait shot of her little boy, his hair neatly brushed by his proud mother – motherhood is international!

China was, in almost every way, a Third World country at the time of our visit. Although its infrastructure was in the infancy of development, its transport network was perhaps adequate for the level of road usage at that time. There seemed to be very few privately-owned cars.

The masses appeared to use bicycles, while trains and ancient buses provided longer distance travel. Taxis were used for city transport only by the rich few. The only other vehicles on the roads were lorries, all resembling old army trucks, but being used for all purposes from supplementing the bus service to transporting timber. This scarcity of motorised vehicles was reflected in the condition of the roads that linked the cities. Of the twenty hours of travelling it took us to cover the two hundred and fifty miles between Guangzhou and Guilin a good fifteen hours were spent bouncing along dirt roads with the wind screaming in through ill-fitting windows. It was clear to me that should the pragmatic approach to governing China's economy prevail and prove successful, then there would be endless work in this country for civil engineers. The luxury of a car for the masses, however, was still a long way off.

Money in China is a fascinating and complex subject. The currency is divided into three basic units; the 'yuan' which is the standard denomination, like the pound, with smaller change being governed by the 'jiao', which is one-tenth of a 'yuan', and the 'fen', which is one-tenth of a 'jiao'. To complicate this further, all three units are typically called by other names, in the same way as we might call a pound a 'quid'. As foreigners, however, we were unable to get hold of this currency. Officially we had to use FEC (foreign exchange currency), which was divided up just as the normal Chinese currency, and with the same official market value. So now we have six basic units, three local and three in FEC. Notwithstanding, the traveller's experience becomes that much cheaper if he can abandon the FEC system and buy into the local RMB (Ren Min Be) system. This is because FEC currency could be used to buy luxury goods such as televisions and stereos in Chinese 'Friendship' stores, whereas this merchandise was usually restricted for the local Chinese – their RMB not being accepted in such stores.

Naturally enough this situation was perfect territory for black marketeering, as people were prepared to pay foreigners well over the odds for their FEC in order to give them access to luxury goods. Thus, having cashed our traveller's cheques for FEC, we then went to the streets to exchange them for RMB at a premium rate of 1.8. The slight catch was that only some hotels were allowed to take foreign tourists, and these were forced by law to accept FEC – fair enough I suppose, since this is all that foreigners were supposed to carry. Elsewhere, however, our Chinese student card (bought on the black market in Hong Kong) came into its own as it gave us that vital 'Chinese link' which enabled us to use RMB to buy train tickets, etc.

To give an idea of what this magic money could buy, a hard-bed sleeper ticket for a 36-hour train journey, such as Guilin to Kunming, was costing us £5 each, while a meal for two could be bought for as little as 70p – beers on top at 15p a litre!

At the end of our second day in Guilin we boarded that train heading for Kunming in South West China. We thought we had bought hard-bed tickets. We ended up with hard seats – all night – and in a carriage so crowded that people were standing in the aisles and sleeping under the seats – a totally repugnant option considering the rural Chinese habit of hawking and spitting. I should have been thankful that we had seats at all! On the upside, with that number of people (most of whom were smoking) it was warm enough to take off our heavy outdoor coats.

At that time there were four classes in Chinese trains. Before 'enlightenment' these used to be called just that; 1st class, 2nd class, etc., down to 4th class. Now, however, they were being referred to as 'soft bed', 'soft seat', 'hard bed' and 'hard seat'. As if to drive home the baseness of the hard-seat class the guard would keep the lights on all night, though at least the music was turned off! Sadly, at six o'clock in the morning, we discovered that this little torture was resumed.

Loud and cheerful sums it up. Imagine 'Puppet on a String' played and sung in Chinese all day long – thump, thump, jolly, jolly! Every now and again, a western tune was played and sung in English by a Chinese voice. Since relations with the west had begun to improve by 1985, a taste for western disco music had developed amongst the young – a kind of vogue. 'Tie a Yellow Ribbon Round the Old Oak Tree' seemed most popular at the time!

When blessed dawn came at last, the pitch black was only replaced by a dull grey. But, despite the weather, the scenery from the train was quite splendid; the same dumpling-like hills as in Guilin sticking out of a flat, fertile land, neatly divided into discrete paddy fields. Every scrap of land that could be used was used, though there were very few people in the fields, which I presumed to be because of the season. Tightly grouped little villages of about a dozen or so houses were seen quite frequently along the route, with smoke rising straight through the roof tiles.

There appeared to be two very distinct types of village. The traditional village consisted of small cottages and farm buildings of wattle and daub construction with thatched or clay-tiled roofs. Occasionally, locally made bricks had also been used to construct the walls. Set against this Tolkien landscape, these small villages provided a 'picture postcard' outlook on the world. Had I been able to get near enough to the window I should have tried to take a photograph, but I fear that the confusion it would have caused in that crowded little space would not have been worth the effort!

The other type of village was post-revolution. These were characterised by drab fifties-style brick buildings constructed around a quadrangle where one of the sides was taken up by a larger communal-type building with a conspicuous red star over the doorway. These buildings would probably have served as mess halls during the heyday of the communes.

China had certainly suffered changes in the fifty years leading up to our visit. Close to Kunming is a village that used to be renowned for its large number of ancient Buddhist temples. But by this time in its history the village lay in desolation, as over two hundred of these ancient monuments were razed to the ground during the Cultural Revolution, a pattern which seems to have been the rule rather than the exception.

As we travelled about the country in 1985, the tone of life felt much more reasonable. Mao's part in that horrible purge seemed to have been largely overlooked, with his wife and three others taking the blame in the famous trials of the 'gang of four' after Mao's death. Mao in the nineteen-eighties was a respected, though not venerated, figurehead. There were no longer the hoards of propaganda banners to be seen draped across train carriages and public buildings, though the 'unit' concept still played an important part in the life of every individual.

Every town dweller belonged to a unit and this governing body was responsible for granting and allocating jobs, and setting and maintaining moral discipline. It also determined such mundane matters as deciding when a person could take a holiday. By 1985, however, its control was beginning to wane. The days when the unit's permission had to be sought before a marriage could take place, was gradually becoming a thing of the past.

In the end, we managed to complete a basically awful journey to Kunming in relative style, as on the evening of our second night I succeeded in bribing the guard into giving us accommodation in the hard-bed section of the train. Travelling in this fashion was far more enjoyable as it gave us room to move about and a small degree of privacy – ideal for changing lenses on the camera without looking like some sort of tycoon! This night of poor-man's luxury was only dampened slightly by a spate of vomiting that I suffered during the night – presumably down to something I had eaten earlier that evening.

With the memory of snow-capped mountains around Guilin still very clear, it was with our coats buttoned up and fur hats on that we stepped off the train the following morning at dawn. But nature can play some wonderful tricks at times. Although on the same latitude as Guilin, the climate in Kunming was as different as it could have been.

The sun rose into a cloudless sky and it was very soon a matter of peeling off the layers and abandoning the coats for the duration of our stay. Our hotel went a long way to making our stay in Kunming a memorable one, as the dormitory, situated on the fourteenth floor, was comfortable, warm at night and with the best view of the city that could be found.

Our guidebook told us that in Kunming one can see the China of forty years ago better than in any other city. All I can say is that there must have been some very beautiful cities back then if Kunming is taken as the yardstick. In place of the drab 'sixties style' housing blocks of Guilin, we found attractive two-storey buildings, wood-faced and shuttered, lining the streets and alleys in the city centre. Down quiet little back streets we discovered markets selling herbs and pet birds in lovely Chinese bamboo cages. Here we also found tea shops full of wiry-faced old men smoking and drinking tea, or just listening to the raconteur who would provide entertainment for clients. These tea shops used to be a national institution, but now sadly they have become far less numerous. In the end it was the sun that caused us to set our seal of approval on Kunming, and we basked in this new-found warmth as we ambled through the streets and parks and then back to our hotel by tracing the canal.

It was as we were walking beside the canal that we came across a most extraordinary sight. A butcher and his mate were disembowelling a cow which had recently been slaughtered right there on the canal path. The carcass lay on its own skin which couldn't have been off the beast for more than an hour. Standing a few yards away, waiting patiently, was another cow – the third in line judging by the skins that were hung out to dry.

Whether you are in the streets of Rio de Janeiro or the back alleys in China, the children act no differently to foreigners, and we soon found ourselves engaged in the tiring but fun game of answering back 'Hello' and 'Goodbye', as often as not used the wrong way round; a 'Hello' as a little boy dived into a doorway, and a 'Goodbye' as he jumped off the wall to land in front of us again.

In Kunming, as in Guilin and Guangzhou, we were struck time and time again by the absence of litter on either the main streets or back alleys, yet this surface cleanliness seemed so incongruous with the Chinese habit of spitting. Restaurants at least provided spittoons at the foot of each table. Friendliness was another thing which impressed us, and in my experience, Brazil is the only other country I have found where the people are outwardly as friendly, or where one feels so free to walk the streets and alleys at night in complete safety.

On our second day in Kunming and with the weather still good, we caught an early morning boat in the town centre and an hour later arrived on the far side of China's sixth largest lake, which lies just west of the town. The object of the trip was to get out into the countryside and to visit some Yuan Dynasty temples.

The land rises sheer from the western shore and we climbed for about an hour, with a good number of Chinese folk who were also out for the day, before we reached the first temple. Why these things have to be made so inaccessible is beyond me! From here, the going got easier and we followed trails through woods and between rocks from one temple to the next, enjoying the fresh air, the sun and the views, and wallowing in the richness and extravagance of the thirteenth century as we relaxed at the foot of Buddhist temples encountered along the way. Fantastic models of fairy tale forms ranging in size from three feet high to thirty feet high adorned the temples. Pillars and ceilings were clad in gilt and incense hung thick in the air.

There were those who came to worship as we stood watching in the shadows but there were many more who, like us, came to stare. I remember one incident in particular.

There were two young lads who came in – both had been drinking. One of the boys (I suppose they were about sixteen years old) obviously knew the routine and seemed quite at home in the temple, while the other gave the impression of being a bit of a 'city lad' with no knowledge of, and no respect for, the temple or the faith it represented. The first boy was demonstrating to the second the various rites which a worshipper should perform at each of the many altars. I had the impression that he must have grown up with these, but like so many English children who are taken to church when they are young, he had never been for any other reason than being forced to go.

Once he had completed his rather dramatic enactment of the rituals, his pal mimicked the routine. Neither boy tried to hide his amusement or derision of the whole affair.

When the boys had finished at each altar an old man of about seventy or eighty came and took their place. For him, his religion was very real and he looked sadly after the two lads who had by then moved on to the next altar. All of a sudden I could see the Cultural Revolution: Mao's Red Army of young zealous men sent out to rekindle revolutionary fervour (which by 1965 had flagged) but who, in their heady misuse of power, sacked and razed to the ground much of the country's religious heritage, while the old and the weak were forced to stand by and watch yet another page in their country's tempestuous history being written. Were those days in China really that different from Germany in the thirties? Although politically the two histories were poles apart, the young zealots who provided cannon fodder for such political activities seemed happy wearing either colour.

We were relatively lucky on the train journey from Kunming to Emei Shan, our next stop on the route north towards Beijing. Since although we had to settle for hard seats for the overnight journey, we had at least been able to sit together and this time we had interesting company. The guy sitting opposite was a technician working for a textile factory in Kunming and because his factory had just purchased and installed twelve British machines his company was sending him on a day-release course to learn English. So, he practised his very limited vocabulary and we plied him with all the questions we could think of that could be presented in monosyllabic English. Liberal use of the dictionary managed to bridge the majority of the gaps.

Most of our enquiries were related to minor events and customs which we had wondered at; like the origin of the tall, rugged people whom we had begun to see appearing at the stations along the route. They were Tibetans who, as a 'minority' were quite strong in that region, Sichuan. However, when we broached political questions his answers became a little more diplomatic, yet he showed no reticence at answering them and made a point of saying that he was quite free to be discussing the subject.

We asked about China's history since 1912 and he confirmed most of what we knew already. Then we asked what the people of China felt about Mao now. 'He was a great man but he made some mistakes in his later life', was his diplomatic answer, which aligned closely with government statements on the subject. As to Mao's mistakes, our friend was quick to condemn Mao for his part in the Cultural Revolution and the sacking of temples and destruction of learning which characterised that period in China's history. I don't suppose it was much of a coup for political journalism, but it was at least interesting to hear it first-hand from a man who had lived through those times.

The scenery as we travelled north slowly began to change, and we passed through a region of mountains and valleys that did not look unlike parts of the highlands of Scotland. Much of the route was tunnelled and we often emerged to find ourselves clinging to the side of a precipitous gorge some two thousand feet deep, with a torrent of green and white water running at its base. I don't think we had passed through a single stretch of boring landscape since our arrival in China.

Late in the afternoon of the 13th of January our train journey from Kunming brought us to Emei, a small town by Chinese standards and somewhat more off the beaten track than the cities we had visited to date. The hotel where we stayed was one for the locals and so lacked some of the little luxuries of the tourist hotels – like heating and individual toilets. I like to think of myself as a fairly liberal-minded person, willing to give most things a go for the sake of a new experience. However, squatting over an open trough in a line with a dozen or so defecating Chinese men comes close to my definition of uncomfortable! I can remember once seeing some 'communal' latrines on a tour of the old Roman city of Pompeii and thinking at the time what a sociable idea they were. It never crossed my mind that I should one day be using one as a matter of course and that, in reality, they were far from the ideal environment for sociable chat!

Human dung is not wasted in China but is collected by women at night and distributed on the soil – hence 'night soil'. In China these women are highly respected for the onerous task which they perform – unlike in India where they would be defined by their caste as 'untouchable'.

That evening we ended up in a local restaurant with three young Chinese 'dudes' who were intent on seeing us 'disco-dance'. I'm afraid we did not oblige. Nonetheless, we had a very pleasant evening bridging the culture gap with a few beers at 10p a litre. Making our way back to the hotel after the meal our attention was attracted by the noise of people and fireworks coming from the street adjacent to our lodgings. Curious as ever we went to investigate.

The Chinese are renowned for their love of fireworks – in particular, firecrackers which you can hear being let off day and night wherever there are people. However, on this particular evening we walked into the middle of a firework street battle. A group of between twenty and thirty Chinese, both young and old, had gathered at each end of the main street and were firing rockets and crackers at each other across the sixty-foot gap! The route which we had taken intercepted the main street in the middle of this battleground and so, quickly realising our predicament and before we became too popular a target, we hurried along to join the 'front' nearest our hotel to watch proceedings. Firework stalls had been set up behind the 'front line' and locals were buying boxes of 'ammunition' and firing at friends in the rival group down the road.

Rockets were not fired up in the air but were laid down on the road and held in place by hand until the fuse was burned down and the missile shot off through the feet of the enemy camp. Then there were the fire-bombs. At home, we would set these in the ground and watch as different-coloured flares were shot up into the air at intervals, ending in a bang. In China, these make excellent 'toys' and are held by the hand and aimed into the mass of the enemy camp to explode either above their heads or in their midst. Occasionally these missiles would go astray and end up going through someone's bedroom window. An indignant face would then appear at the window shouting down at the folk below, only to be answered by a barrage of fire-bombs and laughter from both camps. To round off the armoury there were firecrackers – bangers, as we would call them – and Catherine-wheels which would be lit and lobbed like grenades across the battlefield. I don't doubt that the whole affair was highly dangerous, both from the risk of a direct hit and from the imminent possibility of igniting the open stalls which acted as armouries. Nevertheless, I hadn't had so much fun in ages as we jumped to miss rockets and firecrackers and laughed along with the Chinese at the whole absurd episode.

The morning after the 'battle' we caught an early bus to the foot of Mount Emei. Rising 6,000 feet above the plains to a substantial 10,000 feet at its summit, the mountain must make an impressive sight from afar. Unfortunately for us we spent the whole of the day walking through mists and low cloud. The bus dropped us by the first of a number of Buddhist monasteries that are located on this sacred mountain and we then followed rough paths and tracks for the whole of the day wending our way from one monastery to another, slowly climbing all the time. Life on the mountain reminded me very much of Nepal. The mule tracks provided the only line of communication between the various villages through which we passed, and one always seemed to be walking up an interminably long series of flagstone steps. We even found corn cob stacks, a scene which I shall always associate with Nepal.

By four in the afternoon, we had reached Wanniansi Monastery where we had the option of staying the night, but the cold and the damp dulled our enthusiasm for what in summer or spring would be, I am sure, a very romantic notion. So, after a quick squint at the six-metre-high, Song Dynasty, bronze Buddha riding an elephant (cast in 980 AD) we hurried off down the mountain to catch the last bus back to Emei and thence to Leshan, a nearby market town where we planned to stay the night.

After a quiet night in Leshan, spent in a local hotel for an absurd 50p a head, we got up early and wandered down to the river where we had been told we could get a boat to take us to see the largest Buddha in

China. We were, I must admit, a little sceptical of this claim as it is one which is heard in just about every town you visit. However, when we reached the river we soon found a local ferryman who promptly abandoned his job of ferrying locals across the tributary river, and much to the indignation of those still awaiting his services, launched off with us as sole passengers down to where the tributary joined the main stream. It was still only seven o'clock in the morning and the mist lay on the water as our rickety wooden craft was poled away from the bank. The grey misty light and the shabbiness of our surroundings reminded me of a scene from Dickens's *Great Expectations*, where Pip is attempting to smuggle his convict benefactor down the Thames on just such a morning.

The scene didn't remain tranquil for long, for as our craft (more a canoe than a sampan) neared the junction with the main river, the surface of the water became broken and we were soon shooting through white water at around ten knots with our ferryman fighting to keep a straight course, using his oar as a rudder worked from the sculling point at the back of the boat.

In seconds we shot through the rapids and into the main river like a cork from a bottle.

From that point to the Buddha it was a pleasant ten-minute drift downstream, and as the colossal two-hundred-and-thirty-foot monster of a sculpture came into view, we realised that its claim to uniqueness had been no hollow boast. The Buddha was carved from the river cliff and was portrayed sitting, gazing out onto the plains beyond the river in awesome majesty. Indeed, the statue is so integral to the cliff from which it is carved that the locals have a saying which roughly translates as: 'The mountain is a Buddha and the Buddha is a mountain'. The in-situ statue was completed in the eighth century.

Our ferryman, much to our relief, dropped us on the banks of the main river, but not without a hard wrangle over money. We had committed one of the traveller's cardinal sins. We had not fixed a price before setting off. In the end, a fair price was agreed, and we made our way back to town by an alternative route.

It was time to be moving on once more, so returning to the centre of Leshan we caught a bus to Chengdu where we planned to make a brief halt on our way north to Xian and then Beijing.

Our stay in Chengdu was brief indeed, three hours to be precise. In that time we managed to book a hard sleeper to Xian, take a bus ride round the sights, including the ten-metre-high statue of Mao Zedong in the central square (one of the few that remain in the provinces) and treat ourselves to a slap-up meal in the best restaurant in town at £1 a head!

It struck us as we went from town to town, just how like China is to the world that George Orwell described in his book *1984*. There was a lifeless drabness about nearly all the towns we visited, which came across so well in Orwell's book. The blue uniform, which both men and women wear across the whole social strata, is also familiar in the picture that Orwell painted. Big brother was here too, perhaps not as all-seeing as in the book, but you still got the impression that people guarded their comments and glanced over their shoulders before committing themselves to something controversial.

In *1984* the power of propaganda was demonstrated when, as each time the name of the enemy changed, all records which stated to the contrary were destroyed and you soon believed that Oceania had always been at war with Eurasia and never Eastasia at all. In a way, it has been the same in China. As the government changed hands between the Pragmatists and the Maoists, statues of Mao went up or got pulled down and the art of propaganda became well advanced.

On the train to Xian we were able to chat to a university physics teacher who was sitting next to us. I say chat – she had about as much English as I had Chinese – but with a pen and a sketchpad all is possible.

Our teacher friend was fifty and she earned 94 yuan per month (about £25 on official rates). Her husband earned about the same. On this, they supported their two children and an elderly father. She paid 6 yuan per month rent on her government house and their food bill came to around 30 yuan per head – that was about 160 of the 190 accounted for. That is why, she said, China rides around on bicycles!

During the Cultural Revolution, and for some years afterwards, her university was closed down and she was sent to work in the fields. This was between the years 1966 and 1972. She then returned to junior school teaching until the university was reopened in 1977. She endorsed our previous friend's opinion that Mao was a great man who made mistakes in his later life, and when questioned about the present government she expressed the opinion that although there had been great improvements over the last two or three years it was looking more and more to America. This concerned her as she would have preferred to see China's sights trained equally on America and Russia in these unstable days.

About three hours before Xian we swapped our diesel engine for steam. The sun was shining and the rugged hill country around us had a thin covering of snow. We shivered involuntarily at the sight.

Our mid-afternoon arrival in Xian gave us plenty of time to shop around for the cheapest hotel. Always an irksome task, it was made all the worse by the discovery that nowhere in Xian was cheap, and that the only hotels open to tourists were five star. Ironically it was the best hotel in town that was the only one to offer dormitory accommodation and which, therefore, ended up being the cheapest. The Renmin Grand was a truly palatial hotel with gardens and fountains and some exquisite Chinese architectural follies.

It was also well heated, and this was a luxury that we would have traded all other trimmings to secure!

Xian put us once more on the beaten track and our dormitory colleagues were all Aussies or Americans. Many had made the trek to Lhasa in Tibet and it was now beginning to look possible to make the trip by truck at a fraction of the airfare. I knew we should have gone, but China was beginning to grind us both down, and neither of us felt ready to extend our stay there by a further two weeks – not even for Tibet. Our decision was finally confirmed by a tale told to us by two Dutch girls.

Early on during their travels in China they had met up and become quite friendly with two Canadian lads who were planning to visit Tibet by truck from Golmud. This thirty-six-hour endurance test was the only alternative at the time to flying from Chengdu and, needless to say, it had the great advantage of costing much less than the airfare.

There were two types of truck working the route from Golmud to Lhasa in Tibet; an upmarket, heated Japanese truck and the locally built Chinese one which was a draughty unheated contraption providing an absolute minimum in terms of comfort. When our two Canadians arrived in Golmud the Japanese truck had already left and so cursing their luck, but not wishing to be put off, they set off in an old Chinese lorry, one sitting by the driver, the other by the tailgate in the back of the truck. By the time they reached Lhasa the guy in the back was dead. He had quite literally frozen to death in his sleep.

The Dutch girls met the remaining Canadian again by chance in Chengdu as he was making arrangements for his friend's body to be repatriated. This was a week before our conversation with them. The story was obviously not representative of the norm, nevertheless we began to feel that Tibet in January was not such a good idea and so turned our concentration on Xian.

For most of China's history, from the Zhou Dynasty in the eleventh century BC until the end of the Tang Dynasty in the tenth century AD, Xian was the capital city. Its historical heritage is therefore enormous; but then, unfortunately, so was the destruction it suffered at the hands of the Red Army during the Cultural Revolution. The city of five million was now an important industrial centre and the smog hung thicker there than anywhere we had so far visited. The polluted atmosphere of its cities was (and to a great extent still is) one of China's most noticeable characteristics. We were both told that we would develop colds during our visit, and we both did! By now Laurence and I were sporting a catarrh cold and sore throat and could not foresee losing them until we were out of China.

Since the destruction of the late nineteen sixties, much has been done to try to restore the Ming Dynasty parts of the city to their former glory. These include the city wall and impressive Bell and Drum towers. But Xian's fame as a tourist spot is accredited to a far more recent piece of work. In 1974 during the construction of a farm well, the world's most substantial archaeological discovery of the century was made – the terracotta army of the Emperor Qin Shi Huangdi. Of the 6,000 life-size figures that make up the guard for the Emperor's tomb, only five hundred had been recovered at the time of our visit. The tomb itself lies under a mammoth man-made hill and, at the time of writing, had still not been touched by archaeologists.

Those soldiers and horses that had been recovered stood exactly where they were found, with the earth cleared around them, under the protection of an enormous canopy. Intricately detailed in sculpture and dating back to 210 BC, any one of the figures alone would be considered a major acquisition for a national museum.

The terracotta warriors, and a visit to the site of a 7,000-year-old Stone Age settlement at Banpo, filled one of our two days in Xian. The other was spent touring the city itself.

It was during this wander round that we came across a junior school which by its architecture we had mistaken for a temple. By the time we had discovered our mistake we had become too curious to turn back and so spent a fascinating quarter of an hour wandering in and out of half-empty classrooms and through the courtyard. It was lunchtime and the children were playing 'hopscotch' or just lounging around in the classrooms. Everywhere we went we were greeted with a smile and 'nee-how' (my phonetic spelling of a Chinese 'hello') but no one bothered to challenge our right to be there.

In the streets we found that nearly all the children had at least two or three words of English and so it was interesting to see just how much emphasis was placed on English in the primary schools. Of the two classrooms that we looked around, one had last been used for an English Grammar lesson, and on the notice board, where Christmas frescoes had been drawn, a good third of the space was given up to greetings and poems in English. The classrooms themselves were quite bare and functional, not unlike some of those I remember from my own early school days.

The Chinese attitude to us as strangers was a curious one. They were always very polite and helpful and yet we often had the feeling that we were considered inferior to them. If 'truth' equates to 'belief', then as a foreigner in 1985 China we *were* inferior, if only because one billion Chinese believed we were! This feeling of inferiority combined with the pressure of constantly being the focus of attention was, by this time, beginning to wear us both down. We recognised that in most of the places we visited we were bound to be something of a novelty and yet I was still amazed at the child-like nature of people's curiosity towards us.

Often when I was sitting on a bus I would turn to find the fellow sitting next to me just staring at me, without the slightest show of embarrassment at being caught. On another occasion I can remember squatting by a wall at a railway station trying to sort out some tickets I had just bought, and within seconds there was a crowd of about twenty people gathered around me – just staring! A performance of 'changing the camera lens' was another great crowd-puller. I can remember the same sort of thing happening in India when we were off the beaten track, but this was somehow a far more passive, almost impassive, behaviour than the inquisitive nature I had encountered in rural India.

At the end of our second day in Xian, on Friday the 18th of January, we boarded the train for Beijing (Peking) – another twenty-four-hour steam train journey, but this time with hard-sleepers and an excellent dining car.

The music was less forceful on this journey with a thankful reduction in the amount of Chinese Opera. I don't like to consider myself a cultural 'stick-in-the-mud', but I couldn't help seeing a certain clarity of perception in a description of Chinese Opera which I once heard from an American dorm-mate, who described the art as sounding like a half-strangled cat singing in falsetto while staggering across an open grand piano with cymbals tied to its feet. Perhaps I just needed to give it more time!

For the first part of the journey the scenery between Xian and Beijing was rugged and mountainous. The type of barren, stratified landscape which typified Cape Verde but fifty degrees colder! However, about three hours from Beijing, the scene changed and the land levelled out to flat arable plains. But, with the intense cold, everything outside lay dormant and brown under a clear winter sky.

Lunch on the trains could be truly awful, but on this particular train it was 'a la carte'. Pork was always the most prominent meat, often served shredded with green peppers. We tried to experiment wherever we ate but found it difficult to find anything to surpass good old 'sweet and sour pork', which now became our 'go to' dish.

Arriving in Beijing by train was much like arriving in any capital city, with grim suburban sprawls and light industry. As we emerged from the station the sun was shining in a clear blue sky and the temperature was ten degrees below. We made our way to the hotel we had picked from the guidebook, but on arrival found that they had done away with the promised dorms and were now charging £10 a night for rooms.

This was out of the question and we weren't in the mood for bussing halfway across Beijing in search of something cheaper, so Laurence played his last card and put in a phone call to a contact that he had been given in Hong Kong. The fellow in Hong Kong was hardly a firm friend. Laurence had only spoken to this guy once on the phone, and that was on business, but the name did the job and within the hour we were settling into the hospitality of a Mr Peter Sun, general manager of China's most prestigious hotel, 'The Great Wall Hotel'.

The hotel had only been open eighteen months and was the first Western five-star hotel to do so in China. The centrepiece of the hotel was a seven-storey atrium which housed a stylish coffee lounge, where a string quartet played every evening until ten. At one side of the atrium, glass-fronted lifts serving all twenty-one floors afforded a splendid view of the atrium as they whisked you up through the atrium space before disappearing into the main bulk of the hotel for the remaining floors.

That evening we were invited to dinner, and so donning the wisely-packed white shirt and tie, we joined Peter and four of his staff in one of the hotel's five restaurants. Both the company and the food were refreshingly good. Peter himself was born in China but had been raised and educated in America, and thus provided the perfect middleman for such a project as the Great Wall Hotel. We learned later that his initial task of interceding in China had been made that much easier by the fact that he was the great nephew of Sun Yat-Sen, accepted by many as being the father of modern China.

As guests in Peking, the meal that evening had to be Peking Duck. This famous dish is a real gastronomic experience as it is a series of dishes produced from a single duck. At the beginning of the meal the glazed duck is presented at the table – head and all. It is then taken away, and the skin is carved off and served with a few bean shoots in a pancake envelope – delicious! The meat is then shredded and served with vegetables and rice. While a soup is prepared from the remains of the duck the meal continues with various non-duck-related dishes. Finally, after the soup, the meal is rounded off with a selection of sweets – doughnuts stuffed with lotus seed was a particular goody.

We had given ourselves three days to 'do' Beijing, a programme which meant no messing about, however our first morning was taken up entirely with buying tickets for the following two days. The train tickets proved the most tiresome, queuing for two hours only to find that we had been in the wrong queue in the first place – that's part of the fun of travelling in China on the cheap! In the afternoon we made our way to the centre of Beijing and to the city's main attraction, the Forbidden City.

During the Ming Dynasty (1368–1644), Beijing consisted of cities within cities. In the centre was the Forbidden City, around which was the Inner City, and then around that the Outer City. The two hundred and fifty acres which made up the Forbidden City was home for the Emperor and his court. Today, only the Forbidden City remains intact within its own walls. As we walked into it through the Tiananmen Gate, which now carries a great portrait of Mao facing out into Tiananmen Square, it was incredible to think that even until 1912 this great Imperial Palace with all its opulence and pomp had been used solely by the Emperors and that it was therefore only seventy years before our visit, on the abdication of the last Emperor, that ordinary people got their first glimpse of where we were now walking freely.

Bordering the Forbidden City, and situated south of it, is Tiananmen Square, the largest plaza in the world, and site of the historic Maoist rallies which took place during the heyday of China's recent history. The massive square is flanked on one side by the Tiananmen Gate and the Imperial Palace, to the south by Mao's memorial hall which contains his embalmed body, to the west by the Great Hall of the people, and to the east by the Communist Museum.

That evening, after a brief and unexciting meal, we went to see the Peking Acrobatic Company – an impressive display of magic and acrobatics performed in a nineteen-forties-type provincial theatre, Beijing's best.

On the morning of our second day in Beijing we discovered a little street restaurant serving Western breakfasts, so we stoked ourselves up with fried eggs and coffee before boarding the coach for our day-tour to the Ming Tombs and the Great Wall. This was a tourist coach, and the luxury was sublime in comparison with local buses where even at six in the morning, the conductor is forced to push bodies into the bus in order to get the door shut. If you are unfortunate enough to have been last in, then at the next stop you get ejected onto the pavement as the compact bodies explode out of the bus when the doors open. If it isn't your stop, then you have to fight your way back in again, before you are trampled upon by the rush of new boarders. On our tourist coach however, we had a seat and even legroom.

About twenty miles north of Beijing, the mountains begin, and at the site of the Ming Tombs these mountains had formed a horseshoe shape encompassing an area of the plain about five miles wide. Into the mountainside all around the horseshoe, the Emperors of the Ming Dynasty had built their tombs, facing them with elaborate facades and surface temples. We visited a number of these sites, including one that had been built for the Emperor responsible for the construction of the Forbidden City. This particular tomb was set at the end of a three-mile-long avenue, lined with life-size stone animals – a popular postcard shot.

By lunchtime the tour had reached the Great Wall itself. For the last twenty miles of our fifty-mile journey from Beijing, we had been travelling through rugged, precipitous mountains, frozen and barren in the grip of winter, yet not covered in snow. When I had visited the Taj Mahal in India, I can remember preparing for a feeling of anti-climax and I had been surprised that the reality had proven even more magnificent than my already high expectation. The same must be said of the Great Wall and, in this respect, it must rank as being one of the most impressive sights I have ever seen.

The Wall, some 3,700 miles of it, was begun in the fifth century BC, and was enhanced right up until the Ming Dynasty in the fifteenth century AD. It remains the only manmade structure which is still visible with the naked eye from space – or so they say! Only some twenty feet across on top, it is not a wide wall. Nor is it, in the main, a tall one, at an average of thirty feet in height. It was not built as a thing of beauty, but beautiful it surely is, as it meanders across this rugged scenery, its honey-coloured stone blending in with the surroundings. The weather was clear and crisp and could not have been better as we strolled and climbed the, sometimes steep, paved road which runs along the top of the wall. Truly a highlight of our China experience.

Having arrived back in Beijing by mid-afternoon, we spent the remainder of the daylight hours touring the Temple of Heaven – more Ming architecture – before making our way to a performance of the Peking Opera. This cultural immersion was everything I had feared it would be, only louder! I shall never understand the musical appeal of cymbals and snare drums being bashed simultaneously throughout almost all of the performance. But the costumes were magnificent! We left the Opera at the interval and retired to the hotel to relax for an hour over a coffee, listening to the quartet and writing much-overdue postcards.

Having checked out of the hotel on day three and deposited our bags at the railway station, we set out to cover the remaining sights.

The Summer Palace was first on the list. Built as a summer retreat for the Emperors, this pretty area of temples and Ming palaces constructed on wooded slopes, overlooked a vast man-made lake. The lake, Kunming Lake, was frozen over and dozens of Chinese were ice-skating, giving the place a festive air. After visiting the Summer Palace we made our way back to Tiananmen Square and the Communist Museum. Sadly, this proved to be a frustrating hour, as nothing was explained anywhere in English. 'Exit' was the only word we could find and understand. It had then been our intention to visit Mao's embalmed body, but unfortunately the Memorial Hall was closed and so we made our way to a Sichuan restaurant for a meal and thence to the Beijing Hotel for a pre-departure drink.

Our train journey between Beijing and Shanghai passed without incident. Once again, it was a twenty-four-hour trip, and once again we managed to get hard-sleepers. The routine search for a hotel went off without a hitch, and by five o'clock we were installed in the dormitory of one of Shanghai's mid-range hotels overlooking the river and quite close to the centre of the town.

Shanghai has a curious history. In the middle of the nineteenth century it was opened to European traders as part of the Treaty of Nanjing. As such, the city was divided up into four parts: the British Quarter, the French Quarter, the Japanese and the Chinese.

Trade flourished and grand European-style buildings were erected, notably along the waterfront – an area that came to be known as The Bund. The exploitation of this little colony was ruthless, and hostility between the European powers and the indigenous Chinese was fuelled by such everyday injustices as notices that were erected at the entrances to public parks stating that dogs and Chinese were not allowed. Then suddenly, as a consequence of the Second World War, the British and French were kicked out and the clocks in Shanghai were stopped. Chinese development in Shanghai, of course, continued until the city was changed from a romantic and glamorous consumer city into an industrial metropolis of eleven million people, but during this time all things western were put away – until now.

On our first evening we called into the Peace Hotel which, as the Cathay Hotel during the thirties, had been one of Shanghai's most upmarket establishments. The hotel is situated on The Bund where all the buildings, including the Peace Hotel, could have easily been lifted from central London or nineteen-thirties New York. Inside, the hotel decor was also of that period, and as we entered the lounge for a beer, we heard a jazz band playing 'Little Brown Jug'. Half hidden behind potted rubber plants, the band played music from the thirties and forties all through the evening. The clocks in Shanghai had been started once more.

In many ways it isn't strange that this idea of the West should have lingered so long, to be reincarnated in 1985, since it is all that Shanghai knew of the West. The gradual 'opening up' or liberalisation that the country was experiencing under Deng Xiaoping was challenging this nineteen-thirties image of western culture, but it would be years before Shanghai accelerated into the global city it is today – almost indistinguishable from Dubai. Yet whether one is talking about old Shanghai or its twenty-first-century transformation, it has always been as different and distant from real China as New York is from Delhi.

The following morning we strolled. First to visit a couple of the city's newer hotels, and then back through the old French quarter to the quay and The Bund. Much of the old French quarter was like Kunming and retained the air of mystery, intrigue and shady conspiracies which once were the hallmark of Shanghai. But The Bund with its grand old buildings looking out onto the river will be my lasting memory of Shanghai.

Twenty hours after arriving in Shanghai, we were preparing to leave it. By this stage we were both looking towards the sun. This country needs the patience of Job and, frankly, as we sat huddled up over our coffee with the paper tissues mounting up in our duffel coat pockets from our streaming colds, ours was running out!

Much of the frustration of travelling in China comes from the 'Alice in Wonderland' syndrome that seems to govern life. It's as if everything is done back to front. There never appeared to be any logic to the situation. Some of this apparent chaos was due to the newness of tourism in China, and thus systems for dealing with foreigners simply weren't standardised. But simple prejudice seemed to account for a far greater part.

A classic occurrence happened at Hangzhou station, our first stop out of Shanghai. We arrived in Hangzhou from Shanghai in the early evening and were attempting to buy our onward train ticket in advance, a standard procedure that saves a lot of time and worry later. Having queued for an hour, along with the rest of China, we were told that we could only buy hard-seats for this thirty-six-hour, two-night journey. There were no hard-sleepers available. 'Meiyou' (nothing) was the only response we could get out of the hard-faced counter clerk. Well, we had not arrived in China the day before, and we knew that this wasn't necessarily the last word on the matter, so, the following morning we returned and visited the foreign ticket office which had been closed the previous evening. We quietly explained that we wanted to swop our hard-seats for hard-sleepers, an accepted procedure, and one which we had employed on previous occasions – but this time: 'Meiyou'! It looked as if we really were beaten. But just as we were leaving, a young Hong Kong Chinese couple came and ordered some tickets for themselves. After they had finished at the counter, they came over to us and asked if we had a problem. We were astonished to find that they had just swopped their hard-seats for hard-sleepers on the very same train that was causing us so much of a problem.

We returned to the counter again. Politely we asked the now familiar question and politely the counter clerk took our hard-seat tickets and swopped them for hard-sleeper tickets. No fuss, no explanation.

Our stay in Hangzhou was particularly pleasant, despite its brevity. We had been recommended by a fellow traveller to try the best hotel in town, a large, impressive Country Club type place on the lakeside a couple of miles outside town. Here, they promised, we should find a comfortable but cheap dorm and a restaurant that could make a Westerner feel homesick – the food was so good.

When we arrived we were not disappointed. Nevertheless, getting into the dormitory had been yet another 'Alice in Wonderland' experience. We requested two beds in the hotel dormitory as usual but were met with the now familiar: 'Meiyou'! Experience had taught us that patience and determination were the order of the day in such a situation. We politely

160

declined the offer of a double room explaining that we couldn't afford it, and then we stood and waited, playing the familiar game through, despite our tiredness and desire to rant and rage. The receptionist shuffled papers for five minutes and then handed us the booking-in cards – they had found room for us. No apologies, no explanations, and on our behalf no questions, just time.

The meal that evening had been truly splendid and accompanied by music provided by a local orchestra that played 'oom-pah-pah' type Chinese 'hit' music, the like of which we had become used to on the trains.

Our train for Guangzhou left at nine o'clock the following evening, and so we had the whole day to wander around the town and lake, taking rickshaws whenever we got too tired of walking. In the late afternoon we found ourselves at a Buddhist temple. Dating back to the fifth century, the temple itself was a magnificent building brought alive by the sounds of cymbals and drums and the chanting of the monks and the pervading smell of incense. The more I see of other world religions, with their great variety and complexities, the more I wonder at the sureness with which we sometimes claim guardianship of the true faith. Someone has to be right I suppose, or none of us, or perhaps all of us in part.

Our train to Guangzhou that evening took us back into familiar territory. We were on our way out, and by the end of the second day all the traumas and excitement of China were behind us.

My diary for that last day concludes as follows:

'Over the next fifty years I can see China see-sawing between capitalism with a small 'c' and communism with a big 'C' as it develops its potential as an industrial power. In the end, I think it will go capitalist. Its roots, however, are firmly planted in the communist ideal, and any swift move to the right is bound to be viewed as a betrayal of that ideal, for which the nation has fought and suffered. Some would argue that the policies of its present government are already throwing the country into a western sphere of influence at an unhealthy rate. This rate of progress towards capitalism will, I'm sure, remain the source of great internal wrangling for years to come. I believe the direction is set and is irreversible. The era of Mao Zedong is over. That of the Pragmatists has only just begun.'

Reviewing these impressions thirty-five years on, much still remains valid I believe. China and the Chinese people still embody a capitalist mentality in a communist system. But my prediction of being thrown towards a western sphere of influence has proven a little arrogant! As I sit editing this book in 2020, it would appear that the future will be determined much more by a Chinese sphere of influence, towards which the West will need to bend, rather than the other way around. The Emperors of old have cast a long shadow and China today has no interest in moulding itself on anyone else's culture. It is too proud and too steeped in its own extraordinary history. Moreover, now that Xi Jinping enjoys indefinite tenure (since 2018) it feels rather as if a new Chinese dynasty has begun, and one that will take us to a very different future than the one I had anticipated in 1985.

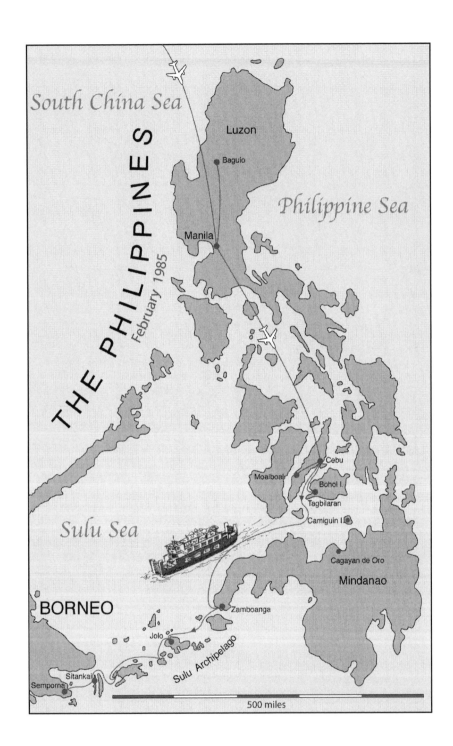

South China Sea

Luzon

Baguio

Philippine Sea

THE PHILIPPINES
February 1985

Manila

Moalboal

Cebu

Bohol I.

Tagbilaran

Camiguin I.

Sulu Sea

Cagayan de Oro

Mindanao

BORNEO

Zamboanga

Jolo

Sulu Archipelago

Sitankai

Semporna

500 miles

164

CHAPTER NINE

The Philippines

During our last day or two of travelling in China Laurence's cold had taken a turn for the worse and the addition of a bout of food poisoning just about laid him out. So by the time we arrived back in Hong Kong, we felt as if we had just been to hell and back. Laurence was coughing blood; he hadn't eaten for two days and was quite pale. I was in much better health, but felt a bit of a social outcast, knowing that I had been travelling and sleeping in the same thermal vest and long-johns for almost three weeks.

Fortunately help was at hand in the shape of Tim and Helen, who we had come to know during our preparation for China. The final struggle through customs and the battle across Hong Kong with our packs had proven the last straw. We knocked on the door of Tim's flat on Lantau Island totally exhausted. Tim and Helen were model rescuers; hot baths, food and then bed – for eighteen hours uninterrupted sleep! When we did awake, we found that Tim had already made an appointment for Laurence to see a doctor who subsequently stuffed him full of antibiotics and sent him back to bed again.

While Laurence was recovering, I followed up some contacts that I had been given in the UK with a view to securing some sort of temporary employment for April through to July. Money was beginning to run out and Hong Kong seemed as good a place as any to claw back a few savings.

In the end, finding a job proved far simpler than I had been expecting and by the time we were ready to leave Hong Kong for Manila a deal was completed with my old firm who had set up in joint venture with a Hong Kong development company. My mind once more at ease, I focused my attention on planning the next two months of travel.

Our intention was to conduct a circular tour of South East Asia, starting in the Philippines and working our way clockwise through Borneo, Singapore, Malaysia and Thailand before returning to Hong Kong in late March. To cover so much ground in only eight weeks was going to require commitment, not to mention stamina. But then neither of us were the type for sitting on beaches while there remained new places to explore. So, feeling much refreshed after our five-day break in Hong Kong, Laurence and I got on a plane and headed south for sunshine, sea and 'jeepneys'.

Arriving in the Philippines after four weeks in China was like taking a breath of fresh air after a stuffy night – there was a sense of freedom which was almost tangible.

The expression *joie de vivre* could have been invented to describe the difference between the two countries. China felt devoid of it; The Philippines had it in abundance. In so many ways the country is like Brazil, and the people themselves strike the first chord of resemblance. The dark complexion – a rich golden-brown skin and black hair with a slight slant to the eyes which was so noticeable in Amazonians.

Secondly, the climate was similar, hot and very humid, and thirdly the two nations shared the same casual play-like attitude to life that shows itself best in the jeepneys of the Philippines.

A jeepney is a mode of transport. In essence, it is a converted US army jeep equipped to seat twelve people, but in appearance it is a glittering masterpiece of brass and chrome, festooned with dozens of aerials, trailing flags, ten times too many mirrors and at least five or six chrome horses fastened to the bonnet. The more stylish jeepneys even have stereos, carpets and curtains. They are even more abundant than London taxis and seeing them all lined up at a set of traffic lights is like waiting for a stock-car race to begin!

However, as a tourist spot, Manila itself did not have a great deal to offer and so, on the morning after our arrival, we caught the bus north to the mountains. The buses were fairly rough and ready but comfortable enough in the warm climate, and by nightfall we had arrived in the provincial capital of Baguio.

The mountain provinces are renowned for their spectacular scenery and magnificent rice terraces. So for the following three days we toured; taking buses along dirt track mountain roads from one village to the next, admiring the lush green flooded terraces supported by their intricate irrigation network. We stopped off at will to swim in the mountain streams, or just to walk, before hitching a lift onwards to the nearest night halt.

Some of the rice terraces around Bontoc and Banaue are particularly impressive; their ancient construction being locally acclaimed as the eighth wonder of the world. Rice in the mountain provinces of the Philippines can be harvested all year round, and so seeing the rice at all stages of development proved an education in itself. These three days were perhaps the most relaxed and enjoyable we had spent in Asia to date. Laurence summed it up quite nicely as we were walking one afternoon, by saying that he could now no longer declare that his native Scotland was the most beautiful place in the world! But travelling around this area was not cheap and so, with great reluctance, we headed back down to Manila on our fourth day and geared ourselves up for touring southwards.

The Philippines consists of over 7,000 islands and so for the second half of our Philippine visit we had decided to do some island hopping. To place ourselves in a prime position for this, and in order to cut down on unproductive travelling, we decided to take advantage of a cheap deal on Philippine's Domestic Airlines and fly the one-and-three-quarter-hours south to the holiday island of Cebu. The cost of the flight was $16.

In Cebu, we had some major decisions to make. The problem hinged around the fact that with diplomatic relations severed between Sabah in Borneo and the Philippines, all legal crossings to Borneo from the southern tip of the Philippines had been stopped.

The question therefore was whether to head north, island hopping back towards Manila from where we could catch a plane into Borneo, or to head south and attempt to cross illegally by ship. Ignoring legalities, the most logical and appealing route was obviously the latter since it conformed most closely with our objective of a 'circular tour'. However, a number of other factors were making the final decision far from easy.

These considerations included civil unrest and banditry on the southern island of Mindanao; piracy in the straits between Mindanao and Borneo; and the risk that even if we did escape the pirates, we could still be caught by the coastguard patrol. If against all these odds we managed to arrive safely in Borneo then we still had to cross a country where there were virtually no roads and where stories of head hunting still abounded.

We had not met a single traveller at that stage who had been able to complete this route through Borneo to Singapore, but we had heard a number of rumours concerning our options. Some of these options were more legal than others and so it soon became clear that a little bit of research would not go amiss if we were to reach a sensible decision on the matter.

Possibly the safest, though least-exciting, option was to hitch a lift with one of the lumber ships that we believed to be operating out of Davao on the east coast of Mindanao. The next option was to travel part of the way down the Sulu Archipelago until we found a barter trader who was willing to help us make the crossing. The 'barter traders' were local merchants who had been granted special licences by the Philippine government to continue trading with Sabah. Their licence, however, specifically excluded the carrying of passengers and so this option would require some careful negotiation.

The third option, and something of a last resort, was to elicit the help of a group of seamen whose profession was the import and export of both goods and people. Smugglers. We had heard it rumoured that such activities were rife in the extreme end of the Sulu Archipelago (Philippine's southernmost chain of islands) but how one went about contacting these people or indeed how safe such a course of action would be was pure guesswork. What we did know, however, was that the real threat to safety, associated with this option, was not from the smugglers themselves but from the pirates who plied the straits feeding off the smugglers!

None of the guidebooks had been able to give any assistance on the viability of crossing to Borneo and official sources, such as tourist agencies or shipping agents, had been equally non-cooperative. In the end we found our most useful source of information on the quayside, talking to seamen and those whose business would have taken them to Zamboanga in Mindanao and along the length of the Sulu Archipelago, bringing them in direct contact with the smuggling racket between the Philippines and Borneo.

With our heads full of tittle-tattle and gossip but still very few concrete facts we retired to Moalboal on the opposite side of the island to consider our decision.

'There is paradise on earth, because I have seen it!' I wrote these words in my diary, sitting in a cane chair on the veranda of our bamboo and cane cottage, on the morning after our arrival in Moalboal. A warm breeze was blowing in from the sea and the sun threw a patchwork of light and shade across the floor as it shone in through the latticework which bordered the veranda. Looking out from where I sat, the world was a collage of greens and reds, pinks and yellows. A large black and white butterfly, contrasting sharply with its surroundings, floated from one flower to the next seemingly unaware of me and the attention I had been paying it. Beyond this Garden of Eden, only some fifty yards away, the ferns and flowering plants gave way to gently swaying coconut palms which gave shade to a white coral beach – nature's 'no man's land' between land and sea.

Moalboal is one of a thousand such places that this country of islands can offer those who are willing to look beyond the sordid bright lights of Manila. It did not have long to work its magic on our weary adventurers. With the knowledge we gained from the dockland of Cebu, combined with what information the tourist organisations could give us on buses and shipping routes in and around the troubled island of Mindanao (of which Zamboanga is the capital), we had reached a number of rather 'thin' conclusions.

Firstly, travel across Mindanao would be quite safe providing we took non-stop buses, being particularly careful not to pick a route which would involve a night halt or even travelling by night. The evidence seemed to suggest that this would be possible for both Davao and Zamboanga. And secondly, we had not been able to find any information to support the rumour that a timber freighter leaving from Davao would be our safest means of crossing to Borneo. There was even talk of the route having been discontinued. Most disappointing was the fact that no one was able to give us any more information on the barter traders or smugglers, other than to suggest that they were 'possible but dangerous' options – wonderfully useful advice! By now though our appetites were whetted and so we decided to head on and test the ground; south from Cebu to the island of Bohol, thence to the island of Camiguin and finally to Cagayan de Oro on the north coast of Mindanao.

The troubles in Mindanao were fundamentally religious. The Philippines are officially Christian, and are the only such country in Asia. But Mindanao has always been a Muslim stronghold and a persistent thorn in the Filipino side. There is a deep-rooted mistrust between the two peoples which is much more profound than the Protestant/Catholic division we were well used to in Northern Ireland at this time.

However, religious fervour was not the only source of unrest in the Philippines during the nineteen eighties. At the time of our travels there existed considerable disquiet amongst the people as a whole, aimed squarely at the government. President Marcos had been in power for over a decade, initially through democratic re-election and then subsequently by means of rigged re-appointment and a systematic crushing of the opposition. The murder of the charismatic opposition leader Benigno Aquino (husband of the later President), on his return from exile in America, did much to highlight the situation in the eyes of the world.

The atmosphere was one of public dissatisfaction. The country's economy was governed by a rich and elite ten per cent, and an absence of social security kept the large number of unemployed on the bread line. And all too many Filipino girls had turned to an alternative means of making ends meet, giving Manila a reputation which made Amsterdam look like a seminary.

I should perhaps say a little more about the prostitution racket in Manila, since to try and understand Manila without a true grasp of this aspect of the city's daily life is to fool oneself about the real problems which faced its people at this time.

It was clear from the outset that the business of prostitution was, and probably still is, very organised – and very public. Filipino girls in their thousands, ranging from the age of twelve upwards, were openly being traded on the streets of Manila for four hundred pesos a night, plus a one hundred and thirty peso 'finder's fee' which went to the business-minded 'mums' who ran the joints. This was equivalent to a total cost of around £25, but terms were more usually quoted either on an hourly basis or conversely for much longer 'holidays' of a week or more.

Wishing to avoid this sub-culture, the careful tourist soon discovers that he is still not 'safe' by keeping clear of the more obvious girly bars and pick up joints, since even in the more respectable cafes where one might retreat for a quiet undisturbed drink, the lid is not off the beer before a young girl would appear 'out of the floorboards' to sit across the table, enticing you to buy them a drink. But the hard-nosed business approach to prostitution is not the whole story. There is a lot of innocence on the streets of Manila. Girls who have come in from the country congregate at the twenty-four-hour fast food outlets in the centre of Ermita, Manila's red light district, and all too soon get drawn into the system, lured by fast and easy money.

The attitude of the girls working in prostitution is very matter-of-fact, and in Ermita there is no shame. Beyond the security of the red light district, however, these girls suffer terribly from the open insults levelled chiefly by Filipino men and boys whenever they are seen in public with Westerners. Sadly, we found this treatment was dealt out to all Filipino girls who accompany white foreigners, whether they were prostitutes or not.

Finally on this subject, I must just relate a little story which reflected this sub-culture. In attempting to leave Manila for Cebu the week before, Laurence and I had managed to miss our plane and so were forced to spend the night by the airport in readiness for the flight the following morning. While I made the necessary flight reservation, Laurence went to make enquiries about accommodation. On asking the taxi driver if he knew of any cheap accommodation nearby for himself and a friend the answer came back: 'OK, no problem, I'll take you there for 20 pesos and the room will cost you 140 pesos for three hours'. Welcome to Manila!

Ever conscious of our tight schedule we prized ourselves away from Moalboal and caught the bus back to Cebu City. From there a ferry took us to Tagbilaran on the island of Bohol and this was followed by another bus ride up into the interior of the island where we booked into a hilltop establishment called The Chocolate Hills Hotel. The travelling had been just about non-stop since six o'clock in the morning – thirteen hours in all. The Chocolate Hills Hotel is named after the region in which it is located, a fascinating landscape of fertile, rice green fields out of which rise innumerable ice-cream-scoop-shaped hills burnt 'chocolate brown' in the dry season but a disappointing muddy green when we saw them. I had certainly not seen a landscape like it, and for that reason, the trip was worthwhile. But it was not a place that enticed one to linger and so, having taken the obligatory snapshots from vantage points near the hotel, we pressed on once again.

As we left the hotel at seven o'clock, we had a sinking feeling that the day was destined to be frustrating and an ultimate waste of time. From the point of view where we were considering its merits, it turned out to be just that, but there were unexpected bonuses.

Our suspicions about the future direction of travel were based on the fact that all the information we could find on ferries from Bohol southward to Mindanao was at the best confused and at the worst, conflicting. It boiled down to a ferry leaving Jagna in Bohol for Cagayan de Oro in Mindanao on either the Saturday night or Sunday night. It was Sunday morning as we weighed up our decision whether or not to risk the long ride to Jagna to find out for sure. We opted to give it a go.

When the bus came into view along the dusty dirt track which passed The Chocolate Hills Hotel we found it to be full, and so opted for sitting on the roof with our luggage. At the time, and it may well remain the case now, this was very much an accepted way to ride throughout Asia, but it was my first experience and I was immediately sold on the idea! The view was magnificent and the warm breeze and space was so refreshing after the hard wooden seating inside these cramped buses.

Two buses and three hours later, we arrived at the little fishing village of Jagna – the ferry had left the previous evening. Somewhat deflated, we sat down for a coke and a bite to eat – fried squid and rice. After a few moments, we were joined at our table by a couple of girls who had been helping out in the kitchen when we arrived. Both girls were in the dreamy little village of Jagna to visit their parents, though they both worked and lived in Manila. Obviously bored by the pace of life on Bohol they were quite keen to play host to us for the afternoon, and soon had the rest of the day planned out for us.

First up: a visit to the cockpit.

Cockfighting is a national sport in the Philippines, and every village, no matter how small, had its own cockpit, where on Sunday afternoons almost all the men from the village could be found. With us as escorts, this was not an opportunity the girls were going to miss, since to have gone unaccompanied would simply not have been proper!

Cockfighting is a gambler's sport, with as much time spent placing bets before the fight as is spent on the fight itself. Even so, the whole cycle of events from shouting the odds to carrying off the two cocks at the end of the fight rarely took longer than fifteen minutes. This cycle would be repeated time and time again, taking up most of Sunday afternoon.

The cockpit itself was a circular bamboo hut, capable of seating about two hundred people, with benches raked back from a fenced-off, sanded square floor in the centre. This is where the cocks fought.

As if pecking each other to death was not enough, each cock had a razor sharp four-inch curved knife blade strapped to its leg – a weapon which seemed to be as lethal and mortally dangerous to its wearer as it was to the opponent bird. With these weapons and a great deal of blood-thirsty encouragement, the two birds would launch themselves at each other in a determined spirit of 'do or die'.

After half a dozen such fights we adjourned and went on a walk to visit one of Jagna's other great attractions – the local church.

Church-going in the Philippines is so popular as to almost rival cock fighting as a Sunday pastime, though no one has ever put this to the test since they are carefully timed never to clash! Our companions had picked this particular church for our walk on account of its hilltop location – the climb to the top being rewarded by a splendid view of Jagna and the coast of Bohol.

At five o'clock our friends put us back on the bus and waved us off for our journey back to Tagbilaran, where it was our intention to catch the overnight ferry back to Cebu.

Once again, we had chosen to ride on the roof, only this time we were in for a bit of a surprise. The five o'clock bus was also the last bus and the numbers that were clambering aboard soon began to reflect this. At its worst our forty-seater bus had its full complement inside, plus twenty hanging on to the sides and thirty more balanced precariously, along with us and everyone's luggage, on the roof. Thankfully numbers soon tailed off as we passed the midway point until, once again, we had the roof to ourselves. With little else to do, the conductor would occasionally appear out of nowhere having swung himself up to the roof for a chat, but on the whole Laurence and I were able to lie back and enjoy the stars and cool night air for the last hour of our journey.

Despite the necessity of our travel plan, the return to Cebu nevertheless smacked of defeatism and our spirits sank as we re-entered the port at dawn the following morning. The ferry had been very crowded and so neither of us had been able to grab more than a few moments kip on the covered deck area that was the entitlement of our second class tickets. I longed to be able to curl up in my own bed at home with the comforting noise of my parents pottering around the house – those childhood associations that represent warmth and security and which, when you are a long way from home and feeling low, take on a special significance and importance. I felt we were slowly being beaten on our quest to reach Borneo. Besides which, I was beginning to feel quite sore from all the sitting around on hard wooden seats, contributing in no small part to my glum feelings.

Thwarted in our attempts to head south via Bohol we resigned ourselves to going direct to Zamboanga from Cebu by boat, missing out the interior of Mindanao completely. But the life of the traveller is like an adventure book, and as you turn each page a new surprise invariably awaits you!

The ferry crossing from Cebu to Zamboanga was a protracted, twenty-seven-hour journey which would have been as boring as it was long had we not met the Falcasantos family. Granny Falcasantos was travelling back to Zamboanga with her daughter and two granddaughters and on learning of our plight she decided to take us under her wing.

When the ferry finally docked in Zamboanga we were bundled into a jeep and whisked off to the family home. It was as if we were being processed; taken in at one end of a conveyor – dirty, shabby and tired – to emerge at the other end clean and refreshed. Our dirty washing was discreetly removed from us on arrival to appear the next day, clean, dry and ironed, and our glass was never more than half empty before someone would spring up and refill it.

We were spoilt to the point of embarrassment. Our meals would be prepared and presented as if we were royalty. We never once saw the rest of the family eat, it was just the two of us who would sit down to the feast while Tonie (Granny) and Gerry (Papa) clucked and cooed over the gastronomic creations which they had placed before us.

The Falcasantos lived as an extended family in a large bungalow on the outskirts of Zamboanga, set in a garden of mango and banana trees.

Gerry Falcasantos had only recently retired from the customs service and was now in the enviable position of being able to spend his days at home with his wife, Tonie, and his children and grandchildren, watching them living their lives around him.

During our stay he played the role of host, chatting and being with his guests or putting the finishing touches to a fish soup or knocking up a coconut vinaigrette to go with the salad, while the humdrum of working life carried on without him.

While we were staying with the Falcasantos family in Zamboanga, we became very friendly with one of the sons whose name was Benjie.

Benjie was about my age and operated a small export business from the family home. From him we learnt more of Mindanao and its problems. As I mentioned previously, the Philippines is predominantly Christian (Catholic) with a Muslim minority which is based almost totally on the island of Mindanao and along the Sulu Archipelago. Until only a few years before our visit, all terrorist activity in the Philippines had been accredited to the Muslim activist group, the MNLF (Moro National Liberation Front), whose political actions were ostensibly motivated on religious grounds. By 1985, this outfit had largely been disbanded by government forces, and in Mindanao it existed only in the form of bandit splinter groups operating from mountain hideouts.

In the Sulu Archipelago, however, the MNLF was still a strength to be reckoned with, and the kidnapping of an American and a German tourist in Jolo during October 1984 provided a chilling example of their style of operation. This kidnapping only made the back pages of the foreign press, since of far greater consequence to the Philippines as a whole was the red terrorist power known as the NPA (the New Peoples' Army). This group no longer operated under the banner of religious fervour but was openly communist.

Between them, these two groups 'ruled the roost' in the Mindanao countryside and throughout the Archipelago. As a consequence, military presence was in evidence everywhere: on the streets of Zamboanga, on the buses, on the boats, even in the shops.

Shoot-outs were not uncommon, and when, one night during our stay, Benjie did not return home on time, Gerry and Tonie were quite obviously concerned. On that particular occasion he had been taking a friend of his to hospital after a gunfight had broken out in the bar where they were playing darts – but it was clear to all that it could have been Benjie in hospital that night.

The Philippines has somehow managed to keep its reputation for gunfights ever since the American withdrawal in 1946. Following the gunning down of Benigno Aquino in 1983 there had been such public outcry in Zamboanga that the mayor, a Mr Climaco, had erected a monument to Aquino openly accusing the Marcos government of his death. His assassination in Zamboanga four months prior to our visit therefore came as little surprise to a community whose disillusionment with the existing regime had reached the point of open hostility. In the end, the struggle for justice and democracy cost the Falcasantos family dearly, when, some months after we had left and just prior to the elections of February 1986, Benjie was caught in a gun battle in the streets of Zamboanga and was killed.

Towards the end of our stay with the Falcasantos family, Gerry introduced us to some of his colleagues in the Customs and Excise office in Zamboanga, allowing us the opportunity to ask one or two deliberately naive questions regarding our proposed crossing to Borneo. Their reply was interesting. 'It's basically illegal, because the only boats leaving Zamboanga for Sabah are owned by barter traders and smugglers and they are clearly not licenced to carry passengers. Therefore, if I stamp your passport I know that you will be attempting the passage illegally. I cannot therefore stamp your passport. Having said this, however, I am aware that some people do attempt this passage – "the back door" – but if you attempt it and are caught, you will be brought back to me and I will lock you in the stockade until an investigation committee of six people can be convened. It would, I think, be embarrassing for all concerned.'

This shed some interesting light on our problems, since it showed us that our real threat was to come from the coastguard patrol boats and not from pirates who, by all accounts, had become less active along the Archipelago in recent years, and anyhow were not in the habit of murdering foreigners.

Bidding farewell to the Falcasantos was a very sad moment as we had both become quite attached to our adopted family. We were still unsure of the way ahead but knew that if it were at all possible to make the crossing to Borneo, then the islands of the Archipelago would provide us with the ultimate answer.

The string of islands that make up the Sulu Archipelago stretch like stepping stones from the southern tip of Mindanao down towards Borneo, and if in the end we were to be forced back to Manila then this would hardly be too great a hardship to endure. The ferry itself was not unlike that in which we had arrived from Cebu. It was about one hundred and fifty feet in length with an upper deck that was open to the air and a lower closed-in deck which took the bulk of the cargo and acted as a stifling overflow for passengers from the upper deck. As a reminder of the ever-present threat from terrorists we carried four armed soldiers onboard this little rust-bucket of a ferry in case we encountered trouble at sea. Navy escort boats were an alternative, often used to accompany the smaller boats making this passage.

Situated only three hundred miles north of the equator, the islands of the Sulu Archipelago are as typically tropical as one can imagine. Each island appears as a sandwich of colour: the turquoise blue of the South China Sea, then a thin strip of gleaming white coral sand topped with an unbroken layer of green (from the thick growth of coconut palms which seem to thrive on the island's gentle slopes), and finally the deep blue of the equatorial sky. As we chugged along calling in at almost every island in the chain, we made our now familiar enquiries about 'barter traders' or alternative ways of getting to Borneo. The answers too were becoming familiar: 'From here, no boats, but there are boats, many boats, which make the crossing from the next island down'. Only, when we reached the next island down, the same tale was repeated and so the pilgrimage continued. Having come this far we were, by now, resolved to go to the very end of the chain and then, unless our luck changed, we would cut our losses and take the little inter-island plane back to Zamboanga and then Manila.

We were both still very new to this game and had much to learn about discretion. Take for example our arrival on the island of Jolo, about halfway down the chain. We had had to abandon our guidebooks by this stage as none of them covered this forgotten string of islands and consequently we were finding ourselves as much a novelty here as we were in China. So, when we disembarked, we immediately found ourselves swamped by the curious. Surreptitiously we tried to make our way round to some small motor launches that were tied up along a quieter quay and which, we had been told, were owned by 'barter traders'. But as soon as we started chatting to their captains, the crowds gathered again. The situation was almost laughable. There we were trying to persuade a guy to smuggle us across to Borneo with half the town looking on. We might just as well have put a call through to the customs house and invited them along too! Needless to say, as the crowds gathered, the captains dropped us like 'hot cakes', so we had to satisfy ourselves with a quick walk around the little town of Jolo before re-boarding the same vessel that we had arrived on, to continue along the string of islands.

There were other interests for us in Jolo however, as this was the island where the American and German tourists had been kidnapped by the MNLF the previous October. During our short walk around the main town we called into a cafe for breakfast and inadvertently stumbled upon the patron of the lodging house in Jolo where the two had been staying prior to their kidnapping. He even had some of their belongings still stored in one of his rooms. It appeared that neither embassy was prepared to pay up and so, as far as our 'patron' friend could make out, the MNLF were still holding them up in the mountains on the island.

This was precisely the information which we had been keen to glean from our short stay in Jolo, and it was good news since while the MNLF had gained nothing from the kidnapping our chances of a safe passage through this far-flung forgotten end of Asia were that much greater. Nevertheless, despite this encouraging news we were aware that our bid for Borneo was not entirely risk free and so, as a precautionary measure against robbery, Laurence and I stitched our dollar cash into our clothing. At that stage I had about $200 sewn into the zip fly cover of my shorts – the remainder of my possessions were insured.

Our conversations with the captains of barter trader vessels in Jolo had been encouraging, despite the negative outcome, because we did at least get as far as agreeing a passage for that evening – and at a fair price – before the gathering crowds scared the captain into backing down. So it was possible!

At the next island down the chain, Siasi, we were told that a small barter trader vessel left three days ago. The island of Siasi would have been a perfect place since it is so small that it has no customs or immigration house. We began to feel that quiet persistence may yet win the day.

Beyond Siasi lay Tawitawi. Another blank! The island of Tawitawi is unlike any of the other islands in the Sulu Archipelago. Its jungle-clad slopes rise almost sheer from the sea, giving the island the appearance of some lost world waiting to be discovered. In this respect, it was by far and away the most beautiful of all the islands in the Archipelago. The main settlement on the island goes by the name of Bongao but compared with Jolo it is still very much a backwater village.

Built on stilts, Bongao functions almost entirely as a trading post; shipping out coconut husks to be turned into charcoal, and coconut flesh to be pressed in Manila to yield coconut oil. It did have boats going to Sabah and we spent an interesting hour making enquiries on a number of dubious looking timber vessels which were tied up alongside this floating village. All the boats' captains were barter traders, and all had opted for postponing their trip until after Chinese New Year (20th February). Even the prospect of a passage to Borneo could not persuade me to waste a week of our travel time sitting in this fly hole, and so we had no option but to press on to the very last island in the chain, and to a tiny village called Sitangkai.

We had dearly hoped to avoid this 'port of last resort'. The barter traders with whom we had been speaking until now were at least undertaking a legal crossing, even if carrying us as passengers would be illegal. However, from what we could gather, the only people who operated from Sitangkai were 'bumboat' smugglers – a very different prospect indeed! It was becoming so difficult to assess all the risks now. Some people said the bumboats made daily crossings and were quite safe, while others maintained that they were too small to make the crossings, being open boats with a very low freeboard and therefore vulnerable to being swamped in anything but a calm sea. To make matters worse they were also an attractive target for pirates; not Filipino pirates as we had assumed, but Vietnamese pirates, who were a known curse to small boats everywhere in the South China Sea.

As the ferry left Tawitawi for Sibutu, the last island before Sitangkai, our 'quest' suddenly experienced the most amazing leap forward. Most of the passengers had disembarked in Bongao and of the hundred or so who had occupied the upper deck to date, only about a dozen remained. We soon got chatting with our new neighbours, hopefully mentioning our search for the 'back door'. 'Perhaps I can help you', one of our new friends replied.

'One of the passengers onboard right now runs a boat to Sabah, and has one leaving this evening'.

'A bumboat?'

'Yes, a bumboat.'

The man, whose name was Seahorn, fitted neatly into the 'gentle giant' category of description. It transpired that he was organising a boat to leave at dusk that evening with a cargo of sundry smuggled goods, Filipino men who were crossing the border for work, and women and children who were making the journey to visit relatives in the refugee camps which were situated in Muslim East Malaysia.

'What are the risks?' we asked naively, 'We are told that there are pirates in these waters.'

'Yes indeed, there are pirates', Seahorn replied gravely.

'Dangerous?'

'Well, it's difficult for me to say', he smiled, 'You see, we are all pirates!'

Frank enough, I suppose. My fault for expecting to see an eye patch and parrot droppings on his lapels! At the time I can remember thinking his comment a little melodramatic, but I began to revise my opinion after we had been in Sitangkai for a while.

As we approached Sitangkai, we passed dozens of individual huts built on stilts in the shallow coral waters stretching for miles out to sea. These huts, we were told, were used as bases for gathering shells and seaweed, the two legitimate occupations of the Sitangkai people.

At about three o'clock in the afternoon the ferry tied up to a group of three or four of these huts, which were located together forming a temporary wharf. This was as close to the village of Sitangkai as our ferry could go because the water from this point on was so shallow as to be only navigable by the wooden, canoe-type launches known as bumboats.

We had agreed a price of 400 pesos (about £20 each) for the crossing, and we were now entirely in Seahorn's hands. As we disembarked from the ferry, Seahorn indicated a private bumboat that we should board and, together with five or six other passengers, we sped off towards the village of Sitangkai.

Never before had I encountered such a village. The whole habitation was on stilts, not a shred of land to be seen. Minutes after entering the village in the boat, we were lost in a maze of ramshackle wooden buildings connected by gangplanks and low rickety wooden bridges. After ten or fifteen minutes we came to rest by one of these dwellings and everyone got out.

In front of the living quarters was a large veranda-type area of planking, upon which were gathered two or three dozen people: men, women and children with sacks of possessions. On the opposite side of the veranda to where we had arrived, a large bumboat lay berthed. The open vessel was perhaps forty feet long and ten feet wide, with a large 145 HP engine mounted about two-thirds down its length. At around four o'clock, we started to transfer to the larger boat. Other smaller boats continued to arrive, their occupants transferring to the new boat until we were about fifty in number – full to capacity and looking more like a Vietnamese refugee boat than a band of smugglers.

However, as we drew away from the landing stage our hearts sank. Instead of heading out to sea, our boat worked its way further into the village until we intersected with the main channel. We then proceeded all the way down the 'main street' until we reached the military police post. This had to be the end of the road for us, since we knew that the success of our crossing into Borneo depended on being undetected when leaving the Philippines. But then everyone else was also leaving the Philippines illegally, so what on earth were we doing sailing straight up the main street and stopping in front of the police headquarters?

The answer lay in the understanding that although the Sulu Archipelago is part of the Philippines, the government's hold on the chain is tenuous to say the least. Thus, our concept of the 'back door' had to be modified from being just a fast boat operating from a smuggler's hideout to something that involved the whole village of Sitangkai, including the military police. Here then was a village where Philippine law had been suspended, providing sanctuary for smugglers, pirates, the MNLF and any other group who swore by the Muslim faith and whose aim was the undermining of law and order and the overthrowing of the Marcos regime.

Back in the police HQ a list of passengers' names was handed over and after a moment's tense discussion about whether they should allow two foreigners in under their umbrella, we were all allowed to proceed.

As we cleared the village and just as we were beginning to believe that we had made it, the boat stopped again. This time we were alongside a solitary hut on stilts that carried a large radio mast. Standing on the landing stage and now peering into the boat were two armed civilians. What their function was we never guessed, but it was obvious that our presence could lead to complications since we were told to keep a low profile as we approached this checkpoint.

A few comments were exchanged between our boat and the men on the platform and then we drew away.

Some twenty yards past this point, Laurence decided to put on my cagoule against an impending downpour. Suddenly the air exploded with the noise of crackling, screeching and banging. There was shouting

183

from the front of the boat and the guys by the engine leapt to the cut-off switch. The engine stopped. The powerful fan from this 145 HP engine had sucked in the cagoule as Laurence was putting it on, and it was now stretched between the water pump and the belt drive on the fan. Barely shouting distance past the checkpoint, we had successfully brought the boat to a standstill! The crew frantically wrestled with the job of dismantling the belt drive and freeing my now completely chewed up cagoule, while two stupid Englishmen sat quietly making apologetic noises whilst also keeping a close eye on the checkpoint behind us.

Within fifteen minutes we were away again and heading out into the night for Borneo.

All we had to watch for now were the government coastguard patrol boats and other pirates – or so we thought. For the first half hour of our journey we made quite slow progress over the shallow waters of the coral shelf, then, safely in deeper water, we increased our speed to around twenty-five or thirty knots, tearing through the night at a frightening rate. But the boat was built for this kind of work and its curved wooden bows cut easily through the relatively calm waters of the Sulu Sea. Despite our overloaded condition, we maintained around one-and-a-half feet of freeboard and remained reasonably dry as we huddled together on the benches that ran along the sides of the open boat. We naturally carried no lights and the overcast skies allowed only the briefest glimpse of any stars. The feeling of being alone in a small boat on a large sea was very, very real – despite my many months of experience on *Morvran*.

About an hour after we had opened up the throttle, we began to close in on a solitary ship's light. Beyond the ship I could see what appeared to be a bank of very low black cloud, but as we drew closer, its true form gradually took shape and I realised that my black cloud was in fact the tops of a line of coconut palms. We were approaching a small island, no larger than a football stadium, with about two dozen coconut palms on it and two or three huts. The ship's light had come from a single boat that was anchored just offshore, fishing for calamari (squid).

Shortly after we had left the police HQ in Sitangkai, a man had jumped onboard from a small boat that had motored up alongside us. He seemed to command the respect of our skipper and, beyond exchanging a few words as he boarded, had sat alone and in silence up in the bows of the boat, nursing a carry-all which he had brought onboard with him. As we touched the beach, now having gently edged ourselves over the reef, this character jumped ashore and was soon met by three or four torch-bearing men from the huts on the island. The bag was opened on the beach and the contents examined before the party, now including our man and his bag, moved back off the beach towards the huts.

We immediately pushed off and began making our way out to sea again past the calamari fishermen. The contents of the bag and the identity of this man, or the true function of this lonely desert island remained open to conjecture.

We continued on through the night keeping a careful eye on the weather which threatened to deteriorate at any moment. Then, without warning, the boat swerved violently to starboard and then to port and then 'crunch', we hit bottom. Shouts and abuse were hurled between those on watch in the bows and those on the helm. The engine was abruptly cut.

With no lights, no stars and no means of navigation, we had drifted off our intended course and were now bashing up and down on one of the many coral reefs that make navigation in these waters so hazardous.

All around us now white spume could be seen through the black night as the sea washed over the shallow coral reef. The boat lifted on the crest of each breaking wave and then crunched down on the coral as the wave passed. Everywhere was black and we were miles from land.

I expected to see the bottom being torn out of our fragile craft at any second. My mind raced as I flashed through the alternatives open to us and what I should do if the boat started to break up. Should I try to salvage my pack? No. Would I be able to stand on the coral and brace myself against the surf? Maybe. Would my flip-flops give me sufficient protection against the jagged coral? I doubted it. And would we be able to last out, stranded in three feet of breaking water until dawn or longer?

It was a curious fear that I felt, not a fear of something unknown, or the sort of fear that can be generated by someone else's reckless driving, but the rational fear that I used to encounter whenever I prepared to launch myself off a slope with the hang-glider, the sort of fear that could be controlled and used to drive the adrenalin. Here was a situation where the danger was apparent but where, if I kept a level head, I had some measure of control. However, just who I thought might be rescuing us, if by dawn the sharks hadn't already finished us, was quite a different issue!

Each time the boat rose on the waves, the crew would pole the boat forward, responding to urgent shouts from the helmsman. Slowly but surely we edged our way off and, ten minutes after hitting the reef, we were in clear water again motoring towards the west.

Had the swell that night been any greater or our boat less sturdy we would surely have never made it.

At about two o'clock in the morning, some seven hours after our departure from Sitangkai, we spotted the lights of Semporna. As we closed in, the engine was cut to a mere tick-over and we edged our way towards the coast. An hour later we lay just off a little village on stilts, similar to Sitangkai, but situated about half a mile down the coast from Semporna. We scanned the shore. A few moments later a torchlight flashed from one of the huts in the village and we turned the boat in towards the shore.

In minutes, we were once again hidden in the depths of a village on stilts, safe from the prying eyes of the coastguard patrol and shore police. People and goods were quietly and efficiently unloaded from the boat and conducted along the planked walkways that connected all the huts. It would not be safe to leave the village until dawn, when the night police patrols had finished their surveillance of the roads into Semporna and so we laid out our carry mats on the rough wooden planking and slept until dawn, Laurence and I taking turns on watch.

At dawn, people began emerging from the huts around us, and we were offered coffee and cakes. We were obviously not what they had expected to find amongst the previous night's shipment! As we chatted, we learned that the village where we had landed was populated almost entirely by Muslim ex-Filipinos and acted as base camp for the MNLF in Semporna, hence the logic of landing here.

One of the main reasons for the antagonism between the Philippines and Sabah was that the Muslim Malaysian government, which held federal power in Sabah, unofficially supported the MNLF in its attempts to overthrow the Marcos government. Indeed, it is said that besides providing a haven for MNLF supporters – such as our hosts on that morning for breakfast – it also turned a blind eye to the MNLF military training camps which, we were told, were responsible for training over twelve thousand MNLF troops in Sabah alone. Anyway, with a coffee inside us, we said goodbye to our hosts and walked into town. It was the 17th of February, and a Sunday. The immigration office was closed and so we found ourselves a hotel and slept until mid-afternoon.

Borneo is made up of four states; the largest, Kalimantan, is situated in the south of the island and is governed by Indonesia. Sabah (formerly known as North Borneo) used to be a British colony but in 1963 it was given independence and came under the governorship of the newly-formed federation – Malaysia. West of Sabah, about halfway along the northwestern coast is the tiny oil-rich sultanate of Brunei, while in the northwest of the island is the state of Sarawak which, like Sabah, is governed by Malaysia.

One legacy of the British presence in Sabah is a large minority group of Christians and on our walk into Semporna in the morning, we had noticed an Anglican church. So, being Sunday, we decided to go along to the evening service. An interesting service was conducted by a Chinese minister who, for our benefit, gave the sermon in both Cantonese and English. It was a most stabilising experience after our traumas the previous evening – and the thought of our last great gamble which was still to come.

This was the sticky business of our 'official' entry into Sabah. Unless we could persuade the immigration people in Sabah to officially enter us into the country all our work to date would be in vain and there would be no option but to turn around and re-enter the Philippines, again by the 'back door'.

As with our research on making the actual crossing, we had made many enquiries regarding the attitude of the officials in Sabah when dealing with circumstance such as ours, but here there was simply no previous experience to go on, and so early on Monday morning we walked over to the immigration office with two local folk who had befriended us on our wanders around town the previous evening.

We went straight in to see the Chief Immigration Officer. The problem was simply this. We had no exit stamp from the Philippines which was proof – if proof was needed in Semporna – that we had entered Sabah illegally. Put another way, it was evidence that the Sabah coastguard had failed to detect us the previous evening. Standing, now, before the Chief Immigration Officer, we were asking him to acknowledge the fact that we had 'outwitted' his own department. Stamping our passports with an official entry visa would be tantamount to admitting this uncomfortable reality.

It was a tricky position to take and we had realised all the time that this morning there was to be no easy victory. We could face imprisonment, or deportation at the very kindest. We were dressed in our best clothes and had a $20 bribe ready to slip into the passport should such a last resort be required to tip the balance. Our reception was understandably cool, and I was surprised by the degree of control that I managed to keep in my voice when I answered the question, 'Where have you just come from?'

We were relieved of our passports and told to wait outside.

For a tense ten minutes we waited on the veranda outside the immigration office, then, 'You two, inside please!' Two minutes later, we emerged with our passports stamped with a one-month visa!

We were legal. We had won! Grinning and laughing at each other, Laurence and I shook hands (as only the English would do) before heading back to collect our packs from the hotel in order to begin the long journey towards Singapore.

There is a traveller's maxim which states that if there are people in A and people in B, there will always be a way of getting from A to B. It may not be easy, and it may cost time and patience, but it will always be possible, somehow.

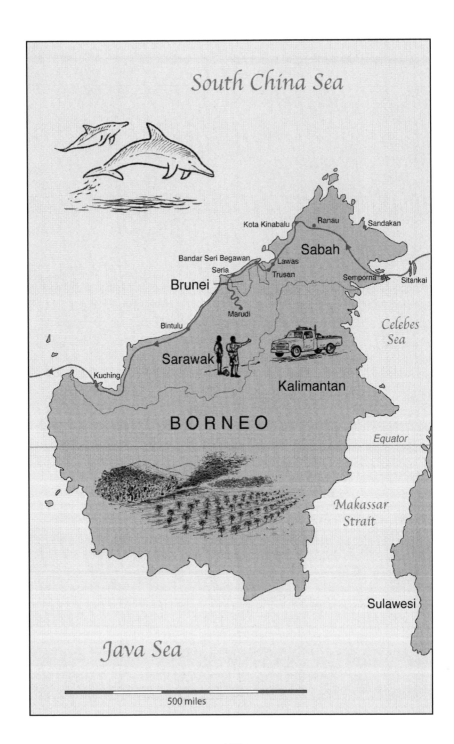

South China Sea

Kota Kinabalu Ranau Sandakan

Sabah

Bandar Seri Begawan Lawas
Seria Trusan Semporna Sitankai
Brunei

Marudi Celebes Sea

Bintulu

Sarawak Kalimantan

Kuching

BORNEO

Equator

Makassar Strait

Sulawesi

Java Sea

500 miles

CHAPTER TEN

Borneo

There was one thing we learned about Sabah very quickly – it was expensive! There were three constituents which went to make up our daily expenses: travel, accommodation and food, and in Sabah any one of these was going to take up the whole of our US$5-per-day budget. Beer was out, cake became a luxury and our diet became simpler – more fruit and vegetables and less meat. However, the greatest saving we could make was in travel. The solution was simple enough, we would hitch our way across Borneo.

This turned out to be a great deal easier than we had expected. Our success was due partly to the fact that people were so unaccustomed to seeing hitchhikers that they automatically stopped, thinking we were lost and asking for assistance, but it was also due to the alarming infrequency of transport. If you are a driver who knows that you are the only vehicle for miles it takes a hard heart indeed to pass by two stupid Englishmen, standing in the heat of the midday sun, when for as far as the eye can see there is nothing else around but primary jungle. Our lifts were mainly in the back of open Land Rovers and the like, with the occasional timber lorry thrown in for variety. By this method, we reached Kinabalu

National Park, near the town of Ranau, arriving at the end of our second day.

In the main, the roads were dirt track and extremely rough, passing through vast plantations of oil palm and cocoa where man had made his mark, and through steaming jungle where the axe had yet to fall. Forty years previously even this dirt track did not exist and the hostile malaria-ridden jungle which covers this land claimed all but six of the 2,400 prisoners of war who were forced to march the one hundred miles between Sandakan and Ranau in 1945.

The Kinabalu National Park exists because of Mount Kinabalu, a 13,400-foot giant of a mountain and the highest in South East Asia. We made it our target for Chinese New Year – when travel would be impossible – partly because it is the number one tourist attraction in Sabah and partly because we had a contact there. Anthea Phillips was the sister of the guy who sold Laurence our cheap airline tickets to Hong Kong – a tenuous link, but good enough to give us two nights free accommodation in the park!

On the 20th of February, as all the expat Chinese were making merry at home, we took a trail from the Park HQ at 5,000 feet, to a point halfway to the summit. The trail which we had chosen took us through some of the less-well-trodden areas and on a number of occasions we found ourselves struggling through undergrowth or across eroded gullies before picking up the path again on the other side. It was on one of these diversions that I picked up a leech on my ankle. These creatures can live for months without a meal but when they do find blood they certainly make up for it! My sock was soaked in blood before I managed to detach the creature's bloated body from me.

After a second peaceful night in the Park we set off once more, making a good day's travel through Sabah's capital, Kota Kinabalu, and on into Sarawak, to a small town known by the name of Lawas.

Accommodation looked a little thin and so we called in on the District Officer for advice. The District Officer in Lawas lived in a large colonial-looking bungalow on the top of a hill overlooking the river. Laurence and I had travelled all that day in the back of a pick-up truck along dusty jungle roads and so it was with some trepidation that we made our way across the neatly clipped lawn to the front door. An elderly gentleman met us and escorted us through to the drawing room where an immaculately dressed District Officer was seated at a table playing bridge.

He greeted us in perfect English and, ignoring our appallingly unkempt state, offered us a seat. I felt as though someone in mixed company had just told me my flies were undone! We politely declined the offer of hospitality on account of our filthy state and posed our questions about accommodation in Lawas. His suggestion sounded just up our street.

We were to take a small riverboat and travel a mile or so upstream to where an Evangelical Mission had been established. They would, he felt sure, accommodate us for the night. Thanking him for his help we left and headed down towards the river, where, as he had promised, we found a small ferry to take us upstream. A few moments later we were in the bosom of Christian fellowship.

Life in the Mission was simple, but there was an overwhelming warmth to the community. That night, before a splendid evening meal of rice and fish, we went down to the river with our host to wash – a delightful alternative to piped water – which soon turned into a luxuriously cool swim by starlight. As we lay in bed later that evening, secure under our own mosquito nets – one of the most useful pieces of travel equipment that we carried – we were gently lulled to sleep by the noises of the jungle and the comfort of a real bed.

At five-thirty in the morning we were up and away again, first of all taking the boat back to Lawas and then a lift in the back of a truck, inland to the village of Trusan. At the time of our adventure, Trusan was a small settlement in the interior, reachable only by a long and dusty dirt road or by river. Travel further west was only possible by riverboat, through the jungle to the coast and then along to the port of Bandar Seri Begawan or BSB, the capital of Brunei.

Our boat ride across the border into Brunei took in some very beautiful parts of the jungle and was one of the better decisions of the day. Stepping off the ferry into BSB, capital of the 200,000-strong country of

Brunei, was like entering another world. All of a sudden there were cars, traffic lights and even white faces. The reason – OIL. This tiny little country was, and still is, loaded with the stuff and consequently its capital resembled Hong Kong more closely than a town in Borneo.

It was our aim to clear Brunei the same day as entering, and so we mopped up the sights in BSB in fairly swift succession; the golden-topped Mosque and the thirteen-hundred-room palace being the two main crowd-pullers and neither warranting much more than a brief visit. The lavish palace is of very recent construction and more closely resembles a modern university campus than anything more regal.

Heading west out of BSB, the first large town – and for that matter the last until the Sarawak border – is Seria. Seria exists purely for the oil, and the 'nodding donkeys' which help pump the oil to the surface appeared everywhere from people's back gardens to garage forecourts. Our lift to Seria was a lucky one as we were picked up by a twenty-six-year-old English engineer, one of ten thousand expatriate Brits who then formed the backbone of the oil extraction industry in Brunei. So here, in this freak country, we enjoyed steak and kidney pie for supper, and bacon and eggs on the following morning for breakfast, not to mention a luxurious dip in the pool at the Expatriate's Club to cool off after the journey.

In the morning Tim, our host, drove us across the border into Sarawak in time for the two o'clock boat up the River Baram to Marudi. This drive was something of a first in itself since, as an alternative to an exceptionally bad dirt road, traffic took to the beach at low tide, bumping back up onto 'terra firma' to clear customs halfway along.

The river trip up to Marudi was not exceptional, but the express launch did at least manage to whisk us some eighty miles into the interior before the day was out. The aim of this diversion inland was to do a little more jungle trekking and to see some Iban longhouses. However, on arriving in Marudi we bumped into three Dutch folk who had just arrived from Brunei. Our interest was piqued when we learned that they had made the journey on foot, through the jungle. Despite the miles we had travelled that day by truck and boat we were in fact only a seven-hour walk from the Brunei border and so, with instructions on how to reach the trail, we took off on foot back towards Brunei, aiming to reach the first Iban longhouse on the trail before nightfall and then to continue the next day for as long as we could before turning back to Marudi. To go all the way back to Brunei by foot was tempting but impractical, since neither of us really fancied either taking our packs with us, or making the lengthy journey back to Marudi to pick them up later.

In the event we did not make the first longhouse that day as a violent thunderstorm forced us to take refuge in a house just before the jungle trail itself began. Seeing our plight, the owners were most eager to take us in and insisted that we stay the night with them instead of forcing on through the jungle in the dark – a prospect which neither of us relished! Our hosts turned out to be of Chinese descent and so we spent the evening enjoying the tail-end of their New Year celebrations as the storm raged outside.

In the morning we resumed our trek and, leaving our packs with our Chinese friends, we set off into the jungle. An hour or so later we passed the longhouse which had been our destination the previous evening.

Put simply, a 'longhouse' is just that – a long house. They are built on stilts with a common veranda which runs the length of the building, and they are the traditional home of the Iban Tribe. The accommodation is divided up into 'two-room' lots, and the whole edifice is constructed from the timber that is felled in order to make a clearing for the community.

The size of the longhouse is described in terms of the number of units or 'doors'. Thus, a sixty-four-door longhouse is one with sixty-four 'two-room' units. Nearer the towns the longhouse folk led quite modern lives, living in the longhouse with the tribe, but working in the town. Some of them even possessed TVs. Further out, however, the traditional way of life was still very strong, and a total twentieth-century take-over was held at bay by at least one generation.

While the young men wore jeans and tee shirts, the older men of the tribe continued to wear the traditional sarong. The women sported a similar garment and remained bare-chested. The practice of elongating the ear lobes was, by this time, no longer fashionable amongst the younger members of the tribe, but all the older folk carried this distinction as a symbol of their Iban identity. During our time with the Iban I saw a number of women wearing large bangles as earrings with their ear lobes extending some six or seven inches below the ear. Another distinguishing feature of the Iban men is a tattoo which they carry on their throats. This practice is of religious significance – similar to the red dot on the forehead of the Hindu – and has its origins in the time when it was earned by an Iban warrior to mark his first kill in battle.

Stopping only briefly at the longhouse, we continued along the trail to Brunei for about three hours before reluctantly turning back towards Marudi. The trail, which was only used by the Iban in travelling between the longhouses in that area of the jungle, was not well defined and we did not meet anyone else on foot in the whole time between leaving 'our' longhouse and returning to it some five hours later. The route took us through swamps and across rivers and along paths made from felled trees, each giant tree calculated to fall in precisely the right place to intersect with the last, forming a zigzag walkway, as wide as the felled tree trunk, through the dense undergrowth.

The tremendous noise put out by the invisible insect world of the jungle was at times so great as to be intimidating, but we had come prepared for those in the animal kingdom who did show their face; we carried salt for the leeches, and good old Boots repellent for the mosquitoes. Wading through the knee-deep swamp using a bamboo pole to steady ourselves, we felt a queer sense of exhilaration from the knowledge that we were actually living out all those childhood fantasies, coupled with a more sobering sense of stupidity, knowing that all this messing about was not actually achieving anything since we would eventually have to turn around and wade all the way back again!

During the walk I saw numerous inch-long soldier ants – the largest I had ever seen – and spotted my first pitcher plant, a fascinating tropical plant designed so as to catch water in which it then drowns unwary insects.

We felt determined to round off this 'expedition to the interior' in style and so, having returned mid-afternoon to our Chinese hosts of the previous evening to wash and change, we set out for a thirty-seven-door longhouse which we had been told could be reached by car along a logging track some twenty miles distant from Marudi. To cut a long story short, or at least down in length, we hitched out on the back of a logging truck and were made most welcome by the chief of the village who responded very favourably to the bottle of whisky we had brought with us as a gift.

After sharing dinner with him – the meal was simple but very strongly flavoured – we joined the family out on the veranda where the old man chatted and smoked whilst the children played a fascinating game with de-winged bugs.

There were two varieties of bug, both of which (in my ignorance) I would have described as looking and sounding like cicadas. The smaller of the two types was green and about one-and-a-half inches long, while the other was brown in colour with a two-inch body (four-inch wingspan). The first task was to catch your bug, not a hard task as they were in abundance, attracted by the light. Then off with its wings and gently squeeze its abdomen. Thus abused, the insect would set up a noisy vibration, rather like a dried pea in a wooden box being shaken hundreds of times a second. This live 'rattle' could now be used for endless happy hours either to throw at friends or to push down your neighbour's trousers or just to hold, using cupped hands to alter the sound of the noise.

Early the next morning after a small breakfast of baked rice and coffee, we bade our hosts farewell and set off back to Marudi and then on down river to the coast road at Miri.

Heading west once again we made good progress for the remainder of the day, ending up with a lift from an oil palm plantation manager who offered us the hospitality of his house for the night. We accepted his offer gladly and were treated to an enlightening tour of his 4,500-acre plantation. Once again, we saw great areas of primary forest being felled to make way for the plantation. As we toured the estate, my thoughts turned to the future and whether there would be anything left of this great jungle and the traditions of its people for my children to visit in thirty years' time?

The following day we completed the one-hour ride and two-hour walk to the Niah caves, one of Sarawak's most renowned attractions.

The caves are located in the centre of a National Park area so the two-hour walk to them through good primary rain forest proved almost as interesting as the caves themselves. From an anthropological point of view the caves are of great significance, since it was here that paintings and skulls were discovered dating back 37,000 years. However, for us the caves' primary interest were the two local industries which they supported, namely the collection of guano and birds' nests, the latter used to make the famous soup.

Buried deep in the jungle, these large caves are home to thousands of swifts which operate by day, and just as many bats that take on the night shift. Together they produce over one ton of guano each day!

As we made our way along the rough wooden walkway into the caves, we were constantly having to jump to one side as local workers raced past, carrying on their backs, sacks of guano or returning with empty sacks to be replenished. This was no mean feat, as the sacks must have weighed many kilos, being filled to the brim with this heavy, wet (and smelly!) substance. But as impressive as this was, the mighty guano harvest was not the main reason that these caves were so highly prized. From a commercial perspective, the nests inhabited by the swifts were the real attraction.

The swifts build their nests by gluing tiny feathers together with their own saliva, the saliva being the major constituent. These tiny scoop-shaped constructions are found high up, glued to the roof of the caves, and so collecting them is both difficult and dangerous. The local solution to this problem is to climb two hundred feet up using a series of slender bamboo poles which are secured to the roof of the caves like so many lianas. Should you ever be tempted to a bowl of boiled bird's saliva, it will generally cost you upwards of £100 in the more respectable restaurants around the world!

Spending that night in the town of Bintulu, we rose early the following day in an effort to make Kuching by nightfall. Kuching represented the end of our trek across Borneo but by sunset we were still some one hundred and thirty miles the wrong side of our destination and a good thirty miles from the nearest town. However, where to stay the night was not our problem, only which offer to accept! Ibans are notoriously hospitable and they seemed to gather out of nowhere when they spotted us standing by the roadside in obvious need of assistance. In the end we stayed with a family of five who had a small but cosy house on stilts nearby. The father of the household worked as a labourer on a rubber plantation.

On the following day, the 28th of February, we completed our journey to Kuching, the capital of Sarawak.

We found Kuching to be a very pleasant town, well laid out with lots of green spaces and an attractive riverfront, giving the place an atmosphere more reminiscent of a fishing village than an administrative centre. The visit to the mosque and the museum were both worth the effort, the latter especially since it proved an excellent documentation of the days when Sarawak was more than just a boring British colony – our guide book put it beautifully: 'Sarawak's history reads more like a Victorian melodrama than hard fact.'

In 1838, James Brooke, a British adventurer, arrived in Borneo with his armed sloop to find the Brunei aristocracy facing rebellion from the dissatisfied inland tribes. He quelled the rebellion and in gratitude was given power over part of what is now called Sarawak. Appointing himself 'Rajah Brooke', he successfully cooled the fractious tribes, suppressed headhunting, eliminated the dreaded Borneo pirates and founded a dynasty which lasted until after World War Two. At this point Sarawak was ceded to Britain as a full colony until the general independence of 1963 when it opted to join Sabah and Malaya (and also Singapore for a short while) in forming the federation of Malaysia.

Our stay in Kuching was characteristically short, but long enough to get a good feel for this one-time centre of the 'Brooke Empire', and to buy our flight out. Sadly, none of the cargo boats that ply between Kuching and Singapore had been willing to take passengers.

By now our hair was bleached and our skin well-tanned by hours of travelling under the full sun in the back of pick-up trucks, along dusty, dirt track roads. We had come a long way towards an understanding of the term 'Wild Men of Borneo'! As with my travels in the Amazon, the urge to invest time and money in a more thorough exploration of this land was strong, and we both felt somewhat frustrated at not being able to have trekked further inland into the areas of this wild country where the twentieth century had yet to disturb the deep-set traditions – traditions which we had only glimpsed in poor reflection. In these parts, the past is preserved not by great distances but by inaccessibility. Therefore until the ubiquitous lumber merchants manage to carve their way into the very centre of Borneo, there will remain a world where the true 'Wild Men of Borneo' – the orangutan – still rule the jungle, and where to be an Iban means more than just being a source of cheap labour.

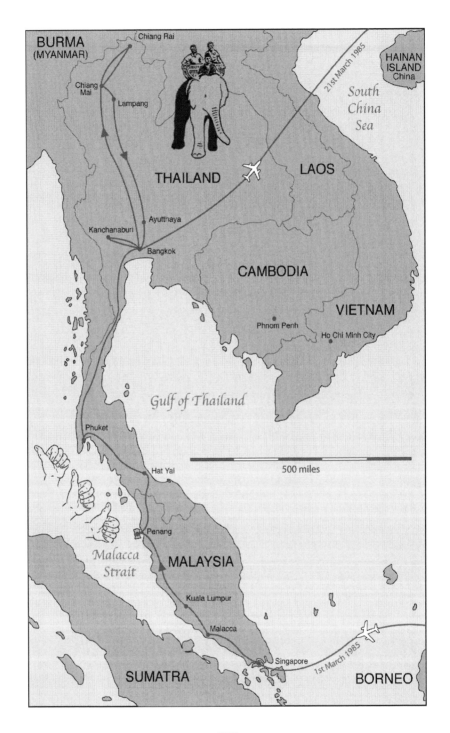

BURMA
(MYANMAR)

Chiang Rai

Chiang
Mai

Lampang

THAILAND

Ayutthaya

Kanchanaburi

Bangkok

Phuket

Hat Yai

Penang

Malacca
Strait

MALAYSIA

Kuala Lumpur

Malacca

Singapore

SUMATRA

LAOS

HAINAN
ISLAND
China

South
China
Sea

21st March 1985

CAMBODIA

VIETNAM

Phnom Penh

Ho Chi Minh City

Gulf of Thailand

500 miles

1st March 1985

BORNEO

CHAPTER ELEVEN

Singapore to Thailand

Coming into Singapore after Sarawak was like a premature homecoming. First, we had completed our overland route across Borneo and were now facing the last and easiest leg of our journey. And second, there was the promise of those little luxuries that had either been out of budget or simply unobtainable. Our euphoria brought on a spate of uncharacteristic rashness and we bought ourselves a bar of Cadbury's chocolate, sampled the celebrated local beer, and even bought cakes, to celebrate our progress!

Singapore began its meteoric climb to fame and fortune in 1819 when an Englishman of the British East India Company, Sir Stamford Raffles, decided that the island was just what he had been looking for as a port and base camp. Full sovereignty was signed over to the British in 1867 and the island remained a British colony until a year after my birth in 1959 when it became independent. In 1963 it joined Malaya, Sarawak and Sabah in the newly-formed federation of Malaysia but two years later, in 1965, decided to change its mind and backed out. Since then, and despite its minute size, it had established itself as a strong economic power – a position which, at the time, was visibly strengthened by fears over the future of Hong Kong.

Wandering around Singapore the impression we got was of a positive, growing city that was less claustrophobic than its big sister, Hong Kong. The pace of life was just a little slower, the streets were a little cleaner, and there was a tangible sense of its colonial past – which we found less striking in Hong Kong. All these differences were perfectly embodied in the city centre on Saturday afternoon where a game of cricket was being played on a large grassed area known as the 'Padang' – an area that had once been an army training ground but which was now surrounded by prestigious banks and skyscrapers. Actually to say that the Padang was surrounded by skyscrapers is a little unfair since, although the 'city' forms a boundary on one side, the other three sides are bordered by a landscaped park, some rather grand Victorian-style government buildings and, a little way off, the famous Raffles Hotel.

The Raffles Hotel is the oldest and most well-known hotel in Singapore and, during the colonial era, served as the centre of high society. The writers' bar was patronised by such people as Conrad and Kipling while the 'Singapore Sling' cocktail was first served in the lounge bar of this historic hotel. Nowadays the hotel relies more on its heritage of tradition than its reputation for excellence. However, it was evident from our short visit that the place still remains popular with die-hard colonials and 'would-be' colonials!

On the night of our arrival in Singapore we met up for a drink with one of Laurence's old university friends, and combined this with a tour of some of the city's newer atrium-hotels. This gave us a good insight into the country and its people.

In 1985, Singapore was riding on the crest of a development boom, largely fuelled by the subtle and not-so-subtle transfer of money and company headquarters out of Hong Kong into the safer, more stable economic climate of Singapore. As a result, the country had virtually no unemployment and a high standard of public service was maintained by a sliding income tax scale from 15 per cent to 45 per cent. Pensions were more than adequately covered by a system of contributions where both employer and employee contributed 25 per cent of basic salary into a private investment account that the employee could use as collateral against a house purchase before retirement, or draw out completely if they left the country. Also, because it was set up as a private account it was unaffected when the person changed company, since every business was legally bound to the same 25 per cent contribution scheme – giving people a guaranteed investment equivalent to 50 per cent of their salary throughout their working life. Time and again throughout Asia we came across this 'private account' attitude towards pension schemes, though not generally at such generous rates.

The other side of the coin in Singapore was that this ideal society was fairly well regimented. Drug trafficking carried the death penalty; you could be fined heavily for dropping litter or jay walking; long hair was officially discouraged; and there was a three-year compulsory national service. But no-one we spoke to seemed to feel that this was too great a price to pay for what was obviously an extremely high and civilised standard of living.

We continued our sampling of the many flavours of Singapore life with a stroll through 'Little India' on Saturday morning, and then a brief look at the touristy playground of Sentosa Island before heading into Chinatown for the evening. It seemed strange, in a country where seventy per cent of the population was Chinese, to see a Chinatown in its capital city but this area was definitely more 'Chinese' than the other parts of the city and, catching the very tail end of Chinese New Year, we were treated to a lion dance through the streets followed by the less appealing Chinese street opera – memories of cats and grand pianos flooded back from our days in Beijing!

The traveller's demand for cheap accommodation in Singapore has led to the creation of the 'crash pad' – a totally illegal but enterprising idea to provide 'shoestring' travellers with a roof over their heads. In essence, the crash pad is simply a private apartment, partitioned off to form small cupboard-sized rooms and dormitories. Because it is unofficial the abuse of space has to be seen to be believed, with people being shoehorned into the most amazing sleeping quarters. However, it was cheap and in the end that was the overriding consideration.

After our second night in one of the many crash pads of Bencoolen Street we took the bus back across the causeway to Johor Bahru on the Malaysian mainland. We had in fact used JB as a cheap place to fly into from Kuching and so, in a way, this was a bit of back tracking.

Once clear of Johor it was thumbs out for Malacca, about one hundred and fifty miles up the west coast of Peninsular Malaysia. Peninsular Malaysia was by far and away the most developed of the three states of the federation. Its major industry was rubber followed by palm oil and coal and so the view from the highway could at times be quite monotonous, one plantation looking very much like another. Generally speaking, the west coast contains all the man-made points of interest while the east coast is less developed and has some of the best beaches to be found anywhere in the world. Since we had already visited 'undeveloped' Sabah and Sarawak and we hadn't time to enjoy the beaches we opted to make our way up the west coast of the peninsular.

Malaysian politics at this time was especially interesting since it represented a good example of what I'm tempted to call a 'guided democracy'. For example, whilst there was the pretence of universal suffrage, the policy (in practice) was very much one that delivered Malaysia for the Malays – which was the main reason why Singapore, with its predominance of Chinese, opted out in 1965. However, the government had only been able to maintain this control over non-indigenous races (that is to say, the Chinese, Indians, etc) by carefully organising constituency boundaries. If the Malaysian Government were ever to be elected so as to reflect the country in terms of race then the Malays would hold a majority of only 51 per cent, jeopardising not only the position the Malays hold in Government but also threatening the religious basis of the country which is officially Muslim (the religion of the country's King).

It reminded me of a constituency shuffle I witnessed in South Africa while I was working there, enacted by the mainly Afrikaner National Party in order to preserve its own future in that 'democracy'.

In South Africa then, whole areas of Johannesburg were populated almost predominantly by non-National-Party English, but this large area formed a single constituency and thus only wielded the same power in government as equally-sized areas out in the bush populated by only a handful of Afrikaners.

In common with South Africa, Malaysia had (and may still have) deep-rooted racial problems. As with so many other countries, however, they go largely undetected by the rest of the world – with South Africa, at the time, acting as a 'scapegoat' for them all. Meanwhile, a Malaysian Chinese student was having to pay for his education abroad because the quota of Chinese places at Malaysian universities was set to favour Malay students. Similarly, Malaysian Chinese businesses were being snubbed in favour of Malay businesses when competing for 'open' contracts, and a Hindu Indian would need to change his religion to Muslim if he wanted to get promotion in his government job.

The first stop on our Malaysian tour was Malacca. This large town or small city was where it all began, first with the arrival of the Chinese during the Ming Dynasty, then the Portuguese, then the Dutch and finally the British – each nation slowly pushing inland from Malacca to develop or exploit the peninsula's interior. By the time Laurence and I arrived, the town had the quiet atmosphere of a seaside town with only glimpses of the past, preserved in buildings and forts to remind you of its significance for the history books of Malaysia.

From Malacca it was on to Kuala Lumpur. Affectionately referred to as KL, it is the capital of Malaysia. The name means 'muddy waters' and referred to the junction of two particularly muddy rivers which acted as a landmark for the tin miners who first opened up the interior of Malaya. Today the city has little to distinguish it from any other city in Asia, though we found it to be clean and quite well laid out with one or two modern yet attractive buildings – the railway station (which looks more like a mosque) and the mosque (which looks like a twentieth-century fantasy) are two examples. The ubiquitous 'Chinatown' is well represented here, and in common with Singapore the red light district sports no red lights whatsoever. Morality, at least on the face of things, was kept under very tight reins in this part of Asia.

After a very pleasant stroll around KL's Lake Garden and a visit to the post office we set off once again, ever northwards. Malaysia must be one of the easiest countries in the world for hitching and within five minutes of off-loading our packs we were picked up by a rather smart BMW heading for the very area we were hoping to visit, the Cameroon Highlands. The car was chauffeur driven and so our host was able to give his full attention to answering our barrage of questions. The Cameroon Highlands has a much cooler and wetter climate than the surrounding lowlands and is ideally suited to growing tea, a tradition started by the British who first developed the area as a hill station.

The road from the lowlands winds up through lush, rainforest vegetation to emerge in an area that bears more resemblance to Surrey than tropical Malaysia. Quiet country lanes connect discrete, plush country homes, once owned by British expats and now owned largely by wealthy Malays and Chinese. Crossed with this Surrey-scene is a sense of Scotland, induced by the misty, rolling hills covered in the lush green of tea plantations and tropical forest that form the backcloth to this very charming spot.

We bathed ourselves in the coolness and freshness of the Cameroon Highlands for a little over twenty hours and then moved on again, this time making for the holiday island of Penang. Penang has a thoroughly British history that started with its discovery by Captain Light in 1786 and ended with the general independence of 1957. There was, of course, one interruption to this period of colonisation and that was during the forties when the Japanese were in possession of the peninsular. The Japanese occupation of British territory overseas is one of those facts that had always seemed of little consequence to me in my appreciation of global political history. However, it doesn't take long when you're in the region to appreciate the weight of importance which is, even now, attached to that period of the country's history. It is the central theme encountered in any museum covering recent history.

The British influence in Penang still came across quite strongly and western travellers seemed to have made it a compulsory stopover whether moving north or south. Bacon and eggs were once more on the breakfast menu and a hamburger (of sorts) made a welcome change from chicken and rice for lunch. Taken in by the atmosphere of the place we decided to take the day off and, booking ourselves into a cheap Chinese hotel for two nights, we spent our first clear day since Singapore relaxing in George Town (the main town) and on the northern beaches of Batu Ferringhi.

Early on the morning of the 8th of March we crossed back to the mainland and continued to hitch north. By lunchtime we had crossed the border and entered Thailand. In just under three weeks we had hitched from one end of Borneo to the other and up the entire length of Peninsular Malaysia. There was less than two weeks left on our schedule and still a great deal of travelling to do. We were hopeful, however, that things would begin to get a little simpler as we travelled further north, since our living expenses whilst in Thailand would be lower, allowing us to resume travelling by public transport.

Fate was not on our side. After an uneventful night halt in Hat Yai we caught the early morning bus bound for the island of Phuket. Three consecutive breakdowns later our seven-hour journey had turned into a fourteen-hour marathon – so much for public transport!

A few words about Thailand. Of all the countries we visited in South East Asia, Thailand is the only one that has remained untouched by the colonial fever which swept through here in the eighteenth and nineteenth centuries. It has nevertheless had its share of turbulence, having a long history of out-and-out warfare with neighbouring Burma (now more commonly called Myanmar). At the time of our journey however, its problems were originating from across its border with Kampuchea (now Cambodia).

It was to general worldwide approval that Vietnam invaded Cambodia in 1978, driving out Pol Pot and the infamous Khmer Rouge to establish the People's Republic of Kampuchea. At the time there was talk of a swift 'Grenada-style' policy of crushing the Khmer Rouge, establishing stability and then withdrawing, leaving the liberated country to rule itself again. By 1985 the world was still waiting and so were the 'liberated' Kampuchean people. Vietnam maintained that the Khmer Rouge were still strong, holding out in little pockets tucked away in the mountains, and that its job was therefore incomplete.

To the world though, the 'liberator' had turned 'captor' and was showing no intent to leave unless forced to do so. This is where Thailand becomes relevant, because in 1979 shortly after the Vietnamese first arrived, the Khmer Rouge (with its leader Pol Pot) fled westwards into Thailand where remnants remain to this day. The Vietnamese 'routing out' exercises therefore involved launching full-scale military actions inside Thailand's borders. The only party not mentioned so far in this little dispute is Prince Sihanouk (the 'rightful' Kampuchean president) and his forces. He obviously would have liked his country back but was too weak to fight the Vietnamese on his own so, as a last resort, was forced to cooperate with Pol Pot and his Khmer Rouge – his once sworn enemy – together with the Thai army (who by now were viewing the situation as a direct threat to their own country's security) in a tripartite counter-offensive against the overbearing Vietnamese forces.

Although our itinerary was keeping us well clear of this border area the great number of military roadblocks we encountered whilst travelling seemed to indicate that this was very much an issue which involved the country as a whole.

On the opposite side of the country to Kampuchea lies the tropical paradise of Phuket and it was here that our trouble-fraught bus ride was taking us. The journey took us past familiar rubber tree plantations and through some beautiful 'Guilin-esque' limestone karst scenery. When the bus wasn't broken down it was being driven at a terrifying speed, which I am told is a memory imprinted on all travellers to Thailand.

I had visited some near-perfect beaches in my few years of travelling and, to our great delight, we found that the beaches of Phuket Island were among the best! By comparison, the beaches of Brazil and the Caribbean must also rate highly in my list of 'perfect spots'. But the beaches of Phuket, with their long sweeps of golden sand shaded by coconut palms and washed by a turquoise sea, were sublime. Yet, being so numerous and existing in such an undeveloped area of the world, they were virtually deserted. How quickly all that has changed. Visitors to Phuket today are bound to find a very different island!

But to us at the time the temptation was too great. We threw caution and our programme to the wind. Hired a motorbike and for two whole days gave ourselves up to sea, sand and sun.

On the morning of the 12th of March we launched ourselves back on the trail once more, with a fifteen-hour bus ride north through cocoa and pineapple plantations to Bangkok, the capital of Thailand.

Up until 1939 the Thai people were called Siamese and their country, Siam. Off and on since the war, and generally more on than off, Thailand has been ruled by the military and this was very much the state of things at the time of our visit. The country has a constitutional monarchy and this has always been a very important part of the national heritage – the Thais are almost as proud of their monarchy as we are of ours. The religion is Buddhism and it is taken very seriously by the people. The large number of saffron-clad monks bore witness to this and almost outnumbered the 'boys in khaki'.

Our first visit to Thailand's coronary-inducing capital was more of a glancing blow than a visit – the aim being to buy air tickets and train tickets, visit banks and the *poste restante* and then continue north to Chiang Mai, leaving Bangkok's wealth of Wats (Thai Buddhist temples) until a subsequent visit.

Our arrival in Thailand's second city, Chiang Mai, on the morning of the 14th of March was something of a disappointment. Compared with Bangkok, we found Chiang Mai to be little more than a village and a rather uninteresting one at that. We had two objectives in coming here, one was to visit the town and the second was to organise a trek into the hills north of Chiang Mai, along the Thai–Burmese–Laos border.

In our 'discovering' of the town, to which end we devoted three hours, we visited its two most notable Wats. During the first of these visits we were invited by two of the monks to join them in their quarters so that they might practise their English. This was a lovely opportunity for us to discover something about the real world of these interesting people.

A Buddhist monk is instantly recognised by the saffron-coloured robes which he wears. His head is always shaven and for shoes he wears leather thongs. The monk's monastic existence is based on a continual striving towards 'nirvana', a state of perfect inner peace and fulfilment which was first attained 'as such' by Buddha in India some five hundred years before Christ. Buddhism might therefore be described as a meditative religion of the here and now. There is no Godhead in the same way as one finds in almost all other religions. In terms of world influence, Buddhism is strong in China, Thailand, Nepal, Tibet and to a lesser extent in India, its country of origin.

As we left our Buddhist friends we headed towards the centre of town to probe our second objective: to organise a trek into the surrounding hills so that we might visit some of the hill tribes. This was the real disappointment of Chiang Mai as what we found was a thoroughly organised tourist racket totally devoid of any individual initiative and priced beyond the reach of the budget-minded backpacker. Deflated but undaunted we gleaned as much information as we could and set about putting together our own trek. To quote a well-used saying: 'We had not come down with the last shower of rain!'

The first leg of our trip involved a three-hour bus ride north to Chiang Rai, a much smaller town close to the northernmost tip of Thailand and equidistant from Laos and Burma. Here we sought out a local guy who spoke a little English and who was prepared to organise the next leg of our little trek for us. This involved a two-hour river journey upstream from Chiang Rai to a village of the Karen tribe. There are five or six tribes which inhabit the hill lands of northern Thailand and they originate from areas of Asia as far away as Northern China or as near as Eastern Burma. I don't aspire to amateur anthropology and so shall not pursue this subject in detail. Suffice it to say that the Karen tribe is of Burmese origin and its people are famed for their skill with elephants.

It was for this reason that we had asked to be taken to their village. Elephants are still used in Thailand to haul the great wealth of teak from the forests but, for a price, these noble beasts could be hired out of their work for the lumber industry to transport Westerners (daft enough to choose them as a mode of transport) along the hill trails that link the villages in the border country.

The river trip from Chiang Rai to the Karen village was undertaken in a small canoe powered by an outboard engine. These river craft are similar to the 'peque-peques' which I had seen in the Amazon; the propeller consisting of a 3-metre-long shaft with a curved knife-like attachment fastened at the end to deflect the shaft in areas of vegetation or shoals and thus to protect the propeller. However, even with this protection, the canoe was not able to negotiate all the shoals, and so on at least half a dozen occasions we would all have to get out and push the canoe through to deeper water.

The moment of our arrival at the Karen village is one I shall remember vividly for some time. The setting was perfect. Half a dozen native huts were standing in a clearing on the riverbank and in the centre of the clearing, partly shaded by the thatched huts, were the dusty grey shapes of two Indian elephants, their loads of green bamboo being unloaded by the villagers in preparation for our arrival.

As Laurence and I took stock of our surroundings, Chat, our guide for the day, prepared some lunch. We were not blazing any new trail or treading where no white man had trodden before – we were well aware of that – and yet there was a feeling of authenticity about this and all the villages we were to visit, which made us feel very privileged to be there. By comparison, this is something I could not have said about trekking in Nepal, where one could almost follow the path by the trail of coke cans and toilet paper where numerous Western trekkers had left their mark.

Here the natives were dressed in their traditional costume, not because it was good for the tourist trade but because it was just the way they dressed and had always dressed. The Yao tribe for instance, who have their roots in Northern China, still wear black fur-collared jackets and head dress despite the fact that their relocation has involved changing to a climate which is considerably hotter than their original Chinese homeland.

With a lunch of rice and dried meat behind us we loaded our bags onto the elephant and climbed up after them, stepping from the veranda of one of the huts onto the animal's forehead and then onto its back. Like white Rajahs, Laurence and I sat side by side on the cushioned seat resting our feet on the elephant's shoulder blades.

'Our man' sat astride the elephant's neck with his feet lodged behind its ears, then with a gentle but persuasive kick and an encouraging shout we were off. As we moved out of the village the countryside began to unfold around us. The border terrain is very gentle. Hills rather than mountains support a dry dusty green scrub, broken up by thick groves of bamboo and pampas grass growing mainly in the valleys.

On a number of occasions the elephant followed the streambed in preference to the path along the bank, making free with the water, in an effort to cool its great bulk. However, as we left the streambed and climbed up out of the valley to cross a ridge, the elephant resorted to sucking up spittle and ejecting that in a fine spray along its flank. Thankfully we were mostly spared from the full force of this inventive water-cooling system!

Now and again the elephant would be troubled by a persistent horsefly and it was much to our astonishment that we noticed a small drop of blood form on the creature's back where a horsefly had just flown off having successfully bored through the elephant's thick hide.

Though slow, we found that travelling in this rather exotic way was not uncomfortable, once we had adjusted to the rocking motion as the elephant lolloped forward. The bulk of the elephant's diet consists of sugar cane and the new shoots found at the top of the bamboo. Occasionally however it would be tempted by a branch of succulent foliage and would snap off four or five feet of sapling, then, treading on the broken end with its foot would strip the branch of its leaves with the curl of its trunk, passing the food to its mouth without so much as a moment's hesitation in its gait.

In time we arrived at the Yao village and dismounted. From here we would have to continue on foot. After sharing some tea with the Yao people we set off, determined to make a Lahu village before dark. The village was some one-and-a-half hours walk away, and we had planned our departure to give us time for a bathe in a nearby waterfall which Chat had told us about. The waterfall was a little way on from the village and tucked away in the privacy of a bamboo forest.

Emerging from the bamboo into the forest clearing, we found ourselves in a pool of dappled light. The water cascaded 30-feet through giant ferns, bouncing off rocky ledges to finally crash into a perfect bowl, carved from the rock before us. The cool fresh water was something of a real luxury and we bathed away our aching backsides and sore feet. Looking for an excuse to stay in the pool we decided to drag our washing in with us and in the abandonment of the moment found that we had discovered nature's very own washing machine. Having soaped our clothes we threw them into the waterfall and waited for the upsurge to deliver the fully rinsed load to the surface again. Sadly, none of our washing reappeared. I suspect that someday there are going to be some very trendy clothes worn in and around the local villages!

Feeling a little foolish and deflated by our loss, but clean and refreshed, we headed back to the Lahu village downstream to look for accommodation. By our arrival we made a sufficient stir to attract the attention of the village headman and, indicating our hope to spend the night with them, we were soon taken into the bosom of the family, enjoying a cup of tea while a room was prepared for us. Throughout our travels in South East Asia we stayed in many such places: in the Philippines, Borneo and on the Peninsular. In essence they varied very little, so that we had now become thoroughly accustomed to the rather primitive yet comfortable accommodation which these native huts offered.

Unlike most African or Indian huts, which are built at ground level and have mud and dung floors, the huts of South East Asia are generally raised on stilts, some to a height of six feet where the threat of flooding is great, and have wooden planking floors. The walls are insubstantial affairs of stripped cane supported on a framework of mature bamboo poles or timber. Windows are not a necessary feature of each room as sunlight filters through the cane walls to provide a dim light. Where a window is included then a hole is simply cut from the completed wall section and the extracted portion mounted on a wooden hinged frame. The roof is generally a thatch prepared from local reeds, but corrugated iron is a preferred alternative where the household is wealthy enough to afford it.

The Lahu headman's house, in which we were staying that night, was typical of others we had stayed in and consisted of a 'living room' (generally a covered extension of the veranda), two bedrooms and a kitchen open to the backyard where a separate construction housed the toilet and wash tub.

The furniture in each room was very basic but functional. The wash tub remained permanently full of water which could then be scooped up to use for either washing or 'flushing' the toilet. The kitchen operated on a coal or wood-fired basis with a single wooden table for preparing food. The washing up was done outside. In the bedrooms the 'furniture' consisted of a simple rush mat for the bed with a mosquito net suspended from the roof to provide relief from the bugs at night. Malaria was still very much a problem in these parts of Asia.

What really surprised us during our travels in Northern Thailand, more generally, was the inclusion of all manner of modern electrical gadgets taking pride of place in the living area. This often included either a colour TV or a hi-fi system which would not have been out of place in a London flat!

These trappings of the twentieth century were usually a privilege of the village headman, or at least that is the conclusion we drew by seeing the hoards of village kids who drifted in when the TV was on, gradually filling the room until we could barely pick our way across the floor. In complete contrast to the TV, the remainder of the living room furniture normally comprised three or four rush mats and perhaps a cane chair or two. Dinner was typically served at ground level.

Lighting had, in most cases, taken advantage of modern appliances and a small petrol generator was often used to work the odd strip light. The TV remained on a 12-volt car battery but, for the less affluent members of the tribe or village group, oil lamps still provided the sole means of light at night. To my mind, the yellow light of oil lamps seen from afar as they twinkle in the doorways of native huts, remains one of the most romantic sights on earth.

Outside the hut lives the household menagerie – a collection of cows, dogs, pigs and chickens, who act as refuse collectors and alarm clocks, as well as providing protein in the diet when wild game cannot be found.

On this particular night, dinner consisted of boiled rice with curried vegetables and pork fat. After dinner the TV was switched on and the villagers once again filtered across the threshold, in what was obviously an accepted routine. Our knowledge of Thai being restricted to a simple 'yes' and 'thank you' we declined the offer of Dallas dubbed into Thai and went to bed, delighted to see that on this occasion our hosts owned the considerable luxury of mattresses which, although lumpy and straw filled, provided a welcome addition to the rush mats.

In the morning, after a much-hoped-for breakfast which never materialised, we set off, but not before we had watched our host, the village headman, address all the village workers, both men and women, and then send them off to their work in the fields – or rather terraces.

After a couple of hours walk through scenery which varied little from the previous day, and a brief halt at an Akha village to admire the costumes the women were wearing, we came upon a dirt road just as a party of four Europeans were passing by. We joined them in the walk to the next village and there, after a short wait, caught the first of a series of trucks and buses that were to take us to the Golden Triangle.

Our short wait was not uneventful as we had stumbled upon the prelude to a local wedding and so were invited to join in the feast and thus lessen the vast quantity of rice wine which they would otherwise be burdened with drinking once the wedding really got underway. How one manages to conduct a wedding when all the guests are either drunk with rice wine or high on opium I'll never know as we were whisked away before we had time to find out!

In days gone by trade in South East Asia revolved around opium. The British were the main buyers and sellers and through their trade in opium with China the foundation stones of Hong Kong's wealth and prosperity were laid. Today the opium market is seen in a different light. In its legal form the opium poppy is used to produce morphine, a cornerstone in the world of medicine and pharmacy. A different process of refinement, however, produces the drug heroin, a product with which the opium poppy is more commonly associated.

Today, as in the early days of the British East India Company, the Golden Triangle is a major producer of the world's opium. The triangle itself is an ill-defined area of Thailand which has as its focus the point where the borders of Thailand, Burma and Laos meet — that is to say, at the junction of the Mae Sai and Mekong (Mae Khong) rivers. This exotic spot is, if you like, the point of the Golden Triangle and it was on the banks of the Mekong River, at this precise spot, that we chose to spend the night.

The accommodation was, if anything, more spartan than that which I have just described, but the view as I lay in bed was unquestionably unique. In one glance I could look upon Thailand, Burma and Laos. Indeed, the Mae Sai River was sufficiently shallow to permit an easy crossing by foot and so, in what was to be our second illegal entry of a country on the trip, we waded across to wiggle our toes on a Burmese beach.

In the centre of the infamous Mekong River, just downstream of the river junction, is an island — well, more of a sandbank than an island. To forty-eight Laosian refugees however, it had been home for a number of weeks. Forced out of Laos by the communists they fled to China where they were also evicted. They then floated downstream on the Mekong — which has its source in China — until they reached this point.

Here they waited for either a rise in the river level or a sympathetic offer of asylum on behalf of the Thai government. In the meantime, a twice-weekly boat organised by the UN was feeding these people.

After one night at the Golden Triangle we moved on again, first visiting Thailand's most northerly point, Mae Sai, and then heading back to Chiang Rai to spend the night at Chat's house.

In the morning we attempted to catch the fast bus south to Lampang where there was a notable collection of ancient Wats. But instead we ended up catching the slow bus, which took a full six hours to complete the one-hundred-mile journey. So rather than temples we saw villages and countryside – arguably a preferable alternative. From Lampang we took the night train south to the ancient Thai capital of Ayutthaya.

When making the decision to stop off in Ayutthaya on our way back to Bangkok we had wondered whether the effort was really justified. It therefore came as a nice surprise to find that what had promised to be a struggle round yet more monuments, turned out to be a very peaceful and relaxed stroll around some of the most splendid examples of ancient Thai temples that we had seen so far. It was as if the whole of Ayutthaya had consisted of temples and palaces, the ruins of which now stood in various states of repair, and free from the hustle and bustle of the new city which had grown up adjacent to the old.

My time being somewhat shorter than Laurence's I left Ayutthaya at midday to complete the ninety-minute journey back to Bangkok, while Laurence stayed on to explore a little more of the ancient capital.

Bangkok really is a dreadful city to get around and so I was determined to pack my sight-seeing into as little time as possible. Parkinson's Law applies all too easily in Bangkok where, if you have time on your hands, the city's transport system will soon fill it for you. I felt certain that this was one place I would be revisiting many times in the future, as it is a stepping-stone for so many places further east. I therefore restricted my visit to the bare essentials and will not insult this grand city by attempting to describe its many temples and attractions from the pace I flew round them.

Having spent barely twenty-four hours in Bangkok, and now joined again by Laurence, our day began with a sense of 'ground rush'. It was the 20th of March, and Laurence's birthday, but it was also my last day in Thailand and so, true to form, we both got on a bus and continued with the programme. There was no time to lose!

One thing which both of us wanted to do before leaving the country was to visit the River Kwai and in particular the famous bridge over the River Kwai. Being only two and a half hours west of Bangkok this made a nice little trip.

Kanchanaburi was the beginning of the 'death railway' which was ordered by the Japanese during World War II to give them access into Burma. In total some 16,000 prisoners of war, mainly British and Australians died during those terrible years. Some 8,000 are now buried in war graves in Kanchanaburi while the remainder were burned in mass graves or just abandoned to the Kwai. The death toll represents around sixty lives per mile of track laid.

In the JEATH museum, constructed on the site of the Kaw Chow camp in Kanchanaburi, the past is preserved in photographs and sketches. Maintained by Buddhist monks the museum takes the form of a faithful reconstruction of the old camp – the exhibition being staged in the bamboo shelters which constituted the dormitories for the POW workers.

Some three miles upstream is the bridge. I have to admit to being a little confused about what we saw but as I understand it, the first construction was a temporary timber bridge, then, one hundred yards apart from this, the concrete and steel bridge which carried the railway was built. In 1945 the Allies bombed this bridge, destroying the central span. What we see now is therefore, either the 1943 bridge, repaired, or a similar concrete and steel bridge built immediately post war. Either way we got a good impression of the site as little or no development had taken place on the far side of the bridge, allowing the imagination to wander back to times for which none but those who actually suffered here can have a full comprehension or appreciation.

That evening we were due to be staying in the Hilton Bangkok on a cheap rate organised by Laurence, but a fully booked hotel meant that that little birthday treat was not to be. So, booking into a somewhat less prestigious but still pleasantly luxurious hotel, the Windsor, we set about celebrating Laurence's birthday.

Early, too early, the next morning I left Laurence at the Windsor and headed out to the airport where a standby place on a Thai International flight whisked me off back to Hong Kong.

Over the three months, Laurence and I had managed to accomplish everything we had set out to achieve, with the exception of a visit to

Indonesia. Given our time again, I believe the only amendment would have been to complete the circular trip by flying Bangkok to Rangoon in Burma and then Rangoon to Kunming in China, and thence Hong Kong. But time and money had by now run out and so Burma, like Tibet would have to wait until a future visit. The second stage of this magical year had drawn to a close and the challenge of hard work in Hong Kong was about to begin.

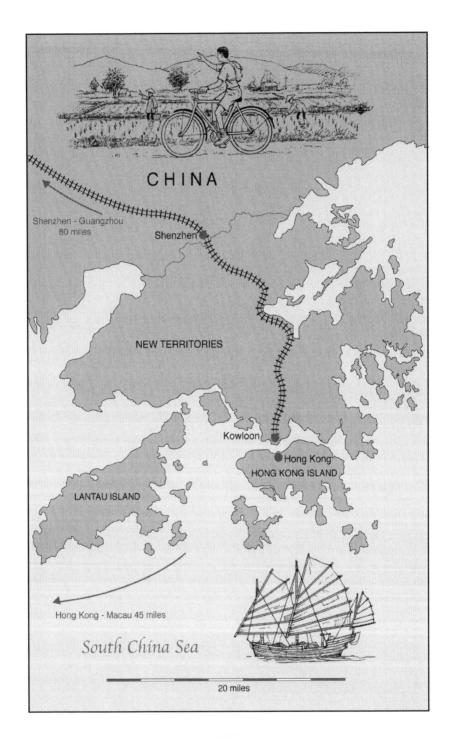

CHINA

Shenzhen - Guangzhou
80 miles

Shenzhen

NEW TERRITORIES

Kowloon

Hong Kong
HONG KONG ISLAND

LANTAU ISLAND

Hong Kong - Macau 45 miles

South China Sea

20 miles

CHAPTER TWELVE

Hong Kong

By the stroke of a pen my life was suddenly changed. A shoestring traveller no longer, I was now a company man. Worries about eating too little suddenly changed to a concern over putting on weight. Where the week before my energies had been taken up with sorting out the thousand and one things in life such as buying train tickets, renewing my visa, finding accommodation or getting a meal, now the company took care of all those things for me. The transformation was alarming in its completeness.

I was now living in a plush new expat flat in Happy Valley, one of many which the company owned on Hong Kong Island. From the lounge balcony I looked out onto Happy Valley racecourse and beyond that to the tower blocks of Hong Kong's central business district. Breakfast was no longer a question of hunting around for something vaguely palatable for eight o'clock in the morning. As a 'company man' my 'package' included an 'amah', or Chinese maid, who took care of all cooking and cleaning for me – not that two shirts and a pair of trousers represented much of a cleaning burden!

One of the most difficult parts of the transition was getting used to taxis. In Hong Kong taxis were very cheap, HK$10 (or 50p) could get you just about anywhere, yet having spent so many months fighting off insistent drivers, preferring to walk and save money, it was weeks before I could bring myself to abandon the crowded trams and buses for an air-conditioned taxi.

Strangest of all, however, was turning up at work in a collar and tie and working from nine 'til five in a clean air-conditioned office. In quiet moments I would gaze longingly out of the windows, reliving the past few months of excitement. In my mind I would be standing on the bows of *Morvran* as we edged our way through an Amazon backwater, or plunging through the leech-infested swamps of Borneo, or simply basking in the sun on a silvery beach in Phuket. The view from our sixty-third-floor office was in itself magnificent, encompassing as it did the whole of Central Hong Kong and Victoria Harbour. Indeed, few buildings on the island could rival such a view, and yet I still felt claustrophobic.

Thankfully not all the work was office-bound and after a month in Hong Kong I crossed back into China to spend a week on site for my employer Hopewell-Costain.

The project on which I was working was an enormous highway network for the whole of Southern China. At the time things were still at the embryonic stage with only outline budgets and rough timetables being agreed. Even the route itself, as it penetrated the Chinese interior, was little more than a series of broad pen-strokes on a largescale map. Nearer to the Hong Kong border the project was further advanced, and by way of a trial run a detailed site survey and investigation was being conducted for one mile of the eventual one-hundred-and-fifty-mile network. I decided to go and take a look.

Unfortunately my opportunity arose at a bad time and in making my way into China I joined the estimated half-million Chinese who were also trying to cross the border that weekend to celebrate Ching Ming – the grave sweepers' festival which that year coincided with Easter. Nobody seeing the thousands and thousands of Chinese of every age who packed the local cemeteries to 'chat' to their ancestors could possibly have doubted the major part that tradition still played in the lives of the Chinese people – communism or no communism.

Although our work in China continued throughout this holiday, Ching Ming did take its toll and amongst the casualties was our van driver. Thus inconvenienced we, that is myself and my two Chinese colleagues who were also involved in the supervision of the work, were forced to improvise.

Spring in Southern China is just about perfect cycling weather and so the half-hour ride to work which replaced the ten-minute drive was more of a pleasure than a labour. The Special Economic Zone of Shenzhen is not the most appealing region in China and at the time I worked there it was undergoing intensive industrial development – which did nothing for its beauty – but one could get away from it all and take a route through paddy fields and along dusty rural lanes. As I cycled my way to work in the mornings, labourers, ankle deep in the muddy paddy fields would unbend from their back-breaking work to stare at me or occasionally wave a friendly 'good morning' before continuing with the planting of young rice shoots. Half the site consisted of this 'picture of rural life', while the remaining half was a collection of duck ponds and fish ponds.

At the edge of the site was a small village, not particularly attractive, but then few towns or villages in China could be described as anything more flattering than drab, and certainly never 'attractive'. By Chinese standards therefore this village was pretty much the norm. However, it had benefitted greatly from the new-found wealth which was flooding into the Shenzhen Economic Development Zone and had decided to invest its new wealth in property. Beyond the tiny nucleus of the old village the villagers had built umpteen new houses, most of which were still empty, but seeing these houses it struck me that we could perhaps adopt one as an office-cum-canteen for use once construction of this trial section of road was underway. I set about making enquiries.

Each village operated as a 'unit' or 'commune', and each 'unit' had two key figures. From a traditional point of view the more senior of these was the village headman, but since the establishment of the 'unit' system the most powerful man was without doubt the local Party Secretary. All decisions went through him, and in village matters he could act with a surprising degree of autonomy. It is he, for instance, who would give permission for a villager to move to any other village, or for a house to be built in the village. It was therefore the Party Secretary who I had to approach in my search for rented accommodation.

Armed with my interpreter, we soon managed to locate both the village headman and the all-important local Party Secretary. The fellow turned out to be most obliging, both then and on the numerous other occasions when we had to return to him for a favour, and I got the feeling that he was as intrigued with the thought of dealing directly with a dollar-wheeling European as I was in dealing with a Communist Party Secretary!

Back in Hong Kong, I spent my free weekends playing 'tourist'. Saturday is a standard working day – or more often, half day – which means that on Sunday just about everyone in Hong Kong seems to evacuate the city 'en masse'.

On one occasion I explored more of the island of Lantau, the island where Laurence and I had spent our post-China days recuperating in Tim's flat. Lantau is in fact larger than Hong Kong and decidedly less populated. At the time (which was prior to the international airport moving to the island!) there were probably more sheep than people. It is also very mountainous and so strolling across its windswept fells it was all too easy to feel oneself in Scotland rather than tropical Hong Kong. I discovered on later trips that the rugged landscape of Lantau Island is not untypical of much of the New Territories – that part of mainland China which was under leasehold until 1997 – and I began to come to the conclusion that to describe Hong Kong as a bustling centre of trade and finance was to tell only half the story.

On another Sunday, I took the one-hour hydrofoil ride across the mouth of the Pearl River to Macau. Macau, like Hong Kong, consists of a piece of Chinese mainland and some islands. However, while Hong

Kong's history goes back to the middle of the nineteenth century, Macau has been a Portuguese colony since the fifteen hundreds.

It is only when you travel to Macau that you realise just how much of a rat race Hong Kong life really is. Macau offered a welcome contrast and its shaded avenues and slow pace made me feel as if I had been transported to the Mediterranean. Much of the architecture is typically Portuguese and, like Malacca in Western Malaysia, it adds a touch of old-world colonial tradition to the town, a quality which is almost completely lacking in all the glitter and brashness of Hong Kong.

The issue of 1997, when not only the New Territories but all of Hong Kong reverted to the Chinese, was less of a talking point than I had expected. In general people seemed to be quite satisfied that the status quo would be maintained at least for a good while into the fifty-year transitional period and, from the perspective of 1985, that was quite a long way off. On the news, however, concern was brewing, particularly over Hong Kong's basic law and the formation of a local political party system, both necessary steps for promoting the 'one country, two systems' approach which forms the backbone of the Sino–British agreement on Hong Kong. Put another way, the question was simply: could the 'two systems' of communism and democratic capitalism co-exist and flourish within 'one country', namely China? It was a 'big ask', and a debate that was only just surfacing in 1985.

Editing this book in 2020 amid the unprecedented level of political street protest, demanding the preservation (or restoration) of democratic rule in Hong Kong, it would seem that the 'concern' we picked up on in 1985 was well founded. Moreover, it evidently still remains a raw and pressing issue for the citizens of Hong Kong to resolve with the government in Beijing, and with almost half of the transition period now expired, the clock is ticking.

One Sunday in late June, I awoke to find the atmosphere in Hong Kong electric with anticipation. What little reserve that normally existed between the expats working and living in the territory had dissolved and people were freely striking up conversations with perfect strangers to learn of the latest development. 'Tai-fung' literally translates as 'supreme wind' but is better known as 'typhoon', and it's as much a part of Hong Kong as mah-jong. Moreover, it is an accepted part of life's 'joss' or 'luck' by all who call Hong Kong home. The radio that morning was broadcasting the news that storm signal 'number three' had been hoisted and the colony was alert, waiting to see if this 'supreme wind' would pass us by or swoop down and wreak the awful destruction of which it had so often proven itself capable.

Precautions for typhoons are well rehearsed. As soon as it has been determined that a typhoon is likely to pass close to the island the 'number one' signal is raised. This is followed by the 'number three' when the typhoon is within twenty-four hours of Hong Kong. As the centre of the typhoon approaches, the wind begins to pick up and white horses start to appear on the normally tranquil waters of the harbour. People will now start to prepare. Windows are taped up and everybody makes sure that there is an adequate supply of beer in the fridge, for when the next signal is raised, the 'number eight', the time has come to beat a hasty retreat as the typhoon is imminent. Two hours after the 'number eight' has been raised, all public transport stops, restaurants and shops close. The city virtually grinds to a halt and everybody is sent home from work.

When the 'number eight' storm signal was raised that afternoon, I beat my 'hasty retreat' to the members' lounge of the Royal Hong Kong Yacht Club. Not surprisingly, one gets a good view of the harbour from there and it added to the excitement to watch the pilot boats and fishing boats scuttling across the usually busy waters, heading for secure moorings in the typhoon shelter.

However, by early evening it had become clear that this time Hong Kong was to escape the wrath of 'tai-fung' and so I wandered home through the strangely-deserted streets of downtown Wanchai with the realisation that there would be work on Monday after all.

During June, July and the early part of August I was joined in Hong Kong by my brother Graham, who, disillusioned with prospects in the UK, had come there in search of 'a better life'. Falling on his feet with uncanny regularity was one of Graham's strong points and within a week of arriving there were two Cottons earning their living in Hong Kong.

His energy and enthusiasm for the good life made him excellent company and together we settled into a routine of sailing on our days off and exploring the nightlife on an all-too-frequent basis.

My time in Hong Kong, however, was drawing to a close. By the end of September I had to be back in England and ready to start my year of study at Cranfield Business School. Keen to complete my travels in style, I made a few brief enquiries and then, in early August, purchased a one-way rail ticket from West Kowloon Station, Hong Kong to Victoria Station, London. It was time to board the Trans-Siberian Express!

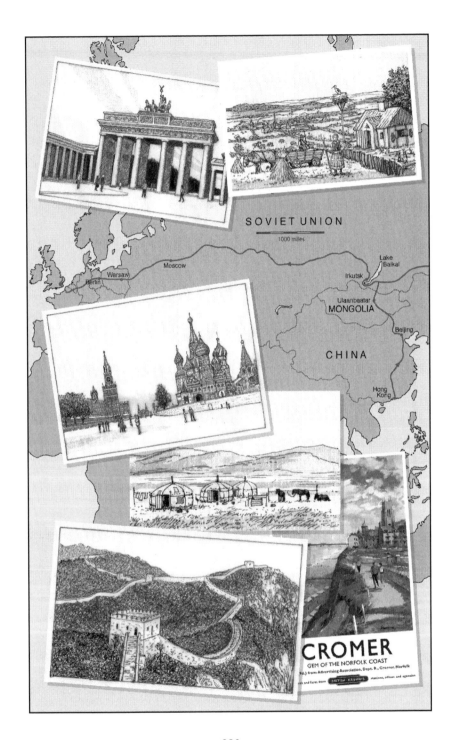

SOVIET UNION

1000 miles

Berlin
Warsaw
Moscow
Irkutsk
Lake
Baikal
Ulaanbaatar
MONGOLIA
Beijing

CHINA

Hong
Kong

CROMER
GEM OF THE NORFOLK COAST

CHAPTER THIRTEEN

The Trans-Siberian Express

Saying goodbye to Graham was harder than I had ever imagined. We had grown very close as brothers in the months we had lived together in Happy Valley and as I completed my last-minute packing for the trip home I felt a very real pang of loss. When it came to it, leaving the security of Hong Kong was not that easy either. There were so many unknowns to face. Although I had purchased my trip home, I had virtually no tickets to show for it, only addresses scattered all over Asia and Europe where my coupons could be exchanged or where a reservation had been telexed in my name. Guangzhou, Beijing, Moscow and Berlin were all potential foul-up points. Nevertheless, two days later, and two contacts successfully completed, I arrived in Beijing.

Beijing represents one of three starting points for the Trans-Siberian Express. This famous railway runs from Moscow to Vladivostok with one spur running south through Manchuria to Beijing and another which runs through Mongolia to Beijing. It was the latter route which I proposed to take. Although I had a ticket for this leg of the journey, I didn't have all the necessary visas and so a two-day stop-over in Beijing was needed to complete the paperwork.

Beijing revisited. I felt sure that my visit to Beijing at Christmas must have been clouded by ill-health and the bitter cold, and that this time around it would be very different. Sadly, however, I found that little had changed in Beijing since that first visit. The buses were still just as impossibly crowded, and the streets were just as shabby and dull. However, the people appeared more colourful, and the blues and greens had now given way to a brighter variety of colours. I could not decide whether this was due to the fact that I was now seeing the place in summer or whether the western influence, which without doubt was becoming more and more prevalent as China opened its doors to foreigners, was simply more noticeable.

Although I bused wherever I could, I found it hard to make that transition from Hong Kong which everyone had warned me about, and consequently found myself resorting to taxis at the smallest excuse. The Mongolian Embassy proved a focal point for those two days that I spent in Beijing prior to my departure for Moscow. Every European in China seemed to be taking the same route home and, as we stood in the pouring rain queuing for our visas, I made one or two good friends. Anita was one. It was her first visit to Beijing and I found it very easy to slip into the tour-guide routine which I so enjoyed, with the challenge of re-discovering old sites without the pressure of having to stick to a fixed itinerary. Having fouled up something wicked on navigating a way to the Heavenly Temple, we then proceeded more smoothly through a night at the Opera, Peking Duck, the Summer Palace – raining this time – and the Great Wall Hotel, which, it appeared, had changed hands since Laurence and I spent three glorious, recuperative nights there. Come Tuesday night we were ready for 'the off'.

Not long after dawn the following morning, I approached the impressive facade of Beijing Railway Station. In contrast to the previous day, the weather had picked up a treat and it was clear that a good, fine day was in the offing. At six o'clock, however, the railway station seemed suspended in a sea of thin mist which later in the day would be burned up and replaced by a haze of Beijing smog. The Orient and his wife were milling around, laden with baggage, while blue-clad stern-faced Chinese ladies officiously checked tickets and the papers of hopeful travellers. As I presented my ticket marked 'Beijing–Moscow', I felt a shaft of excitement. Another adventure was about to begin!

In sharp contrast to my trip up from Kowloon to Beijing, which had been made in the cramped, sweltering confines of a smoke-filled hard-sleeper berth where I had been the only 'foreign devil', the third class accommodation on the Trans-Siberian Express was little less than luxurious. The carriage was divided into four-berth compartments and carpeted throughout. Accommodation had been arranged with cultural division in mind and thus I found myself billeted with European travelling companions for the duration of our six-day journey to Moscow.

Although generally full, the train was fortunately not filled to capacity and I was therefore sharing with only two others – Anita and another English girl, Joanna.

The air was clean and fresh as we left the last of industrial Beijing behind us and headed north, winding into the mountains. By the time we had reached the Great Wall the sun was full in the sky and everybody's spirits were high. Something of a party atmosphere prevailed as people began to relax – the burden of rushing around after tickets and visas and last-minute hassles suddenly lifted. It was wonderful to see that magnificent wall stretching away before us, beckoning us westwards, the treeless slopes which it so precariously straddled now green and luxuriant in contrast to the brown sterile landscape that had so impressed me a few months earlier.

Dipping out of sight and then reappearing, the wall remained with us for many miles, as much a part of China's landscape as the rock from which it is hewn. Eventually, looking out across a large flat plain – green, but for the most part uncultivated – I caught my last glimpse of the Great Wall as it followed a steeply-inclined ridge down to the plain and then turned to skirt the foot of the mountains while our train turned north for the wide open grasslands of Mongolia.

Lunch that day was exceptionally good; shredded pork and bamboo tips, garlic slices and an egg and tomato dish which washed down well with bottles of Beijing beer. I was feeling very happy in myself and more than content with the prospect of five more days of the same. No worries or decisions, just good company, good food and the whole of Northern Asia unwinding before my eyes. The grandeur of the mountains was soon replaced by a landscape of endless plains – not a tree in sight, just a carpet of subtle shades of green and brown with much of the land given over to wheat. The farmers were on horseback.

After dinner at the end of that first day out from Beijing we crossed the Chinese–Mongolian border. The process was somewhat lengthy since a change in railway gauge meant that all the carriage bogies had to be swopped over – a much more satisfactory solution however, than having to change trains.

All during the night the train rattled on relentlessly across the plains of Mongolia while we slept. At the border the Chinese dining car had been replaced by a Mongolian one, but standards had not been compromised and breakfast that morning consisted of fried eggs, bread and jam and Mongolian coffee – an insipid cross between Turkish and Nescafe.

Breakfast was a leisurely affair and another opportunity to chat to fellow Asian travellers. Once again, the weather came up trumps and the view from the carriage window could have been lifted from a movie set. The wheat fields of yesterday afternoon had completely disappeared and now for as far as the eye could see was uninterrupted grassland. Occasionally the train would pass herds of camel, or farmers mounted on horseback tending cattle, sheep or horses. The cattle outnumber the people in Mongolia by a considerable margin. It is an unbelievably lonely landscape and scratching a living from this land must indeed be a Spartan task. God knows what life must be like here in the winter.

There was a noticeable difference in the people now. Both the men and womenfolk wore a rugged complexion, which could only be described as 'Mongolian'. A lot of the folk we passed were dressed in colourful national costume and some of their saddles were works of art. Settlements, such as we saw, were few and far between and more temporary structures were in evidence than permanent towns. Home for these nomadic people is a tent-type structure known locally as a 'ger' but better known to Westerners as a 'yurt'. The yurt is circular and about fifteen feet in diameter. The tent walls are vertical for the first three feet or so then forming a shallow cone to a central point. All those I saw were white in colour and a collection of two or three yurts standing out against the green/brown grassland soon became an accepted part of the Mongolian landscape. The yurt is constructed from animal hides – hence the colour.

The Mongolian lands and people are split into two political regions, Outer and Inner, and for many years these vast grasslands have acted as a buffer zone between the two great superpowers, China and Russia, though largely under Chinese influence for much of its history. But in 1921, as the Qing Dynasty in China was falling apart, Russia helped the northern part of this land or 'Outer' Mongolia to establish pseudo-independence, setting it up as the Mongolian People's Republic, a communist state that would listen to Moscow, whilst the southern part of this territory, known as 'Inner' Mongolia, remained an autonomous region within China. It was not until 1945 that Stalin managed to persuade China to officially recognise the boundaries of this new country and whilst Mongolia is now properly independent, with its own government and economy, at the time of our journey the territory was still strictly controlled by the Russians.

At around lunch time on our second day out from Beijing we arrived in the capital of Mongolia, Ulan Bator (now known as Ulaanbaatar). The Russian presence was very much in evidence as we strolled around the station and waiting rooms. Entering one of these buildings we noticed, in the corner farthest from the door, a group of four or five Russian soldiers, obviously waiting for a train home to Mother Russia. In 1985 the world was still deep in the grip of the Cold War and, for most of us, these were the first real Russians that we had seen face to face; their blue-eyed, blond-haired Slavic complexions marking them out, and for many minutes both groups, equally curious, just stared at each other. We must have looked as odd to them, dressed in our multicoloured Hong Kong cottons as they did to us; their uniforms giving them a somewhat First World War appearance. Eventually our group broke up and moved on without any exchange of words being offered.

Beginning a couple of hours before we arrived in Ulan Bator and continuing until we left Mongolia, the plains had become undulating – though still treeless – grasslands. In parts, the landscape had become quite hilly and once more I was reminded of South Africa or the Western Highlands of Scotland. At nightfall we crossed the border into the Soviet Union.

The crossing was straightforward enough, though predictably lengthy. Passports and visas were checked with a thoroughness I had never seen before and all literature was submitted for inspection. The occasional book would be confiscated and usually these would be Russian novels by 'out of favour' contemporary authors. One or two cassette tapes were also taken and in all cases these items would be signed for and then taken without fuss from either side. I escaped intact.

On the morning of our third day out we awoke to the silver birch forests of Siberia.

The day was a confusing one, due mainly to the rather complicated, but understandable, system of running all trains in Russia to Moscow time. Up until the border we had been operating on Beijing time, which had already become highly inappropriate as we emerged from Mongolia. However, suddenly swapping to Moscow time had the effect of throwing us just as far out in the other direction. For now, instead of it getting dark at nine o'clock in the evening, it was getting dark at half past three in the afternoon!

More alarming still, was that it got light at half past two in the morning! Of course, local Russian time is split into a number of time zones but as we had no idea where we were in relation to those times we soon gave up trying to adapt and gradually settled into a pattern of eating and sleeping according to the sun, whilst keeping our watches set to Moscow in order to make sense of the timetable.

Trees, round-eyes and cheese. The dining car had once more changed hands and as we drifted in for breakfast that morning three buxom

Russian ladies were waiting to serve us. The re-appearance of trees and European faces were two of the biggest differences which struck us that morning. Cheese was the third. Many of us had heard rumours of how bad the Russian food was on the trains – that was on those days that they had any food at all – but breakfast that morning was the most sumptuous meal we had had since departing Beijing. Cheese formed part of this feast, an item of food that had been virtually unobtainable for us in Asia – be it China or Singapore.

By mid-day (sun time), we arrived at Irkutsk, a prominent city in Siberia on the western shores of Lake Baikal. We had been following the southern shores of this lake since dawn. Four hundred miles long and some fifty or sixty miles wide, Lake Baikal, the deepest lake in the world, holds one-fifth of the world's fresh water – more than all the American Great Lakes combined! It is also something of a resort for Siberians. From Irkutsk the railroad turns west, continuing its way through rolling hills forested with silver birch and pine. Towards the end of the afternoon we began to lose the hills and emerged onto the flat lands which would take us all the way to the Urals. In many respects the landscape was very reminiscent of home now, the odd fields of wheat lending a 'Cambridgeshire' air to the place, whilst looking out onto the vast forests of birch and pine I could easily have been standing on some promontory in South Norfolk.

As the morning of the fourth day dawned, we were greeted by scenery that had changed little overnight, despite the vast distances which this journey involved. However, the weather had broken and the skies were now overcast with occasional showers. We were making fewer and fewer stops and saw very little in the way of settlements save for the occasional logging town or isolated timber cabin-cum-single-storey house in forest clearings – 'cricket pavilions' as Joanna appropriately dubbed them.

Since leaving Beijing everyone in our section of the train had come to know one-another quite well and distinct little groups of friends had begun to emerge. We were a mixed bunch: English, Italian, French, American, Dutch and Australian. We were all Westerners though, and in this respect a very definite strategy appeared to have been adopted in arranging the carriages on the train. The Europeans and Hong Kong Chinese formed one group, mainland Chinese another and then additional carriages had been added at the Mongolian and Russian borders to accommodate those nationalities.

After we crossed into Russia, I found that the dining car never became more than three-quarters full. This was no reflection on the food, merely a measure of the disorientation caused by having some watches running on Moscow time, some still on Beijing time and some at all points in between. All meals (i.e. breakfast, lunch or dinner) could be bought at all times of the day and so the adoption of a set eating pattern was not encouraged. I found I was generally taking two meals a day, and life between meals consisted of a quietly determined effort to type or read, but gladly accepting interruptions from friends who would drop in to chat or share a bottle of beer. It was a bit like a six-day-long open house!

The fifth day out from Beijing passed without change to either scenery or routine. The more I saw of Russia the more it struck me as being so much like England, or at least those parts of rural England that I always think of as typical – Thomas Hardy's England.

That night we crossed the Urals and thus made the transition from Asia into Europe.

The stations and towns were more frequent on the sixth day but the overall scenery remained unchanged – silver birch and pine forests, wheat fields, and villages made up of little wooden cottages.

At four minutes past three on that day we came to a halt in Moscow. After five and a half days of travelling the train was one minute early.

Teeing myself up for the next stage of the journey was first on the list of priorities. This took a little while but with baggage stashed away in the luggage lockers of the correct station for Berlin, all the traipsing around Moscow for banks and advanced ticket sales fell hand-in-hand with an improvised sightseeing trip. With train ticket and money finally secured I wandered across to Red Square to enjoy the views in the late afternoon sun.

There are no two ways about it, Moscow's Red Square must rate as one of the world's most beautiful piazzas. Having become used to the vastness of Tiananmen Square in Beijing, Red Square looked at first no larger than an average-sized parking lot and certainly not the sort of place where you might stage the greatest show of strength that the world has ever seen. Big, however, is not always beautiful, and what Red Square lacks in pure size it makes up for in exquisite charm. If imagined as a rectangle with the longer sides twice the length of the shorter, Red Square is a slightly sloping, cobbled area, flanked on one of the two longer sides by the red walls of the Kremlin with its skyline of domes and bell towers and with the very French-looking state supermarket, GUM, opposite. Forming the two shorter sides are the History Museum, looking like something out of Disney Land with its red walls and snow-coloured roofs, and to the south the multicoloured, multifaced Cathedral of St Basil, with its explosion of Byzantine-topped towers. This masterpiece in imaginative design was built during the time of Ivan the Terrible who, it is said, burned out the eyes of his architect when the building was complete to ensure that its secrets were never duplicated. The only hint of Russia's abandonment of the imperialist system that was responsible for these masterpieces is the dull and rather diminutive mausoleum which houses Lenin's body and stands in front of the Kremlin. It is from the balcony of this mausoleum that the Politburo watches the May Day parades.

A group of us from the Trans-Siberian Express had arranged to meet up that evening for a little celebration and so, with the sun setting over the Kremlin, I left Red Square and headed for Gorky Street and the pre-arranged venue. Our meal was sumptuous: caviar, smoked salmon, vodka and white wines. There was a great feeling of good humour and friendship and when, hours later, we emerged to wander back across Red Square, I felt I owned the world!

During our walk through the Square we were approached by a young suave-looking Russian. After the preliminary moves and small-talk we got down to talking about the subject which had been the obvious point of the apparently casual meeting – trade.

Jeans, it appeared were no longer in as much demand as they used to be. Unbeknown to 'muggins' (who had bought two brand new pairs of

Levis in Hong Kong for this very purpose), Russia had begun its own production and just about everybody was now in jeans. However, the market for US dollars was still good and so, in the usual shady fashion, he and I negotiated a transaction. Somewhat to my surprise, the 'going rate' made Russia one of the best black markets for exchanging money which we had encountered, reducing the price of caviar by a third!

That night I, and some others from the 'dinner party', booked into the Hotel Berlin, only a few minutes' walk from the Kremlin. This proved a comfortable alternative to the benches of the railway station, especially since the price of a room came to little more than $10 a head. The hotel had obviously been the house of a very rich and powerful man as the dining room, which had once been the ballroom, more closely resembled the Sistine Chapel than a mess-hall. After a rather weak breakfast the following morning we began a more sober exploration of the city.

I had always imagined the Kremlin to be a single building. In fact, it is a fortress, complete with four Cathedrals, a Palace and all the administrative buildings, new and old, which are necessary for running a government – communist or otherwise. After the Kremlin and a short break for caviar and chicken 'Kiev' (very disappointing), we continued our tour with the Lenin Museum, a ride on the underground (impressive but not as grand as I had been led to expect) and a quick look at the KGB headquarters – exterior only!

In general, Moscow struck me as being well laid out, clean and well organised without being restrictive. Its streets were more like Parisian boulevards and were not overcrowded.

All in all I liked the place, but the question remained in everyone's mind; 'How much of all this was representative of normal life and how much was mere showcase?' From our glimpses of rural Russia we feared that 'normal life' for the average Russian was a far cry from the exotic experiences we were now enjoying.

All the hotels that were open to foreigners were located in the centre of the city, which gave the average tourist very little cause to stray much beyond the central hub.

The shops in the centre were all stocked, although the range of goods was extremely limited, and supermarket shelves were very widely spaced with large queues for anything fresh – especially fruit. But despite the apparent lack of goods, the people in the street looked well fed and were on the whole quite trendily dressed – an image that was in stark contrast to the impression I had built up during the journey, namely, that there were precious few signs of affluence in the country. In many ways it would have been nice to have stayed longer and to have dug deeper, but on the other hand, it was equally tempting to accept it all without question and to sit back and enjoy the grandeur of our surroundings and lap up the vodka and caviar while it lasted.

I had never been a great caviar eater and what little I had tasted I found singularly disappointing. However, during my time in Moscow I found that, as with so many things of quality (French wine being another example), my judgement had been based on an extremely poor sample. True caviar is, I discovered, absolutely delicious!

At eight that evening, after a very full and tiring day, I boarded the train for Berlin.

Of the original group, only my erstwhile carriage companion, Joanna, remained. Anita, brave girl, had left the train back in Irkutsk. Other folk had either taken earlier trains to Berlin or had headed north to Helsinki or southwest to Budapest. Getting out of Russia proved just as lengthy as getting in. The KGB again provided the frontier inspections and were uncompromisingly thorough!

My window view of Poland, as we travelled through on the train, was one of rural landscapes and a bucolic lifestyle. Teams of horses still pulled the ploughs through the multitude of sub-divided fields, and Friesian cows grazed on lush pastures. Only the occasional stork nesting on the top of a haystack gave away the country's identity. The houses were similar to those found in East Anglia's 'fenland' – dull and unimaginative, though occasionally adorned with Catholic regalia. As we stopped briefly at Warsaw station, I thought for a moment that I should really be getting off and taking advantage of the opportunity, but by then the desire to finish the journey and get home was stronger.

Just before midnight on the 4th of September, 1985, we crossed from East into West Berlin. It was a surreal crossing point, buried underground in what must have been part of the city's subway, the train drew to a halt to allow the guards onboard, then proceeded to the next underground station as passports were examined. The atmosphere was charged, and we all felt like characters in a John Le Carre spy thriller!

Joanna and I, being the only two left from the original Trans-Siberian team, agreed to break the journey back to the UK with one day in West Berlin. Leaving luggage at the station we put up for the night in a small 'pension' close to the city centre and the following morning became tourists for the day.

Berlin in the eighties was a phenomenon: a city the size of London with all its roads, railway and tube lines, suddenly cut in half. No continuity, no logic, just roads disappearing into a blank wall. The tube trains still operated but in a most bizarre fashion. Imagine having to cross a national border by taking a five-minute ride on the Circle Line, Piccadilly Line or the Met. Imagine standing outside the House of Commons and looking across to Westminster Abbey, suddenly located in a foreign country. Bizarre indeed, but this was Berlin.

I suppose if asked to summarise my impressions of Berlin, I would pick out three aspects. Its historical buildings, its high-flying standard of living and 'The Wall'. The majority of Berlin's landmarks were, at the time, included in East Berlin. However, famous buildings which were still accessible to us included the Reichstag, or 'seat of Government', and the Brandenburg Gate, although even this was actually just inside East Berlin.

Berlin's main attraction to those who lived there in the eighties, was its phenomenal pace of life. The shops of the Kurfurstendamm were bulging with the latest fashions, lavishly displayed, whilst the street cafes had a quality about them which made many of London's more exclusive restaurants look positively shabby by comparison. The same high standards were apparent on public buses and tube trains, where the latest in passenger comfort had been incorporated at even the most basic level.

The key to understanding Berlin, however, stretched like a dark scar across the full breadth of the city. The Wall, some nine feet high, was fully approachable from the western side and was used by West Berliners as a billboard for popular feelings. Colourful and poignant graffiti covered every inch of The Wall's concrete facade.

On the eastern side of The Wall, however, it was white-washed and bordered by a two-hundred-yard strip of cleared land, mined and peppered with search lights and lookout towers. Beyond this strip of death was a further barrier of mesh fencing and barbed wire.

The message to would-be defectors was clear. A well-documented history of The Wall, and those who had attempted to challenge it, was on display in a museum a few yards from Checkpoint Charlie, the most famous crossing point between East and West Berlin.

After a thwarted attempt to get tickets for the Berlin Philharmonic we repaired to a bar and spent the time before our departure quaffing Berliner Weis, a sweet German beer, whilst tucking into a wide selection of German sausage. A few minutes after midnight, barely twenty-four hours after our arrival, Joanna and I were on our way to London, ETA seven o'clock the following evening.

The train trundled through West Germany as we slept and then on through the familiar landscape of Belgium and France. We chatted for most of that last day, reminiscing about the journey and the life of travel which we were leaving behind. But the pull of home was now strong for both of us.

It was with a glow of satisfaction and a feeling of real homecoming that I finally stepped off the train at Victoria Station – savouring the moment amid the hustle and bustle of life being conducted once more in my sweet mother tongue. Over the previous eleven days I had undertaken the world's longest train journey, some 7,500 miles, crossing ten countries and two continents. However, the longest journey of all seemed that from Liverpool Street Station to the little town of Cromer on the North Norfolk coast.

Conclusion

A week after my return to the UK, I was driving west out of London heading for Plymouth. As I came to the M25/M4 interchange I slowed and pulled over onto the hard shoulder. The M25 was open and the contractor was concentrating on the completion of the slip roads allowing access from one motorway to the other. As I peered over the barrier I picked out one or two familiar faces – engineers who had been my peers fifteen months before. The job had advanced but the work remained the same. Nothing had changed. If there had ever been any doubt as to the value or sense in taking a year out, none now remained.

Yet it is impossible to quantify the value of such an experience. It would be easy to say that, like developing an appreciation for music or art, travel broadens the parameters of one's understanding and insight; but this does not explain the motivation behind abandoning a stable existence for a life of adventure, nor does it help one to justify such actions.

In the end I suppose my motivation was simply a desire to discover the 'inside story' for myself. It is not enough for me only to read about exotic places or different cultures, I have to experience them. Editing this book in the Spring of 2020, as Covid 19 wreaks havoc across the world, the luxury of unimpeded travel feels under threat – at least for the time being. However, I am also aware that the world is fast becoming smaller and more homogenous, lending a sense of urgency to the argument for embarking on adventure. This sense of a 'shrinking world' is partly due to the gradual erosion of cultural differences; the boundary between the developed and non-developed world is becoming very fuzzy. The hill tribesmen of Northern Thailand may not have the luxury of running water but many possess a television and are well aware of how 'they' live in Dallas, Texas.

Without such contact with the outside world the cultural integrity of a country is protected, but it takes only a short while once the barriers are lifted for such innocence to be spoiled. In travelling through China I was aware that barely a year had passed since independent travellers had been allowed the freedom to go where they wished and yet already the impact of tourism and westernisation could be seen; the world of Coca-Cola, tee-shirts and portable music had begun to make its mark.

I suppose it is this desire to catch a glimpse of a disappearing world which, as much as anything, sparked my adventure. However, the true starting point of any adventure is the end of someone else's tale and if this book is to have any purpose beyond simple storytelling it has to be that it might inspire others to take the same gamble and 'take a year out'.

About the Author

CHRIS COTTON is a devoted traveller, having worked in South Africa, Hong Kong and the UK as a civil engineer, and around the world as a management development consultant for over 20 years.

Shortly after the journey recounted in this book, Chris moved to Cornwall where he met and married his wife, Linda. Together they set up in business and raised their three children: Gemma, William and Lucy.

When not travelling for work, Chris and his wife take to bicycles to explore under the skin of different cultures and countries, including much of the Indian subcontinent and South America.

Take a Year Out is Chris's first book and was inspired by the desire to leave a personal legacy for his grandchildren.

He continues to indulge his long-term passion for sailing.

Printed in Great Britain
by Amazon